For Foucault

SUNY series in Contemporary Continental Philosophy

Dennis J. Schmidt, editor

For Foucault
Against Normative Political Theory

Mark G. E. Kelly

Published by State University of New York Press, Albany

© 2018 State University of New York

All rights reserved

Printed in the United States of America

No part of this book may be used or reproduced in any manner whatsoever without written permission. No part of this book may be stored in a retrieval system or transmitted in any form or by any means including electronic, electrostatic, magnetic tape, mechanical, photocopying, recording, or otherwise without the prior permission in writing of the publisher.

For information, contact State University of New York Press, Albany, NY
www.sunypress.edu

Production, Eileen Nizer
Marketing, Anne M. Valentine

Library of Congress Cataloging-in-Publication Data

Names: Kelly, Mark G. E., author.
Title: For Foucault : against normative political theory / Mark G. E. Kelly.
Description: Albany : State University of New York Press, [2018] | Series: SUNY series in contemporary continental philosophy | Includes bibliographical references and index.
Identifiers: LCCN 2016059960 (print) | LCCN 2017054330 (ebook) | ISBN 9781438467627 (ebook) | ISBN 9781438467610 (hardcover : alk. paper) | ISBN 9781438467603 (pbk. : alk. paper)
Subjects: LCSH: Political science—Philosophy. | Political ethics.
Classification: LCC JA71 (ebook) | LCC JA71 .K46 2017 (print) | DDC 320.01—dc23
LC record available at https://lccn.loc.gov/2016059960

10 9 8 7 6 5 4 3 2 1

Contents

Acknowledgments — vii

Introduction: Foucault and Political Philosophy — 1

1. Marx: Anti-normative Critique — 17

2. Lenin: The Invention of Party Governmentality — 39

3. Althusser: A Failed Project to Denormativize Marxism — 59

4. Deleuze: Denormativization as Norm — 73

5. Rorty: Relativizing Normativity — 95

6. Honneth: The Poverty of Critical Theory — 109

7. Geuss: The Paradox of Realism — 125

8. Foucault: The Lure of Neoliberalism — 147

Conclusion: What Now? — 169

Notes — 175

Bibliography — 181

Index — 191

Acknowledgments

If there's a single person who needs to be acknowledged here—other than the spectral figure of Michel Foucault himself, the dedication of the book to him appearing in the title—it's Paul Patton. It perhaps does not come through strongly enough in what follows that his defense of Foucault against normativizing misreadings is seminal to the entire line of thought this book represents. I also owe multiple other debts to him.

I must acknowledge Dimitris Vardoulakis, to whom I also owe much, but in this particular case for encouraging me to take this book forward and making introductions to editors. Dennis Schmidt, my colleague and the editor of this series, also acted as an important conduit in bringing this book to SUNY Press, as of course ultimately did my editor there, Andrew Kenyon.

I acknowledge funding from the Australian Research Council in the form of a Future Fellowship, during which I prepared this book for publication. This book has been long in the writing, however, predating in large part this fellowship. The piece on Rorty dates in its core to 2002. My work on Lenin dates in its beginnings to 2007. The piece on Marx and ethics I began in 2009. My work on Geuss and that on Patton dates mostly to 2011, that on Althusser to 2012, that on Honneth to 2013, and that on Deleuze to 2014.

Particular chapters require their specific acknowledgments. The genesis of the chapter on Rorty dates from a class at Sydney University given by Paul Redding in 2002, and the direction of it certainly begins with Paul's teaching.

Yet another person to whom I am overwhelmingly indebted in life is Jessica Whyte, in the particular case of this book for her help and encouragement in relation to the Althusser chapter.

The Deleuze chapter was initially written with the encouragement of Jeremy Gilbert and Andrew Goffey, to each of whom I also owe other debts dating back several years. I owe thanks for the careful reading of and comments on the chapter by graduate students at the University of Oregon, to Nicolae Morar for penetrating questions and suggestions for further investigation, and to Colin Koopman for orchestrating these encounters.

The chapter on Honneth stems from my involvement since 2012 with the Sydney Recognition Workgroup, which is to say primarily with Jean-Philippe Deranty and Heikki Ikäheimo. I have much for which I should thank them. I was encouraged in bringing the chapter to fruition by Danielle Petherbridge, and should thank anonymous referees for *Critical Horizons* for their feedback.

I also acknowledge the provocatively unsympathetic and uncomprehending audiences I had when talking about opposing normativity at the Australasian Association of Philosophy conference at UNSW in 2010, the Philosophy Department of Cardiff University the same year, and the Sydney Recognition Workgroup's 2013 seminars at UNSW.

An earlier version of Chapter 3 previously appeared as a chapter entitled "Foucault against Marxism: Althusser beyond Althusser" in Jernej Habjan and Jessica Whyte (eds.), *(Mis)readings of Marx in Continental Philosophy*, 2014, Palgrave Macmillan. An earlier version of Chapter 5 previously appeared as an article entitled "Discipline Is Control: Foucault contra Deleuze" in *New Formations* 84/85, 2015. An alternative version of Chapter 6 appeared as an article entitled "Foucault contra Honneth: Resistance or Recognition?" in *Critical Horizons*, 2017.

Introduction
Foucault and Political Philosophy

> With his critique of ideology applied to the bourgeois constitutional state and with his sociological dissolution of the theoretical basis for natural rights, Marx so enduringly discredited . . . both the idea of legality and the intention of natural law, that the link between natural law and revolution has been broken ever since. The parties of an internationalized civil war have divided this heritage between themselves with fateful clarity: the one side has taken up the heritage of revolution, the other the ideology of natural law.
>
> —Habermas 1978, 117[1]

This book is for, and not about, Michel Foucault. I will refer to him often in what follows, and occasionally (particularly in the final chapter, and in this introduction) will slip into Foucault scholarship, but I have already written several books on Foucault, so this one will deal primarily with other figures. Similarly but conversely, this book is against, and not about, normative political theory. This object too will heave into view, but for the most part the book deals with terrain in between Foucault and normative political theory, with a series of political thinkers who contest in various ways the normative stakes of political thought, but retain a normative political-theoretic dimension that Foucault lacks and rejects. I explore and critique their work from a Foucauldian direction, with a particular focus where applicable on their commentary on Foucault.

While I think most readers will readily have some understanding of the term "political theory," the meaning of the term "normative" is trickier. This latter term is bandied about in academic circles with abandon, but it is not often encountered outside of academe, and even within it the meaning of the word can be elusive, as I discovered several years ago when I started presenting papers at conferences and seminars proposing that political philosophy be conducted in a "non-normative" way, in material seminal to multiple of the chapters here. These claims were unpopular with my learned audiences—not merely among those who were practitioners of conventional normative political philosophy, but with almost everyone. Even those who reject conventional normative political philosophy turned out to be attached to some notion of normativity. Some seemed to take everything that is not a physical fact to be "normative," by which measure human life is indeed intrinsically normative. I want to reply now, however, that such a notion of "normativity" is hopelessly inflationary, making the normative coextensive with subjectivity and making the term apply to things that have nothing in particular to do with "norms." By contrast, in my opposition to "normativity" here I mean to invoke a much stricter definition of the "normative," the one operative in mainstream philosophical ethics, which takes it as merely a by-word for prescription, which is to say for "oughts" (Korsgaard 2009). Such a definition may seem no less redundant than the one that identifies it with subjectivity: it's a word of art applied to a well-understood notion, for which we had time-honored names before people started bandying the word "normative" about in the twentieth century. However, I will argue that normativity in this sense does exist in more forms than those imagined by its own partisans, specifically in forms of political imagination that constrain political action through ideas about the way things should be.

Contemporary political philosophy remains in the shadow of an "ethical turn" that happened in political thought in the 1970s, almost simultaneously affecting the main languages of Western philosophical discussion. Raymond Geuss (2016, ix–x) has recently characterized this as a "normativist counterrevolution" that "has been an unmitigated catastrophe." In English, John Rawls revitalized the very marginal field of political philosophy by re-envisioning Kantianism in his 1971 *Theory of Justice*, breathing new life into normative approaches to politics, and refounding political philosophy as a distinctive normative enterprise, linked to—but no longer entirely subordinated to—normative ethics. In German, Jürgen Habermas emerged in the 1960s as the leader of a new generation of Frankfurt School Critical Theory, into which he increasingly injected ethics, and which has become increasingly concerned with normativity ever since. In French, an explosion of Marxist political thought after 1968 petered out by the mid-1970s, and saw thinkers, including many former Marxists, turn to ethics. Foucault might be taken to be a case in point, though his Marxism was thin and youthful, and his late interest in ethics historical: he never straightforwardly advocates a return to ethics, rather treating ethics as an artefact of ancient history, which he, in any case, doesn't understand in a way that is "normative" in the conventional sense.

Rather, against this context of the ethicization of political thought, I will attempt to argue that Foucault pushes in the opposite direction, for a political thought that stands against normativity, while also eschewing the high theoreticism of systems theory. Foucault does not pointedly reject normativity as such, but I think this is in large part because his core political writings—by which I mean *Discipline and Punish* and the first volume of his *History of Sexuality*—were composed before the ethical turn in French thought began, and without any evident contact with the emerging American or German normative political philosophy. Rather, he was working in a context where non-normativity was already quite firmly established as the standard mode for political thought. In what follows—particularly in the first and third chapters—I will give some indication of how this had come to pass, specifically through the inheritance of Marxism's rejection of morality.

Foucault's attitude toward political philosophy, and his ignorance of the formative subdiscipline by this name in the Anglophone world, is indicated in a 1978 paper of his, as yet untranslated into English, that bears the title "La philosophie analytique de la politique" ("The Analytical Philosophy of Politics") (Foucault 1994c, 534–551). Here Foucault imagines what it would be like to think about politics in the style of Anglophone analytical philosophy, which he understands primarily through his familiarity with the speech act theory of John Searle and J. L. Austin. Foucault thus conceives an "analytical philosophy of politics" as an attempt to do with politics what speech act theory does with language. It does not seem to occur to him that there might already be a distinctive form of analytical political philosophy—he (not entirely incorrectly) estimates that English philosophy is essentially apolitical—nor does he anticipate the kind of social philosophy Searle would go on to develop, the analysis of the social and political operation of speech acts, but rather proposes an analysis of politics that begins like speech act theory with an analysis of everyday situations, but with power relations in the place of locution.

Foucault (1994c, 537) situates his proposal for an "analytico-political philosophy" in a long history of the political role of philosophy in the

West since the Greeks. He observes that we have never in the West seen philosophical ideas applied as political practice, however, even though the ideas of philosophers have been politically influential, contrasting this to the situation in the Orient, where Confucianism qua philosophy actually has been the basis of the state form as well as individual conduct. He argues that, since the nineteenth century, we have seen the emergence for the first time of a new "organic connection" of the state to philosophy (Foucault 1994c, 540). The earliest example of this he gives is the relation of Jean-Jacques Rousseau's thought to the state produced by the French Revolution; he goes on to note the links between Karl Marx's thought and the Soviet state, and Friedrich Nietzsche's thought and the Nazi state. The point here is precisely not that the Soviet state represents the fulfillment of Marx's thought any more than the Nazi state represents the fulfilment of Nietzsche's. Rather, the point is simply that a reference to philosophy is part of these states' functioning: the Soviet state, while not representing the inevitable outcome of Marx's thought, nevertheless incorporates Marx as an essential reference point for its operation. In the cases of Marx and Nietzsche, neither thinker had sought any such connection for their work, but were rather anti-state thinkers. They refuse to legislate for the future or to offer advice to power, yet this does not immunize them: indeed, it means there is a lacuna in their thought into which one can insert any reality whatever.

Foucault (1994c, 539) is disturbed by the fact that "philosophies of freedom," as he calls them, have thus given rise to their exact opposite. He declares that philosophy has strayed beyond the area of its vocation, that it should not get mixed up with politics. Instead, he suggests:

> There is still a certain possibility of playing a role in relation to power left for philosophy, which would not be a role of foundation or of renewal of power. Perhaps philosophy can still play a role on the side of counter-power, on condition that this role no longer consist in emphasising, in the face of power, the same law of philosophy, on condition that philosophy stops thinking of itself as prophecy, on condition that philosophy stops thinking of itself either as pedagogy, or as legislation, and that it gives itself the task of analysing, of elucidating, of making visible, and thus of intensifying the struggles that unfold around power, the strategies of the adversaries inside power relations, the tactics utilized, the sites of resistance, on condition in short that

philosophy stops posing the question of power in terms of good or bad, but rather in does so in terms of existence. Don't ask, is power good or is it evil, legitimate or illegitimate, a question of right of morality? Rather, simply, try to rid the question of power of all the moral and juridical overtones which we have previously given it, and ask this question naïvely, which hasn't been posed that often, even if effectively a number of people have been posing it for a long time: what do power relations essentially consist of? (Foucault 1994c, 540)

It is not made entirely clear by Foucault here why this new method he proposes would avoid the fate that befell Marx's and Nietzsche's thoughts. Although this is contentious, I would argue—and I think Foucault would accept—that they already both eschewed any juridical or moral prescription, and indeed I will argue this at length in relation to Marx in Chapter 1. I think, however, that both thinkers in their own way fall short of non-normativity, and I think it is in the end thoroughgoing methodological non-normativity that Foucault is proposing when he talks of a political philosophy that is purely "analytical." That he does not speak in terms of "normativity" as such is unsurprising given that the term had limited currency in French at that time, and that he was not yet faced with a *soi-disant* normative political philosophy.

In Marx's case, I will argue that he fails to be thoroughly non-normative, despite this being his effective intention, because he engages in a prophetic philosophy of history. As for Nietzsche, I will not deal with him in this book, on the basis that he is not a political thinker (Leiter 2011). Indeed, he is precursor to Foucault in this respect, in being a specifically *anti*-political thinker. It is from Nietzsche that Foucault gets the notion of "genealogy" that defines his own political thought (from Nietzsche's *Genealogy of Morality*, no less), and even the very theme of "power" that is central to Foucault's political thought is Nietzschean in complexion, even if taking these concepts in a political rather than personal direction is a signal departure from Nietzsche. Foucault (1988, 251) indeed cast Nietzsche as the main single influence on his own thought. But unlike Foucault, Nietzsche criticizes politics from a distance, in the end advocating a kind of individualistic withdrawal, and proposing a form of personal ethics as an antidote to politics. This leaves Nietzsche vulnerable to being enlisted, against his will, by political ideologies that claim an affinity with his critique of existing political notions and personal values.

Nietzsche (2002) enjoins us to go "beyond good and evil." I read this as an attempt to refuse what we today call "normativity," before that term acquired currency, in favor of a new set of values, which are variable and relative. The fact that Nietzsche does, however, sketch an image of a desirable "new man" is seen by some readers as simply a new normative stance counterposed to the Christian morality that Nietzsche rejects. It also gives Nietzsche's thought a prophetic dimension in relation to the future, a dimension Marx also has, but which Foucault refuses (see Kelly 2014a).

Foucault tells us that Nietzsche started to make an impact on him only once he'd read Heidegger (Foucault 1988a, 250). One interpretation of this comment is that it means that Heidegger's reading of Nietzsche was decisive for the development of Foucault's Nietzscheanism (Elden 2001, 2). Certainly it seems to me that in relation to normativity, Foucault follows the trajectory of Heidegger's reading of Nietzsche, which criticizes Nietzsche precisely for being too normative, instead rejecting all "thinking in terms of values" (Heidegger 1977, 108).

Heidegger's own alternative, thinking of "being," however, is one Foucault is perhaps even less sympathetic to. Neither Nietzsche's "will to power" as fundamental motivation of all life nor Heidegger's "being" appeal to Foucault. Despite the deliberately anti-metaphysical cast of both German thinkers, they retain more than a whiff of metaphysics in their schemata. As I will argue repeatedly in what follows, any ontological commitments of this type can serve to ground a normative perspective, even against the author's intention. I would suggest that Heidegger's "being" ended up, through the search for authentic connections to it, supplying much more of a normative orientation than he expected, making it possible for him to couch his support for Nazism in terms of his philosophical project (cf. Bourdieu 1991). Having said that, Foucault (2008, 374) himself opines that there is no strong link between Heidegger's philosophy and his political commitments, and instead suggests that the essential problem here is one of a philosopher who fails to attend to the practical effects of his thought, of the relation between thought and practice. This failing is indeed why I will not focus on Heidegger in this book, either: he is essentially apolitical, insofar as he refuses in his work to engage directly in detail with politics.

Along with Heidegger, I am also bracketing an entire branch emanating from him. In particular, I will not in what follows look at Jacques Derrida's thought, a notable omission, especially since I spend so much time here on his fellow canonical French poststructuralists, Deleuze and

Foucault. One reason for this omission is that I have dealt with Derrida elsewhere (Kelly 2009, 23–25; 2014b, 40–44). Another is that although I do think Derrida makes moves in the direction of a normative political thought, and which have been increasingly taken up as the basis of a normative political thought by other scholars, I do not think he propounds a normative political theory much more than Heidegger does, even if, to a greater extent than Heidegger, I think Derrida is a fundamentally normative thinker. I however acknowledge that scholars are beginning to articulate a normative political theory on the basis of a certain interpretation of Derrida's thought, particularly in Mathias Fritsch's emerging body of work.

Against Normativity

I think readers will likely already have two questions about opposing normativity. First, I suspect many will simply not understand why it should be necessary or desirable to do so. Second, I expect many will not understand how it could be possible.

Foucault's answer to the "why" question is not entirely clear, though I think he provides several reasons. Foucault in the above long quotation from "The Analytical Philosophy of Politics" seems to base his case against normativity on the possible negative consequences of normative thinking. However, an empirical, consequentialist argument against normativity would itself need to have recourse to a normative standard by which consequences can be judged, so this would be self-contradictory. Rather, I think the case against normativity in political thought must be based on caution and intellectual parsimony. That is to say, it is to be eschewed because there are dangers inherent in pursuing it, no positive reason to engage in it, and also perhaps a pragmatic argument in favor of non-normativity, namely, that normative commitments restrict the possible audience for political thought to those who share them, since those who advocate normativity in political thought have never in any case agreed on what form this normativity is supposed to take.

I suspect it might be objected that, while there are dangers in normative thought, there are dangers in anything, and there may well be dangers in non-normative thought. Indeed, it might be argued that Marx's and Nietzsche's thought was not available for appropriation because of their normativity, but precisely because of their non-normativity—that is, the absence of a clear description of their utopian vision that would make clear that neither the Soviet Union nor Nazi Germany, respectively, bore any resemblance to what they advocated. However, this seems to me mistaken. Some Marxists, for example, have propounded utopian visions of communism (see Chapters 1 and 2), but these have served as justifications for their opposite because the Soviet Union was held to be a stepping-stone to the utopia. As Foucault (1977, 230) has it, "to imagine another system is to extend our participation in the present system." Only a normative utopian vision that condemned absolutely any deviation from it, such as the anarchists', could decisively avoid such a fate, but in such a case utopianism seems to me to have an opposite problem of failing to offer a basis for a nuanced understanding of the present situation, and thus ultimately extends participation in the current system by failing to constitute a serious opposition to it.

By contrast, Foucault's critical analyses of power relations cannot easily be made into a tool of power themselves; rather, they are intended as a tool for those who fight power. This is not to say there is no way it can be co-opted, however. One might use a critical analysis of one problem to distract from another, or as a discursive element of a formation of power that opposes that problem. For example, one might use a scathing analysis of a dictatorship to justify invading a country to depose that regime. Foucault's own critiques of insane asylums served in small part to justify closing those asylums, which was the intended outcome, but in the event formed part of a pattern of cutting funding to mental health services that left former inmates bereft. Although critiques can be targeted in accordance with an analysis of strategies of power tactically toward particular problems, any shift in the situation can change the political valence of these critiques, allowing them to be utilized by power. For Foucault, this simply requires us to continue criticizing as the situation changes. Foucault's name has also been enlisted by power through the false imputation of normative positions to him. I will deal with some instances of this in Chapter 8 in particular.

My final argument against normativity in political thought, elaborated in Chapter 7, is that normative stances have unintended consequences. It seems to me to be a suppressed premise of normative political thought that propounding a normative theory is *eo ipso* a contribution to realizing its normative vision. However, there is simply no reason to believe that that is true; on the contrary, the social effects of propounding a normative viewpoint are radically unforeseeable given the complexity of the social world. Normative approaches are more or less bound to fail to produce what they aim at, and if they can't posit a regular relationship between speaking about their goals and achieving them, I am not convinced there can be any justification for including normative statements in political writing. By contrast, since non-normative approaches do not aim at any determinate result, their inability to foresee their consequences is not a problem for them.

The burden should be on the normativist to explain why normativity is necessary or useful in political thought. It seems to me that no one has ever convincingly managed to do so; rather, normativists simply presume that normativity is required. I will consider various attempts to explain the necessity of normativity in the chapters that follow, particularly in Chapters 5 and 6.

What is the alternative? Simply to analyze things in order to undermine them. I see Foucault's essential, general technique as a kind of partial transcendence of the intellectual conditions in which he lived, through objective analysis, which served political purposes immanent in his life. That is, Foucault investigated specific phenomena, such as the prison, sexuality, or madness, that interested him personally by asking what forces were involved objectively in constituting these phenomena historically, in order to shift outside the usual perspective we have on these things in our culture. Here, we may see Foucault as inheriting Lenin's distrust of "spontaneous ideology," which is to say of the prejudices inherent in our culture. In this sense, one might indeed say that normativity is the default mode of political thought.

Is there not a normativity implicit in the choice Foucault makes of targets for his analysis? Not necessarily: for one thing, the choice of target can be tactical, based on a preliminary assessment of what the crucial points of the accretion of power are in our society. Foucault clearly opposed the institutions he "problematized," which might be taken to imply a normative stance, though I will argue that it does not; in any case, however, even if there is normativity at work in the selection of the object of investigation, the investigations themselves can be more or less objective and historical, aimed at undermining the object by showing its contingency and hidden links to power, rather than applying a normative framework by which any of them could be condemned.

Non-normativity is thus a methodological precept for Foucault. It does not imply that he is personally amoral, nor that he thinks that normative beliefs are not a real social force, nor, least of all, that we should behave directly contrary to the dictates of morality as ordinarily conceived—as Allen Wood (1990, 565) points out, even "to reject morality . . . is not necessarily to reject all the behaviour that morality enjoins and advocate the behaviour that it prohibits." Foucault (2002, 328; 2005, 252) does in point of fact make comments casting doubt on the possibility of any moral or ethical stance today, but I will not explore these claims here, since I am deliberately limiting the scope of my investigation to normativity in *political* thought.

One might argue that to refuse normativity is itself a kind of normative stance. I would argue if this were true that Foucault would be minimally normative, since he would have only one norm in his political thought, which rules out the adoption of any others. And indeed, Foucault (2004, 6) does say "I only propose therefore this single imperative, but this will be categorical and unconditional: never do politics." As I will explain below, I read this comment as a condemnation specifically of normative politics.

I do not believe, however (and nor do I believe that Foucault believed), that it is strictly necessary for us to adopt even a single normative principle. This is because I do not accept that to issue normative prescriptions is the natural mode of political thought, and we must deliberately stop ourselves to prevent us engaging in prescription. That said, inasmuch as the reigning culture in political thought does indeed seem to me to be firmly normativist, today one does need such a heuristic principle to avoid falling back into the spontaneous ideology of normativity. Not being prescriptive only appears to be a stringent limiting condition because of a background culture of prescription. By this token, I think we can say that it is not so much a case that we need normatively to foreswear normativity, as that contemporary political theorists are in the grip of a largely unstated normative metaprinciple that they should be normative. By dint of this unconscious principle, the idea of a non-normative political philosophy simply does not occur to most specialists today, and when they see it, it looks to them like nonsense. When confronted with Foucault's work, most commentators either describe him as incoherent for his opposition to normativity, or attempt to ascribe a deep normativity to him.

In what follows, I will thus use the terms "non-normative" and "anti-normative" interchangeably, since I am simultaneously advocating a non-normative political thought and opposing normative political thought.

Against Political Theory

Opposing normativity in political thought by my lights has far-going implications. It does not mean simply emptying political theory of normative presupposition, but rather rejecting political theory itself as such, since I believe the normative, political, and theoretic aspects are closely interconnected. I will argue, on what I take to be a Foucauldian basis, that thinking about politics should not only be non-normative but should also avoid the temptations of either theoreticism or what Foucault calls "politics" itself.

Regarding theory, it seems to me that Foucault's political thought is atheoretical, eschewing systematization. Foucault (1977, 231) on one occasion declared in response to a Marxist interviewer's assertion of the need for theory that "This need for theory is still part of the system we reject." This does not mean that he resiles cognitive coherence or consistency, only that he refuses to try to produce a totalizing explanation of everything, of "the social" or "the political." Instead, he merely formulates hypotheses. Even his conception of power—in my estimation, his most important contribution to political thought—a very general concept, which is apparently transhistorical in its applicability, is nonetheless not for Foucault (2000, 327) an attempt to produce a "theory of power," but a particular intellectual contribution: "since a theory assumes a prior objectification, it cannot be asserted as a basis for analytical work. But this analytical work cannot proceed without an ongoing conceptualization. And this conceptualization implies critical thought—a constant checking."

Admittedly, Foucault (2000, 327) says immediately prior to this that it "seemed to [him] that economic history and theory provided a good instrument." Foucault's opposition to theory does not imply that he cannot find valuable insights in theoretical work. Foucault (1994b, 523) pointedly provides only a "toolbox," which as such may be used with other ideas, even though these might in themselves both be attempts to produce a totalizing theory, and I believe he approaches others' work in the same light, as a resource.

Foucault (1984, 375) sets himself against "politics" as such because, like theory, it seems to be a matter of "totalization." He indeed suggests for this reason that his work should not even be considered "political"; he questions politics, rather than considering himself part of it. Here, however, "political" and "politics" are invoked by Foucault in a relatively narrow sense. This sense is that of "party politics" and statecraft. Foucault (Foucault 2004, 5–6) expresses his anti-political stance particularly stridently at the beginning of his 1978 Collège de France lectures, *Security, Territory, Population*:

> I think this serious and fundamental relation between struggle and truth, the dimension in which philosophy has developed for centuries and centuries, only dramatizes itself, becomes emaciated, and loses its meaning and effectiveness in polemics within theoretical discourse. So in all of this I will therefore propose only one imperative, but it will be categorical and unconditional: Never do politics.

It is necessary to point out a mistranslation in the English version of this text, where the final word, "politics," is rendered as "polemics" (Foucault 2007a, 4–5). However, the French text indeed says "politics," *politique*, and his enunciation of *politique* is deliberate in the recording of the lecture, 10 minutes and 20 seconds in, an emphatic flourish met with a smattering of laughter from the audience. Foucault (1997, 113) does elsewhere declaim polemics, but here he is targeting politics because of its connection to other things he eschews, such as polemics and theory. His categorical imperative here is in essence synonymous with the minimal normative principle not to be normative, referred to above.

Still, I will copiously refer to Foucault's thought as political in this book in a way that I will never allow it is theoretical or normative. This is because the word "political" has a sense distinct from "doing politics" in the sense that Foucault forbids. Indeed, some use the word "politics" itself to mean more or less the opposite of what Foucault means by it, in particular Jacques Rancière (1999), who in effect uses the name "politics" precisely for resisting what Foucault calls "politics," for which Rancière instead idiosyncratically reserves the term "police."

Although Foucault is against normative political theory, in all three of its dimensions, which is to say, is against almost everyone else within the broad tradition of modern Western social and political thought, he nevertheless remains within that discourse. Similarly, this book pertains only to that discourse, and does not take any position on normativity and theoreticism in other areas, for example in the natural sciences.

This Book

This book is something of an anthology. Each chapter is organized around the thought of a single political thinker, and engages to various degrees in three functions: explaining how a given thinker diverges from normative political theory; criticizing the thinker for remaining somehow normative, political, and theoretical, relative to Foucault's model of non-normativity; and defending Foucault's positions from their criticisms and misinterpretations in the cases where they engage with Foucault. Though a common thematic runs through the chapters, namely, a recurrent and concatenating argument about the superiority of a Foucauldian non-normative perspective in relation to all, each chapter was originally drafted as an individual essay, and a couple of them have previously been published in a different form as such. Readers should therefore feel free to pick and choose which chapters to read.

My title, *For Foucault*, of course apes Louis Althusser's *For Marx*. The reference to *For Marx*, replacing Marx with Foucault, points to a certain rejection or replacement of Marx with Foucault, referring to my engagement in this book with Marx and Marxists, including Althusser himself. There is considerable irony in this reference, however, inasmuch as my relationship to Foucault is not Althusser's to Marx. Being "for Foucault" must mean something very different from what being "for Marx" meant for Althusser. For Althusser, the reference to Marx is a fixed point, around which he nonetheless proposes to articulate a reading of Marx that diverges deliberately from Marx's own position, to construct a kind of "true Marx." To think of Foucault in such a way would be no small irony, given his own critique of the concern with the author principle, and indeed it is a paradoxical position I find myself in, upholding what I do indeed take to be an accurate interpretation of Foucault (more accurate I believe than Althusser's interpretation of Marx—a point I elaborate in Chapter 3), while at the same time disregarding aspects of Foucault's method in doing so: this book is more polemical, with little of the patient archival research that characterized Foucault's work. In these regards, I actually find myself going *against* Foucault in my method.

The book is organized broadly in chronological order of the texts under discussion. It describes something like a kind of progression toward Foucauldian non-normativity, though this is hardly linear. For one thing, half the thinkers discussed are in fact younger than Foucault, and influenced by him, though I will argue they remain theoretically sub-Foucauldian. The chronological order of figures is not particularly clear: Axel Honneth is younger than Raymond Geuss, but I have put the chapter on him before that on Geuss because the texts by Geuss I discuss are on average much more recent than those by Honneth. Indeed, the most significant text by Honneth for my discussion is older than those I discuss by Richard Rorty, who is much older than Honneth, and indeed deceased, but I place Rorty first, in part because Rorty's death means that some of the texts I mention by Honneth are more recent than those by Rorty. Ending with Foucault may also seem grossly out of order from this point of view, but the chapter on Foucault really focuses on recent commentary on Foucault based on lectures of Foucault's that have only been published recently.

The first chapter deals with Marx, whose thought is clearly much older than that of any other thinker dealt with here. However, this chapter is primarily a critique of the attempt in the late 1970s and 1980s in Anglophone political philosophy to rehabilitate Marx as a normative political philosopher. The material for this debate is provided by Marx's own work, though, so it might nonetheless seem that I am, by starting with Marx, following Althusser in positing Marx as a kind of "epistemic break." I, however, follow Foucault in taking an ambivalent attitude toward Marx. I do see Marx as having resiled the kind of normative perspective proper to his German idealist predecessors, which he himself held in his youth, but I also see him as inheriting an ultimately normative theory of history from Hegel. I do think Marx is a supremely significant figure, which is one reason I begin by discussing him, though I think this significance is—to an indiscernible extent—due to accidents of history that have made him a touchstone of twentieth-century politics and thought.

The second chapter deals with Lenin. The case of Lenin, for me, as I think for Foucault, primarily serves to demonstrate the problems with applying to politics the normativity and theoreticism that Marx failed to rid himself of entirely. This leads Lenin to fail to see what he does in practice, namely, I argue, to produce a new form of government that will go on to be used by regimes of various ideological casts over the next century. The focus of the chapter is on a comparative study of Lenin's *State and Revolution* and the historical experience of the Russian Revolution.

The third chapter is on Althusser. I read him as tending toward Foucault's position but held back by a commitment to Marxism and

Leninism that is itself only explicable by a series of incorrect political calculations, ultimately attributable to Althusser's mentality.

The fourth chapter deals with the thought of Gilles Deleuze. I criticize what I see as Deleuze's normative theoreticism. Most of the chapter is dedicated to an extremely close reading of a short but very influential essay of his, the "Postscript on Control Societies," wherein he purports to extend and update Foucault's analysis of modern society. Deleuze was close to Foucault biographically and intellectually, and here tries effectively to addend Foucault's thought seamlessly. I, however, seek to thwart this attempt by Deleuze, arguing that in the end his thought is normative theory rather than a genuine critical analysis of a Foucauldian type.

The fifth chapter is on Richard Rorty and his reading of Foucault. I argue that Rorty badly misunderstands Foucault, and as such fails to see the challenge that Foucault's thought poses for Rorty's "ethnocentric" pragmatist liberalism. I further argue that Rorty's ethnocentric relativism is an incoherent argument for restraining critique.

The sixth chapter is on the contemporary critical theorist Axel Honneth. As with Rorty, I primarily address Honneth's own reading of Foucault, arguing that Honneth fails to understand Foucault's true position, and thus fails to understand how Foucault offers a challenge to Honneth's brand of normative critical theory.

The seventh chapter focuses on Raymond Geuss's recent political thought, which is extremely close to Foucault's, in my estimation. The difference between my position and Geuss's is not so much that Geuss actively propounds a normative political theory, as that he still considers it acceptable for thought to be normative, political, and theoretical, even if unlike almost all other political thinkers today he considers each of these aspects to be optional extras. Against Geuss, I argue that normativity, politics, and theory need to be stamped out, primarily on the basis of their failure to account for social complexity.

The eighth and final chapter focuses on the Foucault scholarship of the Australian philosopher Paul Patton. Patton is a focus because he is the effective originator of the non-normative reading of Foucault that guides this book, while also in more recent scholarship exemplifying the contemporary reassessment of Foucault's stance toward normativity, in particular in relation to Foucault's reading of neoliberalism. Patton is a relatively subtle reader of Foucault as having a certain sympathy for neoliberalism—which would, by my lights, mean that Foucault had, the year after telling us not to do politics, changed his mind and embraced politics and normativity. In this chapter I also repudiate the related claims that Foucault in his later life embraced a form of normativity in his flirtation with the language of human rights.

1

Marx

Anti-normative Critique

> Critique is not, for Marx, the judgement which the (true) Idea pronounces on the defective or contradictory real; critique is critique of existing reality by existing reality.
>
> —Althusser 2006, 17

Introduction

Why does this book begin with Marx? Since ideas do not spring fully formed out of the heads of great thinkers, any starting point for any historical survey is necessarily somewhat arbitrary, as indeed is every point picked out on its trajectory. Still, the choice of Marx is far from accidental. He is a pivotal figure in the history of political thought. This status may itself have been somewhat arbitrarily acquired, inasmuch as there may have been other thinkers whose thought had the potential to have historical consequences as wide-ranging as his, but contingently did not. As things stand, however, Marx's thought has had a political influence no other thinker's ever has: it spawned a political movement, Marxism, for which his writings formed the touchstone in the way no other philosopher's has ever done, and this movement moreover achieved hegemony over swathes of the planet during the twentieth century, constituting the official ideology under which billions lived. Marxism has declined since, but rumors of its demise have been greatly exaggerated: large sections of the world continue to be ruled by parties officially adhering to Marxism, and Marxism continues to be a major oppositional discourse in much of the rest of the world.

I am interested in Marx as a precursor to Foucault in rejecting normative political theory. Historically, Marx represents a sea change away from moralism. As Foucault (1988a, 113) puts it, Marx "refused the customary explanation which regarded [workers'] misery as the effect of a naturally rare cause of a concerted theft. And he said substantially: given what capitalist production is, in its fundamental laws, it cannot help but cause misery. Capitalism's raison d'être is not to starve the workers but it cannot develop without starving them." The point here is that Marx does not morally condemn capitalists for their actions, but analyzes capitalism qua system. One could of course claim that he condemns the system on moral grounds, but Foucault's point is that this would be senseless: the critique of a system works simply by showing how the system cannot but work broadly the way it does.

One can place Marx—somewhat artificially—then as a pivotal figure in the emergence of anti-normative political thought, though he antedates positive use of the term "normative." The turn against normative thought relates, in his own terminology, to his orientation toward materialism in opposition to idealism. Idealism and normativity are close allies, though not synonymous: idealism's faith in the value of ideas makes it apt to see normative principles as the appropriate means for shaping reality. Marx explicitly stood this order on its head, seeing reality as shaping ideas rather than vice versa, a viewpoint from which normative precepts appear to be produced by history rather than offering a way to shape it.

Materialism is not new at this time, however, but a millennia-old viewpoint, and one can find many precursors of the view that morals are not universal. It is my position, indeed, that the moral universalism properly called "normative" emerged only in modernity, and that the importance of Marx is not that he is the first to take a view that is not normative, but that he represents a landmark in the development of *anti*-normativity, which is to say in taking a view that reacts against normative universalism. These claims depend, however, on a full genealogical account of the birth of normativity that I intend to develop elsewhere and cannot elaborate here. Suffice it, perhaps, to say for now that Marx establishes a horizon for political thought, by dint of the significance his thought is accorded during the twentieth century, in which Foucault and most of the other thinkers I will consider here begin to think.

To the extent I am doing intellectual history here, it is, as Foucault would say, a "history of the present"—albeit in a stronger sense than this phrase meant when applied to his work. Where Marx himself both reacted against and thought within a horizon provided by Hegel's philosophy, I, a century and a half after Marx, am defining my position against a neo-Kantian orthodoxy in political philosophy less sophisticated than Hegelianism. The aim of this chapter is not to study the historical appearance of Marx's position, then, but rather to argue against recent attempts to read him as a neo-Kantian transcendental ethicist, though I will also reject Hegelianism. What I mean to do here is to assert a European tradition of post-Hegelian anti-normative thought against the mainstream of contemporary political theory that ignores this tradition, or at least fails to comprehend the radicalness of its alterity.

Speaking within this tradition, Étienne Balibar (2007, 4) says that "*after Marx, philosophy is no longer as it was before.*" This is perhaps true from a French perspective, but "Marx" refers there to a different event to the one that the name refers to in Anglophone or German philosophy. In Germany, Marx's work became fashionable in a period after Hegelianism, in which neo-Kantianism was ascendant. Marx did not in fact change German philosophy decisively, it seems to me. While many philosophers after Marx did engage with his thought in various ways, I do not believe Marx fundamentally altered the course of German philosophy, though Marx was for a time the touchstone for thinkers of the left, and during a different period Marxism was the state ideology of a part of Germany. In France, by contrast, Marx's thought arrived as a shock, because French philosophy had in the nineteenth century largely ignored developments in German philosophy, particularly Hegel, in favor of its own indigenous philosophers. The 1917 Russian Revolution's impact on France, as elsewhere, was enormous, and it was this that decisively brought Marx's thought to prominence in France, with Hegel's ideas spreading there on the back of Marxism, itself primarily a political movement, with intellectual Marxism trailing behind. The role of the French Communist Party in resisting occupation during the later stages of the Second World War propelled Marxism to a general level of prominence and esteem it never had in English- or German-language contexts. In particular, Marx's challenge from his eleventh thesis on Feuerbach, that philosophers have only interpreted the world where the point is to change it, influenced French philosophy to lastingly orient itself toward politics as an ineluctable element of what it means to do philosophy, something that also happened in

Germany at the same time by the need to account for the collaboration of certain philosophers with the Nazi state, but which never happened in English-language philosophy, where rarefied forms of logic and epistemology remain the most prestigious parts of the discipline.

In Anglophone philosophy, things had unfolded in a quite opposite way. Hegelianism had spread in England and America to become the dominant philosophical school in the early twentieth century, a time when its star had waned in Germany. The First World War was the greatest single event in Anglophone philosophy of the century: Hegelianism was abandoned wholesale, displaced by the nascent tradition of "analytical" philosophy that continues to dominate the discipline to this day. This meant that, just as Marxism waxed as a force in the world, the philosophical audience in Britain capable of engaging with its underpinnings disappeared. Marxism came to minor prominence within Anglophone philosophy only decades later, as a marginal school within the marginal subdiscipline of "political philosophy" that had emerged in the English-speaking world in the 1970s, inaugurated by the seminal theory of Rawls—prior to this, political philosophy had existed so far on the margins of analytical philosophy as to be practically nonexistent. In this context, Marxism had to be translated into a neo-Kantian, idealist, universalist political thought.

It is against this background that I begin, seeking to attack this conception of political thought by showing, against the arguments of ostensibly Marxist political philosophers, that it is coherent for Marx to think non-normatively about politics. This endeavor may seem gratuitous to readers from the continental tradition, including mainstream Marxism, because they are not under the sway of the presupposition that political theory should be normative. For those steeped in political philosophy, the point here is to begin to show how non-normative political thought is possible; for those from outside this way of thinking, the point is, conversely, to show how normative colonization of political thought works, before going on to sniff out relatively mere traces of normativity in continental or allied thinkers in subsequent chapters.

Method

I have defined "normativity" narrowly as prescription. It does not seem that Marx prescribes personal conduct in the sense of providing a conventional morality. Rather, what is alleged is that Marx prescribes the kind of society we should live in, morally condemning capitalism and commending communism.

Marx himself wrote in a left-wing milieu in which moralizing was hardly unknown, as he noted (*The Collected Works of Karl Marx and Frederick Engels* 6, 312; henceforth ME). After him, some Marxists sought either to hybridize his thought with ethical theories, particularly German neo-Kantians in the early twentieth century who identified communism with Kant's Kingdom of Ends. There have also been occasional attempts to extrapolate novel moral theories from Marx's thought. However, Marx himself explicitly disavowed morality, inveighing that "communists do not preach morality at all" (ME 5, 247). All commentators agree that Marx, at least at some point in his life, holds that morality is an ideological artefact relative to given modes of production. Conversely, however, all readers of Marx agree that there is some juvenile phase of Marx's thought in which he held opinions that are not those he held later in life, but rather opinions that he would himself repudiate—conventional, bourgeois, idealist opinions. At this early point, he clearly did engage in moralism. Exactly at what point and to what extent Marx breaks with immature views is a matter of intense and longstanding disagreement, though it is generally agreed (even by Althusser, the anti-Hegelian Marxist par excellence) that some of Marx's youthful Hegelianism in particular continued to inform his perspective throughout his life.

My business here is not hermeneutic Marxology: while I do mean to interpret Marx accurately, my primary aim is to argue that it is possible and desirable to avoid normativity in political thought. I cannot engage in a systematic reading of Marx's entire output in this relation—others have attempted this, but it is clearly a matter for entire books—so I constrain myself for the most part here to refuting serially arguments that Marx did have a normative stance. Much of this is a matter of explaining how instances of allegedly moral vocabulary in Marx's work can in fact operate in a non-normative way. There is no question that Marx uses polemical vocabulary, but I question whether it is meant to express anything more than subjective disapprobation.

I focus here on a particular, recent episode of the long history of Marxist or pseudo-Marxist moralizing, namely, Marxist analytical political philosophy since 1970. This episode was contemporaneous and overlapped with a movement called "analytical Marxism," that is, the attempt to inscribe Marxism within an "analytical" framework. Analytical Marxists left behind what they saw as Marx's tendency toward Hegelian mystification, instead reinterpreting Marxism within a framework of "methodological individualism," that is, by starting with individual humans as the basic units of analysis and attempting to justify Marxism as a rational choice. This diverges from Marx's thought in multiple respects. Analytical Marxism is itself primarily a social-scientific movement, only marginally concerned with the question of normativity, hence most of the commentators I will refer to here are not "analytical Marxists" in the strict sense, but rather analytical philosophers who are Marxists, concerned with articulating Marxism as a perspective within post-Rawlsian "political philosophy," understanding it therefore as a normative enterprise, providing a prescriptive theory of social organization, closely related to or synonymous with normative ethics. Thus, Marxism is for them the claim that communism is good and just and right, by contrast with the existing way of doing things, capitalism, which is held to be bad, unjust, and wrong; hence, we have a moral duty to be communists.

It does indeed seem prime facie plausible to suggest that Marxism involves such a normative evaluation of capitalism. Now, it is generally recognized that Marx's attitude toward capitalism is somewhat ambivalent, in that he makes some apparently laudatory remarks about capitalism vis-à-vis previously existing systems, but he nevertheless clearly opposed capitalism in favor of what he calls "communism." However, I will maintain that, with the exception of some very juvenile work, he never normatively condemns capitalism. He did use undeniably normative vocabulary as late as 1847, though not in any of his major works after his 1844 *Manuscripts*. Some scattered normative invocations after this would in any case still be compatible with my claim that Marx's mature political thought is essentially non-normative. But I will argue that even such apparently normative terms as he is alleged to use after 1847 do not genuinely have normative force.

Some interpreters of Marx, particularly in the Frankfurt School tradition, take the view that his early writings hold the key to understanding his thought because they give us the normative basis on which the later work is articulated. At the opposite extreme, in Althusser's interpretation, Marx's early work is considered "non-Marxist" precisely because it contains "humanist" subjectivist concepts, which he was later to jettison. Normativity in and of itself is not Althusser's concern, though anti-normativity is certainly in line with the thrust of Althusser's "anti-humanist" interpretation of Marx, and Althusser (1969, 45) does explicitly reject "ethical" interpretations of Marx's thought as such (see also Kain 1988,

6). A rather different approach is pursued by Foucault (1980, 76), who sidesteps the entire problem by saying that "Marx doesn't exist," in the sense that there is no single theoretical position represented by all of Marx's writings. Myself, I have no horse in the race of Marxology, but rather am concerned only to show against normative interpreters that it is at least possible for Marx to avoid normativity in a sense that they think is impossible.

Vocabulary

I am not aware of any scholar who claims that Marx adopts a straightforwardly normative perspective consisting in labeling certain things "good" and others "bad." In any case, Marx does not do so. If one investigates, for example, occurrences of the word "evil" in Marx's collected works (a term used to translate multiple terms from Marx's original German), one finds it used in a normative sense only in his early writings, for example, in a short set of 1847 notes on wages not intended for publication, where he talks about the "evil" (*Verwerflichkeit*) of wages (ME 6, 436), by contrast with what he calls there the "positive aspect" of capitalism. After this, "evil" does not appear in his works again in such a direct way.[1] He frequently criticizes the use of good and evil as a conceptual pairing, and often invokes the word "evil" to mock his theoretical opponents, particularly the anarchists, especially Bakunin, for deeming the state evil. Most occurrences of the word are in passing, in quoted speech, discussing the views of others, in a loose, idiomatic way of talking, or in private correspondence pertaining to personal matters (Marx more than once calls the moment where his personal financial affairs will collapse into penury as "the evil hour"). There are perhaps only two exceptions, where he uses the adjective in a serious and political context. In *The Civil War in France*, Marx does speak of an "unavoidable evil," but this simply means a thing the Commune would have dispensed with if it could, but couldn't yet; compare Marx's collaborator Friedrich Engels's use of the same phrase, writing about military matters, describing the digging of inadequate trenches as "an unavoidable evil" (ME 14, 546). In a newspaper article, Marx describes Napoleon III as an "evil genius," but this is pure polemic. Perhaps the best candidate for a normative use of the term after 1847 is in an 1849 article in the *Neue Rheinische Zeitung*, where he speaks of "the evil effects of the division of labor" (ME 9, 226). The German word translated as "evil" here is *unheilvoll* (*Marx-Engels-Werke* 6, 420; henceforth MEW), which doesn't mean "evil" in a moral sense, so much as in this case that there are effects for the workers—specifically, in this case, falling wages and lengthening hours—straightforwardly unpleasant for those who experience them.

Alienation

Let us move on, then, to terms that actually are in contention among commentators. Perhaps the most contested of these is "alienation." This concept is often held up as the key normative notion of Marx's entire thought. I regard it, however, as descriptive rather than normative. In this I oppose both proponents of a normative critique of alienation, and Althusser, who deems this concept idealist baggage to be avoided altogether.

Marx's invocation of alienation might seem to involve positing a natural, unalienated state as a norm and then decrying its nonexistence under capitalism. But the basis for his critique of alienation is actually a Feuerbachian conception of humans as having indefinite potentiality (Barbour 2012, 83).[2] Alienation is according to this interpretation ultimately simply a matter of the limitation of potential. Opposing the limitation of human potential might take on the character of a normative value, if it is used to say that any system that limits us is *eo ipso* bad. This is not Marx's position, however; it is rather that limiting human potential means that the system itself will be resisted and overthrown by humans who want to do more than allowed, with a society without alienation the teleological end of the historical dialectic of human liberation this sets up. This is a descriptive thesis, even if it is one that I would reject as speculative. The category of alienation does not in itself imply such a teleology, however. Jacques Lacan, for example, understands alienation (albeit not in exactly the same sense as Marx) to be ineluctable to human experience—in such a usage, it is clearer that this is not a normative concept, but rather simply descriptive.

This understanding of Marx's notion of human nature can also be used to rebuff the claim that his condemnation of capitalism as "inhuman" is normative (Peffer 1990, 57). This might be taken to imply that capitalism is condemned for not according with a particular human nature, but actually it may instead be understood as implying only that capitalism limits humanity.[3]

"Alienation" is a peculiar case of allegedly normative vocabulary in Marx in that he abandons it after a certain point. This seems to suggest that Marx, too, may have thought it normative, or at least otherwise infelicitous. Other normative vocabulary in Marx that is pointed to by normativizing readers is much more circumstantial, consisting of everyday terms with apparent normative force that are used by Marx in passing without any particular thematization. Those I will now consider are "slavery," "theft" (and some closely related terms), and "exploitation." I will focus particularly, but not exclusively, on two texts by Marx: first, volume one of *Capital*, because it is Marx's magnum opus; second, the much more marginal *Critique of the Gotha Programme*, because it is perhaps the clearest statement of Marx's anti-normativism, and from relatively late in his life.

It is worth noting the extraordinary weight put by commentators on circumstantial evidence of allegedly normative vocabulary used by Marx in passing, taking this to trump Marx's explicit disavowals of morality. Norman Geras (1992, 54) argues that since there was no obligation on Marx to use apparently normative vocabulary, such as "theft," since he could use neutral language without any apparent normative meaning, that he uses it indicates an intentional normative alignment. This argument might make sense if Marx otherwise employed only neutral, technical vocabulary. However, Marx's style is not marked by cold restraint, but rather is firebrand rhetoric, rich in metaphor. Of course, Marx's predilection for rhetoric may be seen itself to betoken a lack of neutrality. Non-neutrality, however, is not the same as normativity, because there are reasons other than normative ones for partiality, and moreover even expressing a normatively grounded partiality in writing does not in itself amount to propounding normative claims.

I do not believe that any of those who argue that Marx's vocabulary is ineluctably normative are brought to believe this by the terminological evidence. Geras and others of his ilk do not argue that Marx could have taken the positions he took without taking a normative stance, but just happened to fail to do so because of the vocabulary he used. Rather, they argue that Marx's general position is ineluctably normative, and then seek to adduce lexical evidence of this. It seems to me that their basic premise is that you cannot be critical of something, such as capitalism, without having a normative basis for doing so. I don't accept this premise: I believe antipathy for capitalism need not to be normative, but can simply reflect a non-normative preference. I might not like having my house flooded, might wish it would stop flooding, might analyze the reason it is flooding, and even perhaps engage in political action aimed at getting the state to provide better flood defenses. In order to take systematic action against flooding, I would have to enlist other people to my cause, but this requires only that other people share my preference. None of this implies a normative assessment of flooding as morally bad or positive normative assessment of flood defenses as a moral good. It is perhaps possible to make such assessments—utilitarianism in particular is a metaethics that might allow one to normatively condemn natural phenomena—but not necessary. The same can be said of abolishing capitalism. Of course, capitalism is generically different to flooding: the former is a social order, the latter a physical problem; the former, unlike the latter, has a normative framework internal to its constitution, moreover, as Marx himself allows. Still, I do not accept that this means that opposition to capitalism must itself be normative, and I will in some chapters below, particularly Chapter 6, refute claims that the normativity of society means political thought must be normative.

Exploitation and Justice

The instances where Marx is alleged to use normative terms are always ones where he describes exploitative labor relations. Thus, I will begin by considering the term "exploitation" itself. This is a key concept in Marx's thought, rather than merely a piece of invective. He explains himself how to interpret this term non-normatively.

Marx contends plausibly that workers have the capacity to produce more than they need, and in capitalism that they are induced to produce more than the receive: they are paid wages that are on average significantly less than the value of the work they do, and the remainder "surplus value" is the source of profit for their employers (ME 35, 227). This is exploitation.

Some deem this situation unjust and demand that workers be paid the full value of their labor. In his *Critique of the Gotha Programme*, Marx disputes this, contending that to claim that we are owed all the products of our labor is absurd because it would imply that anything given to unproductive members of society—children, the sick, administrators—is either charity that workers should be able to freely choose to give or not to give, or is itself unjust. Since all labor is itself socially produced, however, caring for society at large is not an optional extra.

The eponymous Gotha Programme, a German socialist manifesto that Marx is critiquing, recognizes this fact formally—if not sufficiently for Marx's liking—demanding that since labor is only possible in society, all value belongs to the whole of society. Marx rails against this, too, however, saying first that workers don't produce all value, since nature already furnishes plenty of value, and that if labor really were the source of all value, it wouldn't belong to the whole of society, but to the workers (ME 24, 81–82). Marx's point here is purely critical, designed not to set up a new criterion for deciding how to distribute nature and society's bounty justly, but to dispose of any talk about a just distribution in opposition to capitalism. He accordingly rails against an explicit demand in the Programme for a "just distribution of the proceeds of labor" (MEW 19, 18),[4] inveighing that, by the standards of the contemporary order, the existing distribution is already just, specifically because the current organization of production (capitalism) is based on this pattern of distribution. He casts "'equal right' and 'fair distribution'" as "ideas which in a certain period had some meaning but have now become obsolete verbal rubbish" (ME 24, 87).

Marx famously imagines here instead an incipient communist society, "emerging" from capitalist society, but "still stamped with the birthmarks of the old society" (ME 24, 85), in which people will have to be paid for the work they do, to be followed by full communism in which such bourgeois hangovers will be dispensed with in favor of a situation where contributions flow "from each according to his ability, to each according to his needs." This slogan might seem like a normative principle for an alternative just distribution, but I read it not as a prescription per se so much as a prediction, and not as a distributive principle so much as the slogan of the abolition of distribution as a problem. Marx allows that practical measures will need to be taken for distributing goods during an interim phase of abolishing capitalism, but this is a pragmatic question, not one of justice. He then gives us the above slogan, which is often interpreted as distributive,[5] but amounts to saying "everyone will contribute what they can, and take what they need." While one could imagine this as a maxim for a police state that will force people to contribute to their maximum ability, and carefully distribute things according to estimated requirements, I think it is clear from the context that this is not Marx's intention, since he believes that communism will also see the state cease to exist, but rather that in a communist society, people will be entirely liberated from any compulsion, and instead will produce freely, and everyone will be provided for by this production. Clearly, this must involve "distribution" in the literal sense of logistical movement of goods, but not in the sense of rationing and formal apportioning goods. Certainly, I would regard this as a dubious prediction at best, but Marx believes he knows this will happen, rather than seeing it as a contingent desideratum to be brought about on normative grounds.

Justice—and more specifically, just distribution—is the primary concept of (post-)Rawlsian analytical political philosophy, so Marx's rejection of the notion in *Critique of the Gotha Programme* is a major obstacle for analytical Marxists trying to read Marx as making a recognizable contribution to political philosophy. If they are not simply to reject Marx's position here, they must read *The Critique of the Gotha Programme* as endorsing some form of distributive justice, despite Marx's explicit claims to the contrary. Geras (1992, 54) cites Marx's (ME 35, 581) use of the term "unpaid labor" here as evidence that Marx did see exploitation as unjust, despite Marx's explicit denial. Does this notion that some of workers' labor is not paid for contradict Marx's position in *Critique of the Gotha Programme* that existing pay rates are just? No, since he never claims that workers are paid for all their labor, only that their remuneration is just. That is, the workers' labor is worth more than the pay they receive, but they are paid a lower amount because it is a buyer's market. Here we see the difference between value that labor adds to a product and the exchange value of the labor: the market determines the rate of pay, justly by bourgeois lights, but labor produces more value than its cost. These indeed are the necessary conditions for the employment of labor in capitalism, and hence for the existence of capitalism.

Slavery

Marx's use of the concepts "exploitation" and "surplus labor" to refer only to profits, and not to the socially necessary use of a productive surplus to support those members of society who are not engaged directly in production that is presumably a feature of every possible society and not just capitalism, might be taken to be a normative distinction. However, this distinction is not ineluctably normative. We can make the distinction on other grounds, for example political ones. It seems to me that this is exactly what Marx does at the end of his *Critique*, by criticizing exploitation in terms not of justice, but as a form of slavery (ME 24, 92).

Now, it is sometimes alleged, for example by Rodney Peffer (1990, 145–146), that "slavery" is itself a term of normative condemnation. It seems to me that this is not always the case: in a society where slavery is legal, to say that someone who is categorized as a slave is indeed a slave is a simple description. However, since capitalism is not a slave society in this explicit way, it might seem that it therefore constitutes a normative condemnation here.

Here, I think much turns on the metaphorical versus literal application of the label. In our society, literal accusations of "slavery" are not so much a moral condemnation as a statement that a particular crime has been committed, violating labor laws and human rights norms. Metaphorical accusations of slavery, by contrast, seem to be normative, accusations that people are being made to work too much or in conditions that are too bad, effectively a matter of rhetorical hyperbole in relation to these accusations.

Now, I hold that Marx means this term literally, not to mean that the juridical norms banning slavery have been violated, but I also do not believe he means the accusation as mere hyperbole. His accusation is rather that the condition of proletarians of his time amounts to objective slavery, even though the law of the day does not recognize it as such, because they are coerced into working. The only way for the working class in nineteenth-century Europe to survive is to sell their labor power, since, unlike their peasant forebears, they have no access to land that they can work to support themselves, so they are not genuinely free to choose whether or not to work for their bosses. While a particular worker might not have to work for any particular employer, and hence is not legally enslaved, the worker must nonetheless work for some or other capitalist—"enslavement to capital is only concealed by the variety of individual capitalists" (ME 35, 609)—the alternatives being starvation or the workhouse.[6] Marx likens the Gotha Programme to a situation where

> among slaves who have at last got behind the secret of slavery and broken out in rebellion, a slave still in thrall to obsolete notions were to inscribe on the programme of the rebellion: Slavery must be abolished because the feeding of slaves in the system of slavery cannot exceed a certain low maximum! (ME 24, 92)

Marx advances no argument however that slavery is bad. His intention is rather simply to show workers something they do not realize about their condition—that is, that it is coerced rather than free, and hence they are actually slaves, though theirs is a "veiled slavery" (ME 35, 747). The normative status of slavery is not decisive here: it doesn't matter whether slavery is considered bad, since workers are unlikely to want to be slaves themselves regardless of what normative gloss is put on the term, and moreover are tricked about this status. Proletarians who, for example, supported the enslavement of Africans, and thus did not regard slavery in itself as morally abhorrent, might nonetheless be appalled to learn that they themselves were enslaved, if perhaps under conditions more favorable than the explicitly enslaved. Of course, by Marx's lights, showing that white workers are also slaves ought to encourage their solidarity with enslaved Africans, since he wants workers to oppose slavery in general. This is not a pious wish of his so much as integral to his understanding of history, by which the working class will be the last class to be freed and will free all classes with them in their revolutionary overthrow of capitalism.

Marx similarly does not condemn "exploitation" as morally wrong or unjust, but rather means it to describe the economic dimension of wage slavery. It is its relation to slavery, which is to say to coercion, that differentiates exploitation from the relation of workers to members of society who must be provided for by their labor but are not characterized as profiting from it: the proprietors hold the whip over the workers, while children and the infirm do not. By contrast, right-wing libertarians in welfare states complain that the state is coercing them to do extra work through taxation, but this notion of coercion falsely imagines that the system of production in which they make money exists indifferently to the existence of the state and the population it cares for.

Theft

Marx's uses the term "theft" on the same pattern as "slavery" and "exploitaiton." This term is different inasmuch as it appears to be an entirely juridical concept, one pertaining to a legal distinction between taking that is legally sanctioned and taking that is not; as Foucault (1980, 36) says, "It is from the point of view of property that there are thieves and stealing." Foucault (1988a, 113) indeed explicitly says of Marx that "Marx replaced the denunciation of theft by the analysis of production." Since Marx demands the abolition of private property, and "theft" is specifically a crime of property, it is unclear how he can consistently invoke theft as a critical concept at all, yet he does sometimes criticize things that are legal in our society as "theft." The answer in my view is that, though he does use the term, it is not a matter of (normative) denunciation, but of analysis. Specifically, I suggest Marx's invocation of theft is best understood as a description of the taking of something through force.

The case of "robbery" (*Raub*), a term that occurs much more frequently in *Capital* than "theft" (*Diebstahl*), is clearer, since "robbery" directly implies coercion: the usual difference between a theft and a robbery is, I take it, that the latter implies accompanying menaces; robbery is a kind of theft, and thus any robbery—a coercive appropriation—is classifiable and describable also as theft, but "theft" may also describe situations where things are taken surreptitiously. This implies that any individual use of the term "theft" might describe a situation of robbery.

Marx speaks, for example, of the "systematic robbery of what is necessary for the life of the workman while he is at work" (ME 35, 429). The things that are robbed from workers—"space, light, air" (ibid.)—they had in their earlier, agrarian existence enjoyed, whereas now they are deprived of them during work hours. This is systematic because it has been wrought societally over a generation through a pattern of action, and it is robbery because it has been done by force without the consent of its victims. Marx even accuses capitalism "not only of robbing the laborer, but of robbing the soil" (ME 35, 507)—that is, taking out of it without replenishing its fertility, forcibly removing what it once had. In both cases, it is clear that Marx is not a neutral bystander, but his partiality is not of a strictly normative type: while one might say that he is holding up the norm that this taking should not be happening, he does not need to have such a normative assessment for him to describe the removal of these things as a kind of robbery, only a descriptive assessment that something has been taken and taken by force.

Turning to "theft," Marx uses the term *Diebstahl* in *Capital* to describe the selling of state lands to capitalists in England, but he is quite explicit that in such cases the sales were strictly speaking in violation of the law (ME 35, 714; MEW 23, 751). He then goes on immediately thereafter to use the word *Raub* (robbery—though it appears in the English translation as "theft") to refer to the formally *legal* "forcible usurpation" of anciently commonly owned lands by acts of enclosure (ME 35, 715; MEW 23, 752).

Geras (1985, 73) claims Marx's use of the term "usurp" (*usurpieren*) itself elsewhere in *Capital* is normative, because usurpation must be illegitimate to count as such (ME 35, 370; MEW 24, 790). But Geras is simply wrong about the meaning of the word: while in English "usurp" usually carries a connotation of illegitimacy, it can be used in English, as in German, as with its Latin root, to mean taking power by force *within* the bounds of legality.

A related term, *entwenden*, or rather its English translation as "embezzlement" (which is a tendentious rendering, since the German word refers fairly broadly to theft), is seized on by Geras (1992, 54) in this passage from *Capital*: "The greater part of the yearly accruing surplus product, embezzled, because abstracted without return of an equivalent, from the English laborer, is thus used as capital, not in England, but in foreign countries" (ME 35, 607). Here Marx is describing exploitation as theft. He similarly in the *Grundrisse* describes exploitation as the "theft of alien labor time" (ME 29, 91—labor here being "alien" in the sense that it is the workers' not capital's).

Is Marx not here finally applying some higher standard of justice, as Geras (1992, 47) thinks? Once again, I think in this case that the concept is invoked, like "slavery," and indeed "exploitation," simply to refer to coercion and the lack of consent of the victim. Keith Graham (1992, 51) argues that we can distinguish between *de facto* and *de jure* senses of ownership and rather tenuously that Marx employs this distinction in a passage in the third volume of *Capital*, where he says that "Landed property presupposes that certain persons enjoy the monopoly of disposing of particular portions of the globe as exclusive spheres of their private will to the exclusion of all others" (ME 37, 609), but that "Nothing is settled with the legal power of these persons" (ME 37, 610). Graham (1992, 112) briefly expounds an argument resembling mine in interpreting Marx on exploitation and robbery. Geras (1992, 63) dismisses Graham's position in a footnote, on the basis of Graham's glib reference to the *Shorter Oxford Dictionary* in determining the meaning of "robbery" and that Graham "does not derive that meaning from anything textually specific about the usages in question in Marx's own work." That we have the dictionary definition of the meaning of words on our side, however, seems to me *ceteris paribus* a point in our favor.

Geras (1984, 66) also mentions the interpretation of Marx's use of "theft" as being about coercion in passing in an earlier article, citing Allen Wood (1979) as its source, but thinks it unworthy of serious consideration. Geras's (1984, 68) counterargument is shorter than a sentence: "'robbery' has a meaning distinct from 'coercion' and we are given no reason to believe either that Marx was ignorant of the distinction or that he chose to overlook it." It is obviously the case that robbery is not the same thing as coercion, but robbery is defined by coercion, in addition to the taking of some thing.

It might be argued that there is an implicit normative condemnation of "coercion" in all this, that Marx is a kind of libertarian, promoting negative freedom as a normative value. Yet Marx does not side with freedom per se, refusing to be "deluded by the abstract word Freedom" (ME 6, 463). The invocation of coercion need not be normative: there is no need to show that coercion is morally bad for people to rail against it in their own case. The desire for freedom thus plays a role in Marx's theory, but as a fact, not a norm. Here, as Foucault (2007b) himself acknowledges, what Marx is doing is very close to what Foucault did a century later in his critical analysis of power relations: Marx shows people hidden connections that affect them. It is perfectly possible for people to object to the operation of capitalism on the basis that they are the ones being exploited, without any normative claim that "there ought to be no exploitation," only a desire not to be exploited. Now, in practice there is often a slippage between the two things. Opponents of exploitation will be tempted naturally to elevate their objection to an ethical cause. Indeed, is an ethical viewpoint not tactically useful to revolutionaries? This is more or less György Lukács's (1971) position in advocating a Marxist ethics—that the workers need to see the communists as principled if the latter are to gain the former's support. But if this is so, it is a matter of the pragmatics of activism, not a necessity in political thought itself. While it might even be argued that a political movement would need to propound some kind of morality, its ultimate grounds for doing so would then be effectively a question of marketing.

Still, it does not seem necessary for a movement to coalesce around normative claims. All that is necessary is a recognition of mutual interest under a slogan like "an injury to one is an injury to all." The invocation of interests here is merely intended as one example of an alternative possibility for the motivation of collective and individual political action; as Marx points out in reaction to Max Stirner, insisting on the selfishness of human motives is itself a normative stance, whereas "communists do not preach morality at all," rather allowing that "egoism, just as much as selflessness, is in definite circumstances a necessary form of the self-assertion of individuals" (ME 5, 247).

This point is relevant in rebutting an argument mounted by Steven Lukes (1985) that members of the middle class like Marx must, unlike ordinary workers, have a moral motivation for their opposition to capitalism, since they effectively are acting on behalf of others. I have certainly argued that Marx appeals to workers on the basis that they are coerced and deceived. Marx's point against Stirner however is that, while one might have selfish motivations, human motivations are not necessarily selfish. With Marx, I would reject an exhaustive dichotomy between self-interested actions and morally motivated altruism.

It is clear enough that Marx could as a young man have chosen to pursue a comfortable legal career, but was seized by a rage against the status quo to which he devoted his life. It is also clear that in his youth this rage found explicitly moral expression. However, it doesn't follow that morality is the key to understanding Marx's decision. While he may not have been a proletarian, there are plenty of reasons for people of more fortunate classes to dislike capitalism too. One might, for example, refer here to Hegel's master–slave dialectic to indicate that not only slaves but their masters are alienated and caught in an experience that is to be opposed.

In any case, the motivational question is strictly speaking extrinsic to the matter under discussion here, viz. the possibility of a non-normative political thought. Even if Marx had moral reasons for engaging in political thought, this does not imply that that thought is itself intrinsically normative, particularly since even by Lukes's lights it aims to appeal to an audience who by and large do not need to have a moral motivation for heeding it.

Allen Wood (1990, 512) agrees that Marx completely eschews morality, but argues that he nevertheless takes a "normative" stance via an Aristotelian conception of human nature, which requires certain conditions to fulfill it. It is beyond my scope here fully to consider the merits of Marxist Aristotelianism, which has in recent decades become a school in its own right, although I think it is worth noting that if Marx thinks we can't use the bourgeois form of morality, it would seem quite odd within his theory of history to instead hearken back to an ethics from antiquity. I would also say, though I lack the space here to make this argument fully, that I do not consider Aristotelian ethics to be normative in the modern sense. Rather, after Foucault, I would deem ancient ethics, including Aristotle's, to be a matter of a style of living rather than of prescribing norms of conduct, as modern "ethics" does. Aristotelian ethics consists in an account of human capacities with the aim of maximizing these "virtues." Such a "virtue ethics" does not involve normative prescriptions in the modern sense, but rather seeks to encourage people to maximize their capacities. While Aristotle's account of capacities may in the end be normative in elevating certain human activities above others, for him, ethics is a practical, therapeutic, and aesthetic art of character based on empirically grounded claims about what is best for particular men. For Foucault, the commitment to ruthless criticism qua the strategic opposition to power via a will to truth itself could be said to constitute a kind of ethics. This is an ethics of the intellectual, of the critic, however, not a normativity inherent in his political thought itself.

Communism

Despite everything, however, I will allege that Marx remains somewhat normative, and condemn him on this basis. Schematically, I think the problem is that, while eschewing normativity, Marx remains theoretical, and one cannot have a political theory without some form of normative presupposition. Specifically, if there is one place where normativity lurks in Marx's schema, it is in his idea of communism.

This is not to say that for Marx communism provides the norm, in the sense of comprising a utopian vision of what should be against which to find other states of affairs wanting. Marx cannot denounce capitalism by contrasting it with communism, because, on Marx's conception of it, we cannot know what will obtain under communism. He takes the position that "The working class . . . have no ready-made utopias to introduce. . . . They have no ideals to realize, but to set free the elements of the new society with which old collapsing bourgeois society itself is pregnant" (ME 22, 355). This neatly encapsulates Marx's position: he in the next sentence mocks anyone who attempts to describe what the new society might look like, but nevertheless believes that we can know that there is a new society in the offing. He posits communism only as the negation of capitalism: "Communism is for us not a state of affairs which is to be established, an ideal to which reality [will] have to adjust itself. We call communism the real movement which abolishes the present state of things" (ME 5, 49). Thus, we can say that exploitation will be abolished, but not what society will look like without it. The two "stages" of communism indicated in the *Critique of the Gotha Program* are merely partial and full abolitions of capitalism.

Sean Sayers (1994) suggests that, while a utopian vision of communism cannot ground a Marxist morality, communism can nevertheless offer an alternative basis for a post-bourgeois normative perspective to the extent that communism is already an emerging reality in our society today, just as capitalism (and with it, bourgeois values) appeared in the towns during the feudal period. While it is consonant with Marx to believe that communism is already emerging in the midst of capitalism, Marx does not himself say as much. It is thus a matter of some debate among Marxists, primarily on the basis of remarks of Engels about socialist morality, whether there might be morality in a post-capitalist society, but it seems to me that Marx's position in the *Critique of the Gotha Program* is that morality is itself as such either specifically bourgeois or at least an artefact of class society, such that he does not believe there is a morality proper to communism that can condemn capitalism.

The problem with Marx's notion of communism from a Foucauldian perspective is quite simply that Marx thinks that communism is inevitable. While its lack of determinate content means it evades the usual objections to political utopianism, Foucault (2002, 285–86) identifies Marx's Hegelian faith in the end of history as nonetheless utopian. Such prediction cannot but slip into normative territory because, though it aims to be descriptive, prognostication outstrips the limits of knowledge. Because Marx can't actually know the future in the way he claims to, but nonetheless claims this knowledge as certain, this belief can motivate action to fit reality to it, on the basis that any action to bring about communism is only bringing about what is bound to happen anyway. While I have defended Marx's anthropology as essentially open in its conception of human nature, his view of history is not so open, and this poses the same type of problem as would a set view of human nature, namely, by demanding reality accord with our idea. Foucault (1994c, 612) reads Marx as having failed to separate out two quite different tendencies found in nineteenth-century socialist thought, one toward prophecy, and the other toward strategic analysis. There is no question with which side Foucault aligns himself.

In the *Critique of the Gotha Program*, Marx doesn't say in so many words that communism is inevitable, though he does say in so many words that certain "defects are inevitable in the first phase of communist society" (ME 24, 87). We could say perhaps that for Marx it is not a matter of what communism definitely *will* look like, but of what it would have to be like were it to exist. In point of fact, however, his discussion of communism in this late document does not speak of it conditionally, using "would" or the subjunctive, nor indeed even predictively in the future tense, but rather definitely, factually, in the present tense. In any case, to the extent that this description is conditional on communism being realized contingently, he nevertheless claims to know what its nature would have to be, which strikes me as problematic, for reasons I will now go on to describe in the next chapter in relation to Lenin's subsequent depiction of communism.

There have been systematic attempts to remove the prophetic dimension of Marxism, specifically Open Marxism. Such a form of Marxism may thereby genuinely avoid normativity, and may also reject theoretization. The self-application of the appellation "Marxism" would seem, however, to betoken a continuing dogmatic fidelity to Marx's thought, which belies its openness—this question of the nomination of Marxism will occupy a major position in Chapter 3.

2

Lenin

The Invention of Party Governmentality

> Marx would be horrified by Stalinism and Leninism.
>
> —Foucault 1998, 10

Lenin and Philosophy

I will now move on to consider the most historically significant instantiation of Marxism, that developed by Vladimir Lenin in the early twentieth century. It would of course be profoundly erroneous to understand Lenin's theory and praxis as the inevitable consequence of Marx's, but Leninism is a descendent of Marx's thought, and hence I believe it does serve to illuminate generic problems in Marxism, as well as having its own novel and particular problems.

I spent some time at the beginning of the previous chapter explaining why I was beginning this book with Marx. Including a chapter on Lenin I expect will surprise readers much more than having one on Marx. Perhaps it will seem natural enough given that the publication of this book follows close on the heels of the hundredth anniversary of the Russian Revolution, along with, I expect, a round of (re)assessments of Lenin's legacy, but my timing is entirely coincidental. Perhaps it will also be concluded that I am a recovering Leninist, but I am not. Rather, I have engaged with Lenin because, even in these allegedly post-Communist times, one finds many Leninists in left-wing intellectual circles. And I can readily understand why Lenin continues to enjoy esteem. I think he is a first-rate political thinker, underappreciated outside of Leninist circles in direct proportion to the degree he is overvalued within them. But Lenin is of course not primarily known as a thinker, and it is in this that Lenin is really a unique case: he was both the leading theoretician of the Russian Revolution and its main mover; he singlehandedly convinced the Bolshevik Party to launch a revolution at a time when they (entirely plausibly, I will argue) thought it was utterly premature. And yet it was successful, at least at putting the Bolshevik Party in general and Lenin in particular in power in Russia. The Russian Revolution is itself an utterly extraordinary historical event. Its spectacular success naturally made Lenin's theory and his praxis the rallying point for leftists worldwide, a status they have never managed entirely to lose in the century since. The Revolution, however, I view as a perverse catastrophe, inasmuch as it undermined and betrayed its own goals.

The October Revolution is a rare world-historical event in the extent to which one man seems to have determined it. So often people imagine themselves "changing the world" in accordance with their personal normative schemata, yet it is hardly ever the case that anyone makes a clear contribution to effecting such a change. By contrast, Lenin appears genuinely to have changed the world, though it is far from clear that this change was for the better, even by his own lights.

Schematically, I want to suggest that Lenin is an important political thinker but a monstrous politico, but that the monstrousness of his practice follows from prima facie subtle flaws in his thought. This diagnosis of "monstrosity" I intend not as a term of normative condemnation, but as a deliberate metaphor to describe the aesthetic effect of the combination of his democratic theory with authoritarian practice in a hybrid that is more disturbing than unalloyed tyranny. In line with the Leitmotif of this book, I will diagnose his mistake as one of doing normative political theory, instead of critically analyzing power relations. Vis-à-vis Marx in this regard, Lenin's thought actually represents a kind of backward step.

Lenin thought he was bringing about communism as Marx had predicted, but I will argue he actually created a society of a new type, unpredicted in Marx's thought or his own. The question of classifying Soviet society, and after it the other states that emulated the model established by the Soviet Union, has vexed Marxists for a century. Lenin invented his own classificatory system according to which the Soviet Union was merely "socialist," as opposed to fully "communist," a distinction not found in

Marx, who nonetheless, as detailed in Chapter 1, allowed for a graduated development of communism after capitalism. Lenin and his heirs acknowledged that the Soviet Union was not fully communist, but held that it was on the way there, in a transitional period identified as necessary by Marx, and was no longer capitalist. On the furthest extremes of the left, encompassing anarchists and ultra-left Marxists, the Soviet Union was decried as continuingly capitalist from the outset, since it still exhibited money, wage labor, and even some private enterprise. Many Leninists acknowledge a restoration of capitalism within the Soviet Union at some point during its history long before its final collapse: Trotskyists in the tradition of Tony Cliff say that capitalism was abolished by Lenin but restored by Stalin; those who prefer Stalin to Trotsky say that capitalism was restored following the former's death. Despite the sophistication of some analyses of the Soviet Union as capitalist, I think there is nonetheless a kind of fallacy of the excluded middle at work here, which is to say that most Marxists consider only the possibilities of communism or capitalism to describe the Soviet Union, because these are the only applicable categories found in Marx. Most Trotskyists characterize the post-Stalin Soviet Union as a "degenerated workers' state," which still excludes the middle, since the only alternatives are capitalist states and "workers' states," with the latter prone to degrees of degeneracy or deformation. It seems to me, however, that the Soviet Union was a society of a new type, a fact that few Marxists have managed to grasp, one in particular being the Trotskyist Hal Draper with his notion of "bureaucratic collectivism."

One reason for their failure here is perhaps that Marxists are committed to understanding society from a primarily economic point of view as a system of production, and politics as a system for organizing production. Foucault criticizes Marxism effectively in two directions at once in this regard, accusing Marxists (along with everyone else) in the first volume of his *History of Sexuality* of paying too much attention to the state, but later accusing them of failing to acknowledge the specificity of statecraft and its autonomy from economics, conceptualizing the latter with his notion of "governmentality," articulated in two annual lecture series at the Collège de France in 1978 and 1979, now published as *Security, Territory, Population* and *The Birth of Biopolitics*. Toward the end of the second of these series, Foucault notes the existence of what he dubs "party governmentality," the mode of government proper to one-party states. He announces his intention to study this phenomenon in the lectures of the following year (Foucault 2008, 191), but completely abandons this plan in favor of a return to ancient texts. Picking up Foucault's thread here, I will locate a seminal moment in the genealogy of party governmentality in Lenin. His Bolsheviks were hardly the first political party, but no political party had before Lenin's innovations been so disciplined or militarized. Lenin's Soviet Union was also the first "one-party state"—previous authoritarianisms had not been based around a party. In both respects, the cadre party and the identity of the party with the state, the Bolsheviks provided the template for one-party governments of both left and right.

The political party first appeared in the context of contesting elections. One aspect of Lenin's breakthrough was to make the party a machine for contesting power outside of the electoral system, a quasi-military, quasi-clandestine model. This is not to say, however, that the model of the party developed by Lenin made party governmentality its inevitable telos. Parties on his model have operated in situations of democratic pluralism, and have won and given up government peacefully within such contexts—the recent history of Nepal provides a case in point, with multiple Leninist parties peacefully contesting power through the ballot box, even against a background of civil war.

Theory

I will focus in this chapter on a single text by Lenin, *The State and Revolution*. This is a monument in the development of a Marxist theory of the state, via close readings of Marx and Engels's writings. It represents the crucial intersection of Lenin's theory and practice, being written early in 1917, the very year that Lenin would later lead the revolution. It sits in tension with the consequences of that revolution, however. In what follows, I will first outline Lenin's theory of the state, then contrast this with the practice of the Bolsheviks' seizure of power in Russia, before moving on to consider what I see as the textual basis of compatibility between Lenin's theory and practice, dismissing various explanations proffered by commentators for the apparent disjuncture between them.

The central concept of *State and Revolution* is that of the "dictatorship of the proletariat" (Evans 1987, 4). This notion was originally coined, albeit marginally, by Marx. It has been widely misunderstood to imply the personal dictatorship of a single man in the name of the proletariat, a misinterpretation Lenin himself at one point in his life subscribed to, though in the *State and Revolution* he correctly interprets Marx's phrase to mean exclusive control by a single *class*, hence Marx's designation of our current situation as a "dictatorship of the bourgeoisie," the rule of the capitalist class, disguised as democracy. A dictatorship of the proletariat, by contrast, put the workers in control of the state as a new ruling class, asserting itself over the bourgeoisie. This dictatorship of the proletariat is for Marx incipient communism, leading ultimately to its own supersession with the final abolition of the state.

Marxist orthodoxy in Lenin's time cast this shift as requiring only the takeover of the existing state apparatus. Lenin argues, however, that the state that exists today is inherently bourgeois (Lenin, *Collected Works* 25, 387; henceforth L). According to Lenin, the dictatorship of the proletariat will not, strictly speaking, constitute a state at all, but would rather be so democratic as to constitute only a "semi-state," always already in the process of withering away to nothing. Lenin believes that the existing state must be smashed (414–415), and hence that revolution must be violent (400). To understand what a dictatorship of the proletariat would look like, Lenin draws primarily on Marx's account of the 1871 Paris Commune, the only actual example of a dictatorship of the proletariat Marx identifies as such.

Lenin, after Engels, describes the state as essentially consisting of two "departments": an organization of armed men on the one hand, and "public power," involving all other institutions of state, on the other (L 25, 388–389). Lenin argues that each of these departments must be smashed and replaced, as they were by the Commune. In his introduction to Marx's account, Engels calls the measures taken by the Commune to replace these departments "infallible" (ME 27, 190). *Pace* Engels, however, surely no scheme can be known to be absolutely fool proof, and the Commune is no exception.

In the case of public power, both bureaucrats and politicians were replaced with workers' delegates, elected by universal suffrage and subject to instant recall, who would act only as a mouthpiece for their electors and be paid as much as ordinary workers. Since such delegates have neither discretionary power nor privileges, they have no interests distinct from, nor can they take any actions against, those of the people who elect them.

The other department, the repressive apparatus, is to be replaced by the proletariat itself, under arms. This does not mean that no element of the old apparatus could survive: Lenin, for example, notes that the police were converted to the purposes of the Paris Commune rather than abolished (L 25, 418–419).[1] This conversion was possible because the police were subordinated to the authority of the proletariat, which had replaced the former primary repressive apparatus, the army (419).

Without this abolition of the specialized repressive apparatus, one could easily imagine that both delegates and electors could be menaced such that democracy would be subverted. Conversely, the proletariat under arms qua repressive apparatus constitutes a means of keeping the behavior of delegates in check. However, even with this measure, the proletariat itself may be misled. One might refer here to the importance of what Louis Althusser would later designate as the "ideological state apparatuses," which include what Lenin calls public power, but also institutions such as the family, religion, and education, which all contribute to producing people's attitudes and prejudices.

Of course, none of this is enough to constitute socialism: this requires a transfer of "ownership of the means of production" from "private" to "social," in addition to the "political reorganization of society" (L 25, 421). The economy thus also comes under the control of the proletariat through the delegate structure. This is necessary for the mutual reinforcement of the other measures, since allowing the economy to remain private leaves the bourgeoisie with inexhaustible fiduciary resources to bribe delegates and militia. Unless and until the bourgeoisie is completely abolished via the seizure of all its financial reserves, its capacity to corrupt remains. One reason these measures, even taken together, are not quite "infallible" is that we cannot presume that they will all be instituted simultaneously, perfectly, and without remainder. Still, it seems plausible to think that, taken together, they would imply the decisive abolition of domination by the capitalist class.

Lenin here derives from the Commune a schema for the political conditions of possibility of the abolition of capitalism, rather than an empirical claim about what measures would be efficacious (a claim that would be very weak since it would be based on only a single observed instance). This procedure strikes me as essentially similar to Marx's pronouncements about what would be necessary in incipient communism, albeit that Lenin goes further than Marx in describing it and does so on the basis of a concrete case study. In any case, Lenin's procedure is hardly a safe one, and amounts to a case of Marxist theoretical prognostication, which then carries a danger of slipping into normative claims that accordance with this model is good and anything that runs contrary to it is bad. This slippage does indeed occur, but proceeds in a surprising way.

Practice

In the October Revolution of 1917, the Bolsheviks, led by Lenin, smashed the core of pre-existing Russian state power. What replaced it, however, diverged from the schema Lenin had expounded earlier that year.

The political justification for the Bolsheviks' seizure of power was their control of the majority of the soviets. The soviets were councils with a delegate structure, hence the assertion of soviet power over parallel parliamentary bodies, first over the Duma in 1917 and, later, in 1918, over a freshly elected Constituent Assembly, neither of which were dominated by the Bolsheviks, might seem like proletarian direct democracy triumphing over bourgeois representative democracy. There was, however, no attempt to make good the slogan "All power to the soviets," by which power was seized. The Bolsheviks used their domination of the Congress of Soviets to elect an executive council, the Council of People's Commissars, and did not allow their domination of either body to be challenged in any way thereafter.

The Bolsheviks quickly began to lose grassroots support after the Revolution (Pavliuchenkov 1997, 142), with their Menshevik and Socialist-Revolutionary opponents winning majorities in the soviets of every provincial capital for which records exist in the elections of spring 1918 (Brovkin 1987, 159). The Bolsheviks disregarded these elections and dissolved the relevant soviets (Brovkin 1987, 137–138, 140–141, 143–144, 158; see also Pirani 2008, 96). The soviets were relegated to—at most—administering decisions made at the center rather than making policy.

It is generally argued by defenders of Lenin that this suppression of democracy was a temporary expedient necessitated by the civil war in the midst of which the new state was being built. Most of parliament sided with the counterrevolutionaries from the start. Some sympathetic parliamentary forces, primarily the Left Socialist-Revolutionaries, did ally with the Bolsheviks, but they soon rebelled too, which in turn led to their large-scale suppression. Tony Cliff (1960) argues that it was the rebellion of all other parties against the Soviet state that caused Russia to become a one-party state. However, one could argue, conversely, that the Bolsheviks forced all remaining legal opposition parties to rebel by stymying democratic challenges to their rule. The argument that Bolshevik political repression was necessitated exceptionally by conditions of war is belied moreover by the fact that they did not reverse this repression as the war ended, but rather began to repress even those who had engaged in no military opposition to their rule (Pirani 2008).

Lenin was largely absent from public life by the end of the war, incapacitated due to illness from 1922 until his death in 1924 (Lewin 1969, 34), but the threat to the revolutionary government decisively declined before 1922, with White and imperialist forces largely defeated, yet Bolshevik repressiveness continued to increase continuously. There was increasing intolerance of dissent even within the Party itself: opposition was banned, purged from the Party, and many Party members were arrested. A specialized repressive state apparatus had been created early in the Revolution, first in the form of the Cheka to enforce internal control, followed by the Red Army in January 1918. These organs replaced the Red Guards, the military wing of the Bolshevik party. The Red Army was immediately used to repress proletarians, including Red Guard units (Pavliuchenkow 1997, 143). While these repressive bodies were more proletarian and democratic than the armies of the Whites, they were no "armed proletariat," nor indeed even in the initial stages of the Revolution was the proletariat as such under arms in charge.

Thus, the Bolsheviks failed in perpetuity to implement the two cardinal measures of the dictatorship of the proletariat identified by Lenin himself. We could also mention his considerable vacillation on the question of control of the economy: capitalism was reintroduced under the New Economic Policy, but this was a genuine change of tack that reflected a compromise in the face of necessity, whereas the repressiveness never wavered.

Substitution

It has been argued that *State and Revolution* is simply an anomalous, utopian work of Lenin's that one should not take seriously (Evans 1987).[2] It is anomalous in his corpus, however, only by dint of the fact that it deals with theoretical questions he does not ask elsewhere. It is indeed the only place he states what his revolutionary aims were, or to what his frequent later references to the dictatorship of the proletariat are supposed to refer. Without this work, his political project would be vacuous.

Still, his later practice could be taken to indicate a serious change of mind. Simon Pirani opines that "the ideas in Lenin's *The State and Revolution*, which was written under the influence of the surge of soviet activity in 1917 and extolled popular participation in government, were dumped." Yet, as Ralph Miliband (1997, 525) notes, Lenin never explicitly disavowed the book.[3] Indeed, it was first published only *after* the October Revolution, which in itself seems to indicate a continuing relevance of its contents for Lenin, and I will argue that his post-revolutionary praxis does have a certain subliminal compatibility with *The State and Revolution*. As E. H. Carr (1950, 248–249) argues, it would "be a fundamental error to suppose that the experience of power brought any radical change in Lenin's philosophy of the state . . . in so far as this was inconsistent, the inconsistency was fundamental."

My contention is that the fundamental inconsistency in *The State and Revolution* lies in an ambiguity. This ambiguity relates to two major facets of the prospective revolutionary situation in Russia that Lenin ignores in the book, dealing rather only with generalities. These facets are the existence of the Bolshevik party, and the fact that the proletariat was only a small minority of the Russian populace.

The first omission is odd given that Lenin believed that proletarian revolution was only possible via a disciplined democratic centralist party, which in Russia meant the Bolsheviks. Democratic centralism entails that the leadership and platform of the party are decided democratically by the membership through the election of delegates to party congress, with the day-to-day running of the party entrusted to the thus-elected leadership, who have military-style authority over the party.[4]

Miliband (1970, 313) notes that there is "scant" mention of the party in *State and Revolution*, with only three direct references, of which only one says anything revealing, namely the following passage:

> By educating the workers' party, Marxism educates the vanguard of the proletariat, capable of assuming power and *leading the whole people* to socialism, of directing and organising the new system, of being the teacher, the guide, the leader of all the working and exploited people. (L 25, 404)

This passage is of crucial importance as the only point in the text where Lenin explicitly relates the party to the dictatorship of the proletariat.[5] Here, he affirms the importance of the party to revolution, but he signally fails to demarcate its precise role.

Miliband points out that it is ambiguous in this passage whether the "workers' party" and "the vanguard of the proletariat" of the party are supposed to be the same thing (I would add that this ambiguity, like the others I will discuss, exists in the original Russian). This makes it unclear whether it is only the party or some wider section of the proletariat that is to be educated and, in turn, to seize power.

I would furthermore point out that the phrase "vanguard of the proletariat" is ambiguous in itself: it is unclear whether this phrase means the proletariat itself qua vanguard, or a vanguard section of the proletariat not identical with the party (which may or may not include the party, and may be smaller or larger than the party), or is simply a synonym for the party.

Like the word "party," Lenin uses the term "vanguard" in *State and Revolution* only three times, the first being in the passage just quoted. The third is approximately as ambiguous as the first (L 25, 461), but Lenin's second use of the term in *State and Revolution* does unambiguously call the revolutionary proletariat itself the "armed vanguard of all the exploited and the labouring" (L 25, 425–426),[6] which is to say of what Lenin calls "the whole people," which in his lexicon specifically refers to the proletariat plus the peasantry (L 25, 416).[7]

The vanguard status of the proletariat is a basic tenet of Marxism: capitalism creates this dispossessed, predominantly urban class of propertyless wage-workers, who are in their density able—and in their penury and relatively high education inclined—to organize around demands for a new society. Thus, capitalism produces its own gravediggers. Though Marx does not describe the proletariat as a vanguard,[8] Engels does in an 1847 letter:

> The industrial proletariat of the towns has become the vanguard of all modern democracy; the urban petty bourgeoisie and still more the peasants depend on its initiative completely. (ME 6, 295)

Now, the metaphor of the vanguard strictly speaking only implies being at the forefront of the fighting. The proletariat is clearly placed in this role by Lenin, and indeed it took this role in the October Revolution.

Hal Draper (1987, 84) points out that Marx spoke of the dictatorship of the proletariat as a "movement of the immense majority," yet Lenin points out in *State and Revolution* that Marx lived in an age when the proletariat was a minority in every country (L 25, 416). This offers us two obvious alternative interpretations: either Marx didn't think the proletariat was ripe for revolution during his lifetime; or he thought that the dictatorship of the proletariat would involve the wider people, but the proletariat would be its prime movers. The former interpretation was that of most Marxists of Lenin's day; Lenin took the latter position.

Lenin had long argued against the majority of Russian Marxists that the small size of Russia's proletariat did not preclude launching a socialist revolution there. At the time of the 1905 Revolution, Lenin suggested that Russia might take an unorthodox course to socialism via a combined dictatorship of the proletariat and peasantry. In April 1917, Lenin claimed that this combined dictatorship had already been accomplished by the bourgeois revolution of February 1917 (L 24, 44–45). The task that remained was thus the establishment of the dictatorship of the proletariat proper, by breaking up the coalition of proletariat and petty bourgeoisie (in which latter category Lenin, following Marxist orthodoxy of the time, included the peasantry).

In *State and Revolution*, Lenin maintains a notion of a "people's revolution," in reference to the situation in France at the time of the Paris Commune,

> ... actually sweeping the majority into its stream, could be such only if it embraced both the proletariat and the peasants. These two classes then constituted the "people." These two classes are united by the fact that the "bureaucratic-military state machine" oppresses, crushes, exploits them. To smash this machine, to break it up, is truly in the interest of the "people," of their majority, of the workers and most of the peasants, is "the precondition" for a free alliance of the poor peasant and the proletarians, whereas without such an alliance democracy is unstable and socialist transformation is impossible. (L 25, 416–417)

While Lenin thinks this class alliance is necessary to make revolution, he defines the post-revolutionary government solely in terms of the proletariat. While on the cusp of his revolution, in September 1917, Lenin argues that "Only if power is based, obviously and unconditionally, *on a majority* of the population can it be stable during a popular revolution, i.e., a revolution which rouses the people, the majority of the workers and peasants, to action" (L 25, 367), this does not imply that the proletariat will share *leadership*. Similarly, he glosses his contemporary slogan of "power to the soviets" as meaning a "popular ... democratic apparatus ... i.e., the organized and armed majority of the people—the workers, soldiers and peasants" (368). He at this point calls for a "dictatorship of the proletariat and the *poor* peasants" (373)—apparently implying a shared leadership with some portion of the peasantry, namely, the least petty bourgeois element—this still leaves the possibility of excluding much of the peasantry, and differentiates this proposal from the situation of combined dictatorship he argued already existed before October.

How do we interpret this apparent vacillation? My interpretation is that it is possible because the underlying ambiguity of the concepts involved, specifically of the notions of vanguard and dictatorship, allows a free slippage between defining control by the people, by the proletariat, and by the party. Here we see a tendency in Lenin's thought identified by Leon Trotsky (1904)—as early as 1904—as Lenin's "substitutionism,"[9] the substitution of the party for the class, then ever narrower party layers for the layer below, leading to the final substitution of a single dictator for the people. Substitutionism is made possible not by an explicit identification, claiming that the party leadership is literally the same thing as the proletariat, which would be patently absurd, but rather by a slippage introduced by the logic of leadership, by which the leaders of the party lead the rest of the party, which in turn leads the proletariat, which in turn leads the people.

This slippage is observable in the Bolsheviks' revolutionary praxis. They consistently favored the proletariat over the peasantry. They seized power on the basis of the domination of a Congress of Soviets in which proletarian districts received representation five times higher in proportion to their actual population than rural ones. That is, the Bolsheviks dominated the Congress only because it was skewed toward their urban support base. The Bolsheviks lost the constituent assembly elections held after the Revolution because the peasants had more representation (though still not equal to that of the proletariat).

However, the Bolsheviks ultimately respected the will of the proletariat no more than that of the peasantry. Rather, they consistently interpreted "dictatorship of the proletariat" as synonymous with a dictatorship by the party, and indeed with the will of the party executive. Democracy was trumped by centralism both inside and outside the Party. Lenin banned factions within the Party, with party congresses becoming rubber stamps for the decisions of the center.

Étienne Balibar claims that Lenin consistently attempted to transfer power "to organizations of the masses of the people" (1977, 118–119).

His best evidence for this claim is that Lenin moved from demanding the subordination of the trade unions to the state and Party to encouraging their independence, with Balibar mentioning but dismissing an obvious alternative explanation that this move simply coincided with the New Economic Policy, in which unions again had to negotiate with capitalist employers. The overall picture, however, suggests that that alternative explanation is more plausible. Unions were certainly never allowed to challenge Bolshevik power.

Cliff, following Trotsky, lays great weight in explaining the side-lining of the proletariat on the relative destruction of that class during the Civil War, meaning that the proletariat was simply not extant to play its historical role, and thus that the party had to substitute for it. However, Pirani shows that as the proletariat began to reconstitute itself in the aftermath of the Civil War almost nothing was done to give it any more power. A rare partial exception was the People's Commissariat of Workers' and Peasants' Inspection, which worked on soviet elective-delegate principles as an anti-bureaucratization force from 1920 to 1923, championed personally by Lenin (Carr 1950, 226–228), but this commissariat did not comprise a mechanism for proletarians to exercise control over the state apparatus.[10] Ultimately, the people exercised influence only as a consideration of the state, that is, to the extent that the executive of any state must take into account the temperament of the ruled. All evidence suggests that the Bolsheviks lost the active support of the proletariat even by the narrowest definition of that class almost immediately after the revolution; they were compensated for this by great growth in support among white-collar workers within the state apparatus they constructed.

Lenin accepted that he had installed a dictatorship of the Party, but he saw this as simply the manifestation of the dictatorship of the proletariat and not in conflict with it (Miliband 1970, 314). Substitutionism stopped just short of the final substitution of one man for the whole during his lifetime, but paved the way for that substitution afterward.

Lenin notes that the majority of the proletariat have never joined a revolutionary movement in any country in the world. The German Social-Democratic Party, the largest workers' party that had ever existed at that time, organized only one in fifteen wage-workers in Germany. Lenin sees this as inevitable under capitalism: even where workers are enfranchised, they lack the time and energy to participate in politics due to the drudgery that characterizes their life under capitalism. He also mentions the function of the media in capitalist society and myriad other factors. Thus the conscious minority, which is to say the party, will have to take the lead in making revolution, since the majority are incapable of coming to desire it. This is a separate point to Lenin's controversial position on the necessity of the intervention of intellectuals in the working-class movement in his *What is to Be Done?*[11]—as Robert Mayer (1996, 1997) has shown, this argument was abandoned by Lenin, to the extent it was ever held, well before 1917; Lenin's position by 1917 is not that the working class need help from outside, but rather that the conscious minority of the working class must lead the whole.

This might seem to contradict his claim that power should be based on the support of the majority of the population. However, support does not require party membership or ideological adherence. This is concretized in the Bolsheviks' demands for "peace and bread" in the run-up to their revolution, which garnered support on a non-ideological basis.

Since Lenin believes a successful revolution must be based on majority support, logically he can infer from the success of a revolution that this support exists. However, Lenin's premise is wrong: a successful revolution does not require this level of support. While it seems unlikely that revolution could succeed where the immense majority actively *oppose* it, meaning that in a sense they must tacitly consent, such consent, which any state must effectively have in order to continue to exist, does not imply active support, since the great majority can simply be indifferent: all that is required to win a revolution is that the revolutionary forces defeat those of reaction, but all those involved in active contestation of power might together comprise only a small minority of the population. In the Russian Civil War, much of the population, the great majority of whom were peasants, were indeed not direct participants.

Alternative Explanations

Miliband (1970, 315) claims that Lenin did "question the identification" of party and proletariat, becoming obsessed with this by the time of his death. The only citation Miliband offers in support of this claim, however, is to Moshe Lewin's (1969) account of Lenin's last years, in which there is actually nothing to support Miliband's claim. The change of heart Lenin had in his last days was not about substitutionism per se, but really in the opposite direction: in 1923, days before his final incapacitation, Lenin suggests belatedly that the Russians "lack enough civilization to enable us to pass straight on to socialism" (L 33, 501). This resembles the longstanding position of the Mensheviks that Russia was not ready for revolution, but Lenin concedes only the lesser point that the post-revolutionary road to socialism in Russia was more tortuous than he initially envisaged.

Miliband (1970, 314–315) takes up this thesis, arguing that not only in Russia, but in general, Lenin failed to appreciate the problem of "political mediation." Miliband (318) holds that it was impossible to produce a dictatorship of the proletariat in 1970 when he himself was writing, let alone in Russia in 1917. He argues that a period of party government is a necessary transitional step to the dictatorship of the proletariat (317). He thinks that Lenin's determination of political mediation in terms of a single party is the core problem, that this is the fault of both Marx and Lenin for leaving the question of leadership "in abeyance" (314), and that one needs to make "adequate provision for *alternative* channels" to avoid single-party dictatorship (316).

Miliband here dismisses the solution of the problem of mediation to which Lenin himself actually refers in his writing, the Paris Commune, which operated without the party form through the delegate system. Miliband disqualifies the Commune by referring to Marx's diminution of it as a limited and mostly non-socialist rising, to the fact that only Engels and not Marx described the Commune as a "dictatorship of the proletariat," and to the fact that Engels, while taking the Commune as the archetype of a dictatorship of the proletariat, also said that the dictatorship of the proletariat must take the form of a democratic republic. Each of these considerations is unconvincing, however: that the Commune was mostly not socialist should make it all the more convincing as an example of the possibility of doing without political mediation, because it was able to achieve coordination despite a lack of an ideological consensus; that Marx did not sanctify it with the appropriate designation did not prevent Lenin from taking it up as a model; and that the Commune remained confined to Paris rather than taking place at a national scale was due primarily to the siege of Paris that prevented it from linking up with forces outside and does not preclude it from serving as a model for more widespread socialist government.

Moreover, Miliband does not explain how party government can lead to communism. Lenin conceives of an automatic transition between the dictatorship of the proletariat and full communism because the abolition of class distinctions renders the state progressively unnecessary, "the withering away of the state" envisaged by Marx. This process can hardly be expected to be uncomplicated, but Lenin in *State and Revolution* envisages the decisive step to abolishing the state being the revolution itself. If the revolution does not do this work, which it did not in the Russian case because a new state was created to replace the previous one, and would not on Miliband's model, then would-be revolutionaries seem to still face the problem of having to abolish the state. Miliband's solution, an open political terrain in which dissent and opposition parties are allowed, might remedy the ossification encountered in Russia, but would not much differ from the situation found already in a "democratic" dictatorship of the bourgeoisie. One might refer here to Balibar's (1977) thesis that the state form is intrinsically bourgeois and the proletariat will always have to struggle against state power even under socialism. Balibar's formulation here is an attempt to reinterpret Lenin's conception of the withering away of the state so that Lenin's construction of a new state can be said not to contradict his socialist ambitions, when it actually belied them.

Both Cliff and Draper (1987, 100), following Trotsky, explain Lenin's failure to realize his schema for the dictatorship of the proletariat with the fact of the Bolsheviks' international isolation. Draper argues that no Russian Marxist had ever thought that a dictatorship of the proletariat could exist inside Russia alone, and argues that indeed it could not, making the defeat of a genuine socialist revolution confined to Russia inevitable.[12] While Lenin did believe that a socialist revolution would occur more broadly than just in Russia, he never expressed a conviction that revolution elsewhere was necessary for revolution to succeed in Russia. He does not mention the international dimension of revolution in *State and Revolution*, nor in his other 1917 statements on the ability of the Bolsheviks to retain state power in Russia (L 26). He argues rather that the conditions are already present in Russia for soviet power to be "incomparably more powerful than previous forces," while also being the most democratic state apparatus ever seen (L 26, 103–104). He moreover never retrospectively invoked international isolation as a factor to explain the failure to establish the dictatorship of the proletariat in the years following the Revolution. Indeed, he could not, because he consistently maintained that the dictatorship of the proletariat had been achieved. One could argue that this was a rhetorical necessity, since the notion of proletarian rule was necessary to legitimate Party rule and prevent the collapse of the state, but there is every indication Lenin believed his rhetoric.

One might try to excuse the Bolsheviks' retention of power on the more modest basis that the likely alternative to it was the restoration of capitalism. Given that the Russian Revolution ultimately led to a restoration of capitalism by 1991, however contingently, this justification cannot any longer hold water, inasmuch as their actions failed to prevent this, such that the Russian Revolution seems with hindsight to have been pointless or counterproductive from the perspective of abolishing capitalism in the long term. As Pirani argues, "Socialism was damaged not only by the choices the Bolsheviks made, but by their sincere insistence that those choices were the continuation of the revolution, and by the powerful influence of their ideology on subsequent movements of social liberation" (Pirani 2008, 241).

Conclusions

Cliff (1960) claims that substitutionism can be avoided only if certain "necessary . . . objective conditions" are met, namely, those set out by Trotsky in 1903, that the "great majority" of "the working class" should be united in demanding socialism. Cliff thus implicitly rejects Lenin's position that achieving a conscious proletarian majority is both impossible and unnecessary.

Cliff's conditions are neither necessary nor sufficient to avoid substitution, however. They are not sufficient, because no matter how large the party, the substitution of the leadership for the party can still occur within it. Moreover, neither a conscious nor a proletarian majority is a necessary condition of a non-substitutionist dictatorship of the proletariat. To suppress counterrevolution, one needs only enough strength to triumph over whatever counterrevolutionary forces assert themselves. To have direct democracy, people need only to take part in running their own affairs; they do not need to be politically "conscious" or proletarian.

For Cliff (1960), the problem with attempting to build socialism from a combination that involves the peasantry is that, whereas the proletariat want to abolish private control of industry in favor of workers' collective control, the peasants desire private property in land. However, even to the extent that one can make statements about what peasants generically want, a desire to hold personal land rights does not prima facie constitute a roadblock to the abolition of private ownership of the means of production or to the democratic control of the economy. Lenin, in his final 1923 reflections on the Revolution, blames the impossibility of building socialism on the low level of "civilization" in the countryside.

But it is not clear which element of the *State and Revolution* dictatorship of the proletariat would be made impossible by "uncultured" peasants. The peasants had participated in soviets, and elected mostly socialist delegates—if not Bolshevik ones. In the absence of the old authority, the pre-existing social form in the villages involving peasants running their own affairs was identified explicitly by Marx as a possible basis for a socialist society in Russia (ME 24, 346ff.). Peasants could also participate in the armed suppression of counterrevolution. It is not necessary for them to support the abolition of all forms of private property, because that is needed only for full communism, not a transitional dictatorship of the proletariat.

We cannot know then whether it was possible to have socialism in Russia with delegate democracy and the absence of a specialized repressive apparatus in 1917, since this was never attempted. Even had it failed, perhaps the attempt to realize it would have done more for the proletarian cause than the dictatorship of the party that eventuated.

The problem here is not Lenin's model of party organization, democratic centralism. Much of Lenin's defense of democratic centralism in *Left-Wing Communism: An Infantile Disorder* can be accepted while rejecting substitutionism. A dictatorship of the proletariat constituting itself through delegate elections might contingently coincide with the political rule of the Party, since the people might overwhelmingly elect Party members. Even if we grant Lenin's position that without the Party the workers are incapable of making revolution, this does not imply that the Party must substitute for the class, nor that it automatically represents their interests. The Party can lead, can be a vanguard, without dictating. We can invoke here, as Cliff (1960) does, Marx's *Communist Manifesto* statement that Communists "have no interests separate and apart from those of the proletariat as a whole" (ME 6, 497). A party subordinating itself to these interests, avoiding substitution, could lead the proletariat in the direction of its own self-organization as a class. The problem arises when the *Manifesto* statement is fallaciously read backward, to infer that whatever the communist party's interests are, they must therefore be those of the proletariat.

Lenin poses the problem of how socialists can govern. Foucault (2008, 92) claims in his 1979 Collège de France lectures that "there is no governmental rationality of socialism," which is to say that socialists do not govern in a distinctive way, but rather only use governmentalities that are not intrinsically socialistic. The first socialist governments used liberal governmental methods, and then Lenin invented a new one, what Foucault (2008, 191) calls the "governmentality of the party," which I think I have demonstrated actually has little to do with socialism. It is unclear whether there is such a thing as a governmentality proper to socialism. Miliband effectively simply commends liberal governmentality to communists. By contrast, Balibar seems to say that the point of communism is in the end to oppose governmentality altogether. It seems to me that what Lenin outlines in *State and Revolution* similarly comprises not so much a distinctive governmentality as the abolition of government. It is as such, I think, that a Foucauldian can be sympathetic to it, even if its presumption that it is possible to abolish government is tendentious and prophetic, because it is essentially directed at the negation of existing relations. However, into this nullity, Lenin inserts the germ of party governmentality.

Lenin's vision of the dictatorship of the proletariat is an attempt to delineate the minimum conditions that would have to obtain for capitalism to be abolished. There is a difference, however, between the Commune's exemplary development of these means as a way of dealing with the situation after abolishing the old state, and Lenin's production of a positive theory based on this example, which serves not even as a dogmatic guide as action, so much as a normative cover for doing something different, as an excuse for being inattentive to the reality around him. To this extent, Lenin's is a classic example of normative political theory in action, with a utopian vision covering reality. In this relation, I would invoke Foucault's own remark on the Soviet experience:

> I think that to imagine another system is to extend our participation in the present system. This is perhaps what happened in the history of the Soviet Union: apparently, new institutions were in fact based on elements taken from an earlier system-the Red Army reconstituted on the model of the Czarist army, the return to realism in art, and the emphasis on traditional family morality. The Soviet Union returned to the standards of bourgeois society in the nineteenth century, and perhaps, more as a result of Utopian tendencies than a concern for realities. (1977, 230–231)

Foucault's Marxist interlocutor here tellingly responds by reference to the vicissitudes of the Russian Civil War.

From the perspective of this current book, Lenin represents an awkward position between politics and anti-politics, theory and anti-theory, and normativity and anti-normativity. Lenin realizes that his task is to smash politics, and dispense with morality, but he, like all Marxists of his time, regards Marxism as a total theory, and theory as an appropriate guide to action, and precisely by theoreticizing anti-politics turns anti-political principles into a politics and norm. Marx's teleo-eschatology is at least partly to blame here, whatever Marx himself would have thought of Lenin. Though some of the assumptions made by Lenin were not Marx's—Marx did not prescribe a revolutionary method—the Bolsheviks' confidence in the progress of their revolution was a case of Marxist historical determinism in practice.

3

Althusser

A Failed Project to Denormativize Marxism

> Althusser freed the traditional Marxist interpretation from all the humanism, from all the Hegelianism, and from all the phenomenology that burdened it, and thus made possible once again a reading of Marx that was no longer an academic reading but a truly political one. But as important as these Althusserian readings were at the start, they were quickly outstripped by a revolutionary movement that, although developing among students and intellectuals, is, as you know, an essentially antitheoretical movement.
>
> —Foucault 1998b, 422

Lenin's name was an odd term in our sequence in that it is generally not included in the canons of either continental philosophy or political theory. Our third name sheds some light on Lenin's inclusion, however, since it is that of a canonical figure in both sequences—Louis Althusser—who himself explicitly positioned himself as a Leninist. I read Althusser as attempting to get out of the problems of both Marx and Lenin's normative-political-theoretic entanglements, but ultimately failing to do so precisely because of his commitment to Marxism-Leninism.

It is perhaps worth noting the temporal distribution here. The *Critique of the Gotha Programme* and *State and Revolution* were written more than three decades apart. Lenin's and Althusser's main works are separated by more than four decades. In turn, Althusser's last philosophical works were written forty years before the present day. All of our remaining chapters will deal with discourses of the half-century leading up to the present—which makes them more or less contemporary by the standards of the history of philosophy. Althusser is then effectively the first of our (near-)contemporary thinkers here.

Althusser represents Marxism's and Leninism's maximum proximity to Foucault, both intellectually and personally. I will argue that Foucault and Althusser pursued the same basic intellectual trajectory in relation to Marxism, one starting from but leading decisively away from Marx, but that Althusser was stymied in this trajectory by his adherence to the French Communist Party, leaving Foucault to fulfill it.

Althusser's project for most of his working life was to purge Marxism of Hegelian metaphysics while remaining Marxist-Leninist. Foucault, by contrast, though a Marxist and close to Althusser as a student, broke with any adherence to Marxism early in his career. Althusser did repudiate strict adherence to Marx late in life, in particular in a book-length essay in 1978, "Marx in His Limits," though this was published only posthumously, appearing in 1994 in French and only in 2006 in English. This shift in Althusser's position thus remains relatively unappreciated.

I will argue that Althusser's long-held Marxism amounted to a strategic decision to tailor his arguments to suit his context. I will further argue that this was a mistake. By contrast, Foucault, by breaking with Marxism early in his career, produced something more appropriate to the times in which he wrote, and *a fortiori* to us today.

A Tale of Two Philosophers

Althusser and Foucault met as students at the École Normale Supérieure in Paris in the late 1940s. Foucault was only two years behind Althusser at the school, but this belied an eight-year difference in age: Althusser had spent the war as a prisoner in Germany, and hence began his higher education only at its end. The older man effectively became the younger's mentor, influencing him to join the French Communist Party (PCF). Foucault also followed Althusser in writing an undergraduate dissertation on Hegel's thought (see Macey 1993, 32). Both of these commonalities reflected a shared adherence to Marxism, the first explicitly, the second because, in France, at this time, Hegel was read and appreciated largely through the historic prism of Marxism, and to study Hegel in France in the 1940s indicated at least a proximity to Marxism.

Foucault was never properly active in the PCF (Macey 1993, 38–40), and left after just two or three years.[1] He continued briefly thereafter to adhere to Marxism theoretically, but ceased to be a Marxist altogether by the end of the 1950s, before he wrote his major works. This contrasts with Althusser's ongoing ultimate fidelity to both Party and doctrine. However, Foucault and Althusser did not break with one another personally, though they grew apart to an extent, Foucault spending most of the 1960s outside France while Althusser remained in Paris. Foucault's life partner Daniel Defert tells us that Althusser "assented" to Foucault's leaving the Party (see Foucault 1994a, 20). Theoretically, Foucault and Althusser remained close intellectually too, as part of the same broad academic movement in France in the 1960s, what is often called "French structuralism," though both Althusser (1970, 7) and Foucault (1970, xiv) rejected this label. It would be more accurate to call the tendency they both belonged to "anti-humanism," since it rejected the centrality and sovereignty of human subjectivity, instead emphasizing our constitution by anonymous structures outside of our control. For my purposes, I believe I can fairly say that this tendency is also anti-normative: it is not going too far, I think, to identify "normativity" today as analogous to the "humanism" that Foucault and Althusser encountered as the dominant and essentially conservative way of thinking shared by both left- and right-wing ideologies.

Althusser's anti-humanism sat awkwardly with his Marxism, inasmuch as both the PCF and Marx's early works took a humanist perspective. Althusser, however, saw Marx's economics-based analysis of class society as anti-humanist, and rejected Marx's early, more Hegelian output, with its emphasis on the alienation of the human subject in capitalism, as not properly Marxist.

Foucault, for his part, hardly mentions Hegel at all in his published work, positively or negatively, but then there was no reason for him to, since he was not trying to detach Marx from Hegel. Rather, Foucault simply rejected Marx's economic theory itself as a relic of the nineteenth century. Foucault (1998b, 281) identified the main point of difference between Althusser and himself as being that Althusser saw Marx as representing an "epistemological break" that decisively broached a new way of thinking, while Foucault himself saw Marx as a thinker stuck in the nineteenth century. Still, while unlike his close associates Althusser and

Gilles Deleuze, Foucault declares no hostility to Hegel, his rejection of nineteenth-century thought implies *a fortiori* a rejection of Hegel, and indeed he regards Marx as something of an advance on Hegel, inasmuch as Foucault (1970, 335) accepts Marx's position vis-à-vis Hegel that economics is a more historically important discourse of the nineteenth century than philosophy. Nevertheless, Foucault deems all nineteenth-century thought, be it philosophy or economics, Hegel or Marx, obsolete after Friedrich Nietzsche, on the basis that pre-Nietzschean nineteenth-century thought understood history as having an end and its own logic. For Foucault, by contrast, the point is to acknowledge the open-endedness of history and humanity. Althusser does not disagree on this point, only on its historical pedigree. For Foucault, Nietzsche looms large as the originator of anti-humanism, while Althusser sees his own perspective as originating in an "underground current," stretching via Marx back to Spinoza and even back to Antiquity.

It is important to emphasize, however, fundamental continuities of Foucault's thought with certain aspects of Marxism. In an untranslated 1971 interview, Foucault (1994b, 170) clarifies that the Marxism he condemned in *The Order of Things* was not Marxism *tout court*, but specifically humanist Marxism. His break with Marxism is itself Marxian: like Marx, he eschews metaphysical philosophy in favor of objective historical analysis. Foucault retains class analysis (while abandoning the philosophy of history that gives class a privileged role)[2] and a sympathy for revolution under the right circumstances (while abandoning any insistence on the inevitability of revolution or any other historical event).[3] Foucault's overall project of critical analysis of thought and society resembles nothing so much as Marx's early declaration for a "ruthless criticism of all that exists" (ME 1, 344). Foucault extracts this critical kernel from Marxism, freeing it from its constraining nineteenth-century husk.

Althusser

What is the difference between Foucault and Althusser such that one left the Party and one stayed, such that one was aloof and the other committed? I will conclude, following Althusser's own remarks, that his loyalty to Marxism was essentially a case of psychological insecurity trumping theoretical consistency, via a mistaken strategic assessment of the political situation. This is not quite to say that this is the only thing separating

Althusser and Foucault theoretically: Althusser's fidelity to Spinoza puts him on a different metaphysical basis and in a different historical frame to Foucault's Nietzscheanism. That said, with Althusser it is not possible categorically to state that any part of his thought exists independently of his commitment to Marxism, so pervasive is it to his intellectual practice.

Althusser's core philosophical project was to reconstruct a scientific "structural" Marxism, centered on *Capital*, bracketing Marx's early Hegelianism from consideration. The ultimate problem with this approach is that *Capital* is itself widely acknowledged to be profoundly influenced by Hegel. For Althusser, the co-presence of materialism and Hegelianism is a central contradiction in Marx's thought. Althusser meant to do away with this contradiction by expunging the Hegelian influence, to produce a purely materialist Marxism. His procedure for doing this, however, namely, to distinguish a "Marxist" late Marx from a Hegelian young Marx, was flawed inasmuch as this distinction was never as clear-cut as Althusser claimed. Late in his life, Althusser (2006) admitted as much—that is, that *Capital* was substantially Hegelian, albeit only in texts that were published posthumously.

Althusser's insistence on a non-Hegelian late Marx in spite of evidence to the contrary was bound up with his adherence to the PCF. As Jacques Rancière (2011, 24) puts it, "Althusser's theoretical and political project . . . is staked on the bet that it is possible to effect a *political* transformation inside the Communist Party through a theoretical investigation aimed at restoring Marx's thought." The immediate obstacle facing Althusser in these aims was the Party's intolerance of dissent. A frontal attack on the tenets of Marxism-Leninism, or on the hierarchy of the Party, would have simply resulted in Althusser's expulsion. Althusser thus adopted a strategy of attacking the Party only at the level of philosophy, and by reference to Marx or, less frequently, other canonical figures, such as Lenin. As long as Althusser couched his anti-humanism in terms of an adherence to Marx's thought, it was hard for a Party to silence him, since it was committed to conforming to Marx (Althusser 1993, 196). That said, the Party did not disguise its hostility toward his interpretations, explicitly rejecting them.

Althusser's strategy implied considerable compromises. He had to maintain not only a public silence about the deficiencies of the Party, but also about deficiencies in Marx's and Lenin's thought. As he himself admits, it is surprising that he chose to remain within the Party at all, given not only his considerable differences with the organization's ideological line and political behavior, but that during his earliest days as a member, the woman who was to become his wife was persecuted by the Party for reasons he clearly saw as spurious (Althusser 1993, 203). Indeed, Althusser was ordered to stop seeing her, and he refused. He gives us several reasons for nonetheless remaining.

Throughout his life, he regarded the PCF as the sole serious force on the French Left. He thus argues that being in the Party was the only possible way of affecting the "course of history" (Althusser 1993, 240). Particularly prominent in his retrospective defense of his strategy is his claim that the PCF had the crucial weight that could have turned the "Events" of May 1968 into a full-scale social revolution (230). This claim is of course an untestable counterfactual, but it is not entirely implausible. Althusser does not, however, consider the possibility that the PCF's size was directly proportional to its lack of revolutionary inclination—that is to say, that the Party was as big as it was because it was a component of the status quo, and that taking a more revolutionary line might have cost it mass support. I'm also dubious about the capacity of a party that failed consistently to win a national election to launch a revolutionary seizure of power, but it is impossible to rule out that a more radical line could have earned it more, not less, popular support.

The ultimate problem for Althusser's strategy, though, was that there was no route to changing the party line. There is no indication that philosophical criticism could affect the Party's theoretical tenets, let alone its political practice. The Party's proletarian members cared little about philosophy, Althusser (1993, 179) notes, while its intelligentsia were comfortable toeing the Party line and had scant interest in new interpretations. Moreover, by his own assessment, he was the only person mounting such an internal opposition within the PCF. While he points to the level of concern the Party leadership had about him as an indication of his significance (233), this does not imply they thought he might actually be able to change the Party. Rather, I think their concern was that Althusser would have precisely the effect he did have, namely, corrupting the youth and cause them to shun the Party—relatively few of those who were sympathetic to Althusser's ideas followed him in joining the PCF (228). From this point of view, the Party's strategy of condemning Althusser while allowing him to remain a member was eminently sensible; it was quite likely Althusser would do more damage to them from the outside, serving as an alternative pole of attraction, and allowing his dissent to an extent allowed the Party to seem much more open-minded than it really was.

Althusser's followers chose to operate outside the Party because they saw the PCF as insufficiently Marxist, an irony, inasmuch as the conception of Marxism they got from Althusser had been developed by him primarily as a tactic for doing business within the PCF. As he had in Foucault's case, Althusser (1993, 233) accepted their stance toward the PCF as reasonable: "The rule I adopted was that each person had to make his own decision." Indeed, speaking of the departure of his student Rancière from the Party, Althusser (228) noted that Rancière's action seemed more consistent with Althusser's theory than his own behavior was.

Althusser (1993, 204) admits that in the end he remained in the Party for psychological reasons: it allowed him simultaneously to satisfy his desires to resist and to be protected. Althusser was hardly comfortable in this situation, however, given that he swung continuously between hospitalizations for psychotic episodes and frenetic scholarly activity, a pattern that culminated in his homicide of his wife.

The Party did change, but in the opposite direction to the one Althusser wanted. Althusser fought a desperate rear-guard action to stop the Party abandoning its official commitment to a dictatorship of the proletariat during its 1970s rightward drift into "Eurocommunism." Althusser failed in this effort, too, and the Party abandoned even its formal adherence to core tenets of Marxism. The game was over, inasmuch as Althusser could no longer hope to leverage those tenets to radicalize the Party. The strategic logic of Althusser's strict adherence to Marx evaporated. Not unconnectedly, I would suggest, in 1976, Althusser suggested publicly for the first time that adherence to Marx has limits. One must note, however, that it was only Marx, and neither communism, nor Marxism, nor the PCF, that Althusser criticized at this time. He always retained a commitment to communism, defined as the abolition of market relations (Althusser 1993, 240), and Marxism. He did ultimately quit the PCF, but tells us that this was only because, after he notoriously killed his wife in 1980, he felt his continued membership would bring the Party into disrepute (241).

This is not to say that Althusser fell into line with the PCF's break with Marx. He rather broke with Marx in the opposite direction. Much of "Marx in His Limits" is devoted to upholding the Marxist-Leninist theory of the state, including the notion of the dictatorship of the proletariat. It is rather that Althusser widens the scope of his "Marxist" critique of Marx's non-Marxist moments to criticize elements of *Capital*.

Althusser casts "ideological state apparatuses" (ISAs), in which category he includes political parties, as a battleground in which Marxism fights bourgeois ideology. This is consistent with his project to reform the Communist Party. We may contrast his perspective with Foucault's (1998a, 100) insight into what he called "the tactical polyvalence of discourses," by which apparently opposed discourses can support one another in strategies of power produced by the complex interplay of power relations. This insight can be applied both to understanding the PCF's position in French society, and to understanding Althusser's position within the PCF. While the Party explicitly advocated revolution, it in practice was a component of a relatively stable French social system, and it in fact never seriously threatened the status quo. Althusser's view that the Party is itself a venue for class struggle allows that this is the case. However, he takes the strategically naïve position that putting forward an anti-humanist discourse within the Party put pressure on it for change. In spite of the Party leadership's chagrin at Althusser's contradiction of their line, they nonetheless tolerated this because it served to create an impression of a Party that was open to debate, giving it a veneer of intellectual credibility. Moreover, by playing the game of Marxist orthodoxy, Althusser quite explicitly supported the basic dogma of the Party, strengthening orthodox Marxism's status as the horizon of left-wing thought.

This is not to say that Foucault's thought has been more effective at changing society than Althusser's. In point of fact, Althusser's uncompromising Marxism immunized his work from the appropriation that has befallen Foucault, whose name is often invoked in contemporary academic discourse to support banal forms of self-reflection, and increasingly, even neoliberalism. The point is rather that there is no guarantee of efficacy for any tactic, and for this reason there is no justification for compromising oneself in the way that Althusser did, since the political ramifications of philosophizing are profoundly unpredictable. Althusser's late position, "aleatory materialism," according to which politics is a multidimensional field of aleatory encounters, is very close to Foucault's in this regard, implying similar conclusions.

Althusser (2006, 255) compares himself to his great influence, Spinoza, a philosopher who was under extraordinary limitations in what he could say. However, by contrast with Spinoza, who had to work within the limits of an intolerant religious society in order to avoid the harshest punishments, Althusser's submission to the *diktats* of the Party was quite voluntary. Foucault's break with Marxism was, by comparison with Althusser's subservience, relatively courageous, given the scale of opprobrium he attracted from preeminent, Marxist intellectuals. It must be distinguished from the easy anti-Marxism found in the English-speaking world, where there was no powerful Stalinist party, and where intellectuals were always predominantly anti-communist. That said, Foucault's marginalization within the Party for his homosexuality might have made remaining within the Party more difficult.

Foucault beyond Althusser

Foucault rejects key aspects of Marxist thought that might be said to harbor Hegelian or metaphysical tendencies outright in a way that is difficult for Althusser: the notions of dialectic and totality, and the metaphysics of the last instance. Althusser struggles to free himself from each of these, and does not manage to completely. He does renounce the eschatological view of history by which communism is seen as history's "inevitable end," but retains a minimal image of communism as an aim; he redefines the dialectic, the totality, and the last instance, but feels bound to keep using all three phrases.

To take the last example, Althusser retains the orthodox Marxist position that the economic infrastructure "determines" the ideological "superstructure" "in the last instance." In his most widely cited piece of writing, "Ideology and Ideological State Apparatuses," he argues that ideology is essential to the reproduction of any economic system. He then ties himself in knots trying to square this claim with the notion that ideology is a superstructure. Due to the significance of ideology in his schema, as a materialist he is compelled to posit ideology as itself material (Althusser 1971, 165). He maintains the base–superstructure distinction on the basis that the degree of materiality of superstructure is lesser than that of the material objects, and that the superstructure is ontologically dependent on this materiality (Althusser 1971, 166). While ideology surely would indeed not exist were it not for the existence of matter in the strict sense, this does not itself imply a priority of economics over ideology within the social form, which is what the base–superstructure model is supposed to indicate. In "Marx in His Limits," Althusser (2006, 61) allows that the superstructure can continue to exist even if the base be taken away, and that ultimately "anything can be determinant in the last instance." This makes a nonsense of the architectural metaphor, however, which clearly implies that the base is needed to hold the superstructure up, and not vice versa. Althusser now interprets this dependency diachronically, instead of synchronically—that the base is needed to raise the superstructure, but not to sustain it after it has been raised. The appropriate metaphor for this, however, would be scaffolding, not base and superstructure. Althusser (2006, 263) ultimately, in interviews in the mid-1980s, stops asserting any priority between infrastructure and ideology, only on the priority of the material element within each of them.

Foucault, by contrast, does not engage in this kind of ontological speculation. Where Althusser sought to provide a "missing" philosophy for Marxism, Foucault eschewed both Marxism and philosophy *sensu stricto*. In this respect, Foucault was more Marxian than Althusser: like Marx, Foucault was an academically trained philosopher who turned himself to the study of disciplines outside philosophy.

Foucault's opposition to Marxism was far from total. While he rejected Marx(ism)'s philosophy of history, there was much in Marx that he admired. After the anti-Marxist tone Foucault set in *The Order of Things*, in his next book, *The Archaeology of Knowledge*, he takes a rather more sympathetic view of Marx. It is worth noting perhaps that in this latter work, unlike the former, Foucault (1972, 5) references Althusser's first book, *For Marx*, which appeared just before *The Order of Things*. One is tempted to conclude that Foucault was brought (back) to a sympathy with Marx by reading Althusser's work in between writing *The Order of Things* and *The Archaeology of Knowledge*. However, Foucault's line on Marx in *The Archaeology of Knowledge* is very similar to sympathetic comments Foucault made about Marx in "Nietzsche, Freud, Marx," a piece roughly contemporaneous with *The Order of Things*. As in *The Order of Things*, he in that essay understands the nineteenth-century episteme as concerned with concealed profundities, and sees Nietzsche as breaking with this. Unlike in *The Order of Things*, however, he also casts Marx's *Capital* in this vein, indeed casts Marx as of a piece with Nietzsche (and Freud) in disrupting the Western worldview. He concludes, however, by contrasting Marx with Marxism as a tendency that closed down Marx's critical opening in favor of "a reign of terror" (Foucault 1990, 67).

In *The Archaeology of Knowledge*, Foucault (1972, 14–15) echoes Althusser by alleging that Marx has been distorted, viewing the humanist interpretation of Marx as an attempt to restore what Marx had decentred. He identifies Marx as a seminal figure of an "epistemological mutation of history" (Foucault 1972, 12–13). Foucault thus interprets Marx as a partial break with nineteenth-century thought. In response to a question about the applicability of his *Order of Things* critique of Marx to Althusserian Marxism in 1971, Foucault makes clear that the former does not apply to the latter (Foucault 1994b, 170).

It is tempting to read Foucault as vacillating in his position toward Marx, but actually Foucault's pronouncements on Marx and Marxism (as on other things) are coherent: Foucault lauds certain aspects of Marx, while condemning others, hence Foucault's (1980, 76) dictum that Marx, *qua* coherent, unitary thought, "does not exist." Foucault sees Marx as a precursor to new ways of thinking, but does not see Marx as the decisive figure that Marxism, including Althusser's, insists on making him.

Early in 1976, Foucault (2003, 13) points out the inadequacy of the Marxist view of power, or "at least a certain contemporary conception that passes for the Marxist conception." Later in 1976, he reads *Capital* as containing an embryonic version of his own pluralist conception of power, formulated in his *Will to Knowledge*, published that same year (Foucault 2007b, 157–158). Thus, Marx is pitted against Marxism.

For Foucault, renouncing Marxism as such is in fact a route to recovering a useful kernel from Marx's thought, without the constraining baggage, without a name or an agenda, within a genuinely radical political stance that is neither Marxist nor communist. Where Althusser tries to rid Marxism of Hegelianism, Foucault moves one step further.

Foucault approached Marx and Marxism much as he advocated his own thought be taken up: as a kind of conceptual "toolbox" from which one should pick what one needs to suit one's critical tasks. Foucault (2003, 6) indeed claims Marxism can provide tools only when its theoretical unity is ripped up.

This led Foucault largely to elide Marx's name itself, to avoid sanctifying him. This tactic of Foucault is seen most clearly in the game he plays of including unreferenced quotes from Marx in his books (see Foucault 1980, 52), and it can also be seen in an outburst in which he refused to talk about Marx (see Eribon 1991, 266). Naming Marx plays into Marxism—the point is simply to use his insights, not to name-check him. Foucault vacillates between refusing to speak about Marx, because the signifier has become so overinvested as the Lacanian phallus of Marxism, and trying to detach Marx from Marxism, a castration that Marxism could hardly allow. Foucault (1977, 220) makes the point that Marx's name is effectively one of a host of concepts that serves "to dispel the shock of daily occurrences . . . to exclude the radical break introduced by events."

That is to say, that Marx's name refers us back to a theory that saves us having to attend to the complexity of what is happening around us.

There is an argument for retaining Marxist dogma: Marx's thought functions as a theoretical lodestone, a way of checking we are on the right course. Foucault points out, however, that Marxism has a bad track record in this regard. Rather, the insistent reference to Marx's works by Marxists has functioned as a guarantee that their course, whatever it might be, is correct. It thus serves as an excuse not to pay attention to new realities or new theories.

What differentiates Foucault's thought from Marxism, including Althusserian Marxism, is that Foucault does not insist that others follow his methodology in their analyses. Foucault leaves no dogma, but rather offers his work as one possible view, to whomever finds something useful in it. This has allowed many to utilize his name for purposes quite foreign to his intentions, but we must remember that Marx suffered the same fate, as Lenin noted (L 25, 385), despite any amount of attempted orthodoxy.

One might argue that it is more Marxian to repudiate Marxism than to cleave to Marx's works as a doctrine. One may refer here to Marx's dictum that he was not a Marxist. Althusser papers over this hole in the center of Marxism, insisting that Marx was a Marxist (see Althusser 2006, 15). His reasoning for this claim is that Marx was quite consciously embarking on an epistemological break, propounding a radically new form of science. We must insist against Althusser that nothing is more glaringly un-Marxian than the attempt to canonize a single man, to declare Marx himself to be the fountainhead of a profound and specific wisdom, accessible only via knowledge of his writings. Here, we can say that Althusser did not stray sufficiently far from his youthful Catholicism, from which he had converted to Marxism, and indeed that Marxism in general retains a certain religious impulse. To hold that one finds a peculiar doctrine laid out in Marx's work that must continue to serve as our evangel ought to stretch the credulity of avowed atheists. Now, Althusser does in effect want to propound a living Marxism that exceeds what Marx wrote and in certain aspects breaks with Marx. What he in his last work identifies as his "aleatory materialism" is a matter of an epistemological break effected again and again over thousands of years down to the present, of which Marx is but one historically significant exemplar, hence it no longer seems appropriate to call it, as Althusser does, by the name of "Marxism."

Marx's own method is to challenge orthodoxies by reference to political reality, to history, to empirical facts, and so on, not by reference to a canon. The very fact that the only way to challenge Party orthodoxy was by reference not to reality but to Marx is indicative of a doctrinaire formation not receptive to new ideas. While one could say that Althusser's invocation of Marx undermined Party orthodoxy and allowed him to refer to realities ignored by the Party, playing this game could be said to reinforce the basic principle that there is a Marxist orthodoxy to be found in Marx, which in itself is a force for ossification and dogmatism.

Repudiating Marxism has a bad reputation among leftists because it typically coincides with a move to the right, but I would suggest that Foucault breaks with Marxism to the left. He has been adopted by some to the right of Marxism, by commentators who are liberals, sometimes in name and sometimes not. Foucault's criticisms of Marxism made him useful to anti-Marxists within academe. He has been accused of courting such attention, specifically because of his closeness to the French "New Philosophers," former young Maoists who had converted to anti-communism during the 1970s. While Foucault was close to some of them, I think it is unfair to conclude from this an endorsement of all their views. Rather, I think this should be seen as a matter of a friendly and encouraging relationship with young philosophers, which he had forged when they were Maoists, though he disagreed with much of their perspective then, and maintained after their dramatic shift to the right, during which process his thought served as a point of support for their newfound anti-Marxism. In opposing the French prison system in the early 1970s, Foucault had been in coalition with Marxists. When it came later to opposing martial law in Poland, or exposing human rights abuses in the Soviet Union, some of the same people—though they now held opposite views in some ways—remained natural allies.

This is in itself a difference between Foucault's modus operandi and that of many Marxists, including Marx. Foucault did not make collaboration with others contingent on the coincidence of his "line" with theirs. Rather, multiple discourses may be in play, but the question is one of the resistance to power relations these discourses animate, how this resistance operates tactically in relation to power. Marxism is in some situations a discourse of resistance, but in others, though making the same formal statements, a crutch for power; the same can be said of Islam, for example, hence Foucault's enthusiastic commentary on the Iranian Revolution hardly makes him an Islamist.

Conclusion

I want to conclude that, *to the extent that he remained in the PCF*, Althusser was stymied in achieving things (though he may still have had an enormous influence), because it was based on an incorrect strategic assessment by him, whereas Foucault's efficacy was amplified by his decision to leave the PCF. I cannot claim that Althusser's Party affiliation had negative consequences (since this would imply a normative assessment of certain consequences as bad); I rather claim that his own purposes were not served by this affiliation. I indeed cannot claim anything about the consequences of his action per se at all, since this would call for an impossible counterfactual knowledge of what would have happened otherwise as a frame of comparison. Rather, I question Althusser's assessment of the tactical possibilities that obtain contemporaneously. Certain compromises might be justified through an accurate assessment of the field of possibility—it is not the case that one should always say what one thinks even in the face of probable persecution and exclusion for saying it, since we can pick our battles. Althusser's tactical calculus does not stand up to examination, however, even on the basis of the information that was available to him at the time.

To couch this conclusion in the terms of this current book, Althusser commits to a kind of normativity, which resides in his being theoretical and political. That is, for the sake of an involvement in an organized state-oriented politics, he commits to following a particular theoretical path. Now, Althusser is a theorist through and through, in a way that Foucault is not: Althusser is committed to articulating a philosophical position that is genuinely theoretical and even in a certain sense metaphysical. As G. M. Goshgarian (2003) points out, Althusser moves in a Foucauldian direction as he takes a less theoreticist orientation over time, from thinking naïvely of practice as the application of theory, thinking theory as scientific verification, thinking in terms of a unified theory, to thinking of philosophy as a "continuous break" with existing reality. This for Goshgarian (2003) is closely correlated to a change in Althusser's orientation toward the Party after it became clear, as early as 1966, that its theoretical line would not be reformed.

4

Deleuze

Denormativization as Norm

> The pairing Deleuze/Foucault, even if its empirical virtue—their friendship and admiration—is incontestable, nonetheless is philosophically empty.
>
> —Badiou 2012, 85

Our next thinker, Gilles Deleuze, can be understood as a further step in our departure from Marxism, though I do not think he necessarily takes us further toward Foucault's position. Deleuze, a French contemporary of Althusser and Foucault, sitting between the two in age, if much closer to the latter, was much less vehement in his adherence to Marxism than was Althusser, but nonetheless retained an affinity for it that Foucault resiled. He also retained a commitment to philosophical metaphysics, indeed to a greater degree than did any of the other thinkers to which a chapter of this book is devoted.

It is often assumed that Michel Foucault and Gilles Deleuze have compatible philosophical perspectives. There are both biographical and textual grounds for this assumption. I want to suggest, however, that the two were rather far apart in a number of ways, including on each of the three axes with which we are dealing in this book: Deleuze is more normative, more political, and more theoretical than Foucault. That is, Deleuze's thought is animated by clear normative preferences, which are cast in theoretical terms and used as the basis for the development of a philosophical system.

Biographically, the two men were close friends during the early 1970s. This was a relatively brief association, however, that ended apparently because of political differences between them, specifically over Deleuze's signing in 1977 of a petition that described the West German state as fascist and appeared to support the Red Army Faction's armed struggle against it (Macey 1993, 294).

Textually, one reason the two are taken to be aligned is their explicit commentary on one another's work. Deleuze wrote an entire book on Foucault's thought. He also wrote some relatively brief and informal remarks concerning Foucault, including the focus of this chapter, his "Postscript on Societies of Control," which takes up and expands upon elements of Foucault's conceptual toolkit. For his part, Foucault wrote a couple of short pieces on Deleuze. The first was a 1969 review of Deleuze's *Difference and Repetition* (Foucault 1994a, 767–771), followed in 1970 by a review essay, "Theatrum Philosophicum," treating that book together with Deleuze's follow-up, *The Logic of Sense*. These two books by Deleuze, published only a year apart, in 1968 and 1969, respectively, represent his main attempt to articulate his own distinctive philosophical position. Foucault's reviews are enthusiastically exegetical; this was the era of the burgeoning of their personal friendship, originating around their shared interest in Friedrich Nietzsche's thought (Grace 2009, 54).

Foucault (1971b) goes on briefly to incorporate some lexical elements from his review in his inaugural Collège de France lecture later the same year. Here he largely restates his 1960s research program, albeit in a somewhat politicized form. He also takes up positions he had previously identified in the review as crucial components of Deleuze's *Logic of Sense*, namely, advocating a philosophy of the "event" concerned to give materiality to the "incorporeal"—though he admits in his review that the concept of "incorporeal materiality" he derives from *Logic of Sense* is not one Deleuze would assent to (Foucault 1998b, 346). In any case, any influence on Foucault's thought itself here is overdetermined, inasmuch as it is already accounted for by other influences such that it is impossible to say that the influence of Deleuze was decisive in influencing Foucault to make any particular claim here: Foucault's *Archaeology of Knowledge*, released the same year as *Logic of Sense*, can already be described as attempting to give a material reading of incorporeal language through the notion of the statement, and the word "event" is already almost as prominent in Foucault's book as in Deleuze's. One might suggest Deleuze's attention to ancient Greek thought influenced Foucault to conduct research in this direction in 1970, opening a research program he would return to in force in the 1980s, yet Foucault's longstanding interest in Nietzsche already provides a basis for this turn; Foucault and Deleuze indeed became friends partly because of their mutual interest in Nietzsche's thought.

Foucault also wrote an enthusiastic preface to the English translation, published in 1977, of Deleuze and Félix Guattari's first collaboration, *Anti-Oedipus*. Like Foucault's earlier review, this is a case of laudatory exegesis, but in neither case does this imply complete agreement. Indeed, there are reports that Foucault actually disliked the book (Dosse 2010).

Anti-Oedipus is, as its title indicates, aimed at usurping the psychoanalytic notion of the Oedipus complex. This was a cause that Foucault and Deleuze had in common: in the first volume of his *History of Sexuality*, Foucault criticizes Freud for reinforcing the patriarchal family as an institution via the notion of the Oedipus complex, at a time when paternal authority was otherwise under attack. Foucault and Deleuze also both criticize psychoanalysis for overvaluing sex itself. However, the pair ultimately have almost contrary positions regarding the question of sexuality, due to a broader difference concerning the nature of social power. As I have argued elsewhere (Kelly 2013b, 26), Deleuze and Guattari's position is very close to Foucault's main critical target in his book, what he calls the "repressive hypothesis," since they view the things they oppose as repressive, whereas for Foucault the key problem of sexuality and modern power is that it is productive, not repressive. Deleuze still cleaves to the idea that power is essentially negative, something we need simply to be liberated from. Relatedly, he still cleaves to a certain kind of Marxism (Deleuze 1995, 171), whereas Foucault pointedly abandoned any explicit fidelity to Marxism decades before.

More prominently, and not unconnectedly (since it means positing a nature that can be liberated from contingent distortions), Deleuze aims to produce a materialist metaphysics, whereas Foucault's project is explicitly purely critical. Now, Foucault cannot completely eschew ontology in the sense of not positing anything, and to the extent that he does posit things, they seem to be entities that would be at home in Deleuze's metaphysics. Foucault and Deleuze both emphasize the body, for one thing. Deleuze's emphasis on "desiring-production" in *Anti-Oedipus* is, however, a concept lacking any equivalent in Foucault. Deleuze yearns to liberate desire and its productivity, while Foucault is deeply suspicious of desire precisely as a driver of what he sees as a productive form of power. Foucault, for his part, advocated the use of pleasure as a counterpoint against desire, something Deleuze opposed in turn. It should be noted, however, though this point is often misunderstood, that pleasure for Foucault is only ever a *point d'appui* for resistance to refer to, rather than something that can actually be liberated to exist in a raw state (Kelly 2013b, 117). This opposition of desire to pleasure is the closest thing to an explicit philosophical disagreement between the two thinkers, since they both commented on the divergence as such—although both tended to deflate its importance by suggesting that the problem really amounted to one of terminology.[1]

I believe that the basic divergence between Deleuze and Foucault, underlying Foucault's opposition to both desire and metaphysics is that, whereas Deleuze believes that there is no intrinsic problem in using language to couch desires or describe ontology, Foucault sees language as leading to inevitable problems. This is not to say that Foucault opposes the use of language, but rather that he takes both desire and ontology as inherently problematic enterprises of which we should be wary and critical as philosophers, because trying to think either our desire or our being in words inevitably means doing a violence to their richness. By contrast, Deleuze posits an inherent oneness of thinking and being, even if he thinks each of these things in terms of multiplicity (Deleuze and Guattari 1994). As Peter Hallward (2000, 94) indicates, this makes Deleuze fundamentally Parmenidean. Foucault, by contrast, is Heraclitean, asserting that rupture of being with itself is an essential characteristic of thinking.

In Foucault's writings on Deleuze, this basic disjuncture between the two thinkers' positions remains concealed due to the brevity and exegeticality of these publications. Deleuze's writings on Foucault, however, have a different character. Deleuze's monograph on Foucault is vastly longer than anything Foucault wrote about Deleuze, and the very brief "Postscript" goes far beyond exegesis. That major differences between the two thinkers do not shine through in these works may be attributed to Deleuze's characteristic modus operandi, which involves minimizing any differences he has with thinkers he discusses in favor of the ventriloquization of his own views.

Chronology

I have just outlined what I take to be the deep general philosophical differences between Foucault and Deleuze: the former aims to demolish existing strategies of power through critical analysis of their operation, whereas the latter aims to build up a new positive account of reality in order to free constrained creative forces. These two projects in principle could be compatible, and I think Deleuze believes them to be. From a Foucauldian perspective, however, Deleuze's project is misguided, even if Foucault himself remained open-minded enough and anti-polemical enough not to condemn Deleuze's thought explicitly. Foucault did not, however, live to see—and he could not, I think, inasmuch as this was a deliberately posthumous act—Deleuze's appropriation of his own thought. Deleuze's main appropriation of Foucault is of course his book on his friend's thought, which does more or less what Deleuze always does with his books on other thinkers, a kind of productive deliberate misreading. This is primarily a matter of providing Foucault with the ontology that Foucault in fact deliberately refuses to formulate. This is tremendously interesting nonetheless, but because its gesture is to infer from Foucault's relatively political output toward the metaphysical, it speaks only obliquely to my concerns in this book. A rather more apt document for my purposes in this book is Deleuze's "Postscript on the Societies of Control."

This piece is extremely brief—only a few pages long, containing fewer than two thousand words—and relatively obscure in terms of its publication origins.[2] It might indeed for these reasons seem unfair to focus on it to the extent I do, but I believe such focus is necessary because of how influential this text has been, despite how unimportant it might have been from the perspective of its author at the time he wrote it. I should admit that focusing on this piece cannot allow me to substantiate my broader critique of Deleuze's thought sketched above. Indeed much of my criticism of the "Postscript" is relatively independent of my criticisms of Deleuze. What I in the end do here in relation to the "Postscript" is much more modest than refuting Deleuze: it's an attempt to detach a coupling that Deleuze has attempted to forge between his thought and Foucault's in relation to analyzing contemporary political reality. I do this on the basis that Deleuze in the "Postscript" first misinterprets Foucault's notion of discipline, and then moves on to advance a thesis that is partly redundant, inasmuch as he is talking about things already covered by Foucault's notion of discipline, and partly simply false, describing as changes things that are either not new or are simply not happening at all. Some of his errors here I do read as symptomatic of deeper problems I see in his thought, but this reading is dependent on my prior diagnosis in relation to his thought. Still, there is a particular value to this exercise, namely, that Deleuze's foray into Foucault's idiosyncratic array of critical concepts in the "Postscript" does allow a uniquely direct comparison between the two thinkers on the same terrain.

Deleuze begins the "Postscript" by correctly characterizing Foucault as saying that discipline displaced an older form of power, sovereignty, in a move from a reductive power of death to a positive and productive power. An extraordinary omission, however—the first of several but perhaps the most glaring of them all—is the absence of the word "power." Deleuze thus sidesteps Foucault's main political insight, namely, the importance of power as an overlooked societal dynamic. Rather than identifying discipline and sovereign power, as Foucault does, as "technologies of power," he uses the terms "sovereignty," "discipline," and "control" adjectivally, speaking of "disciplinary societies." This allows a serious divergence from Foucault's position to go unmarked: Deleuze takes these notions as essences of societies, whereas for Foucault there is no limit in principle to how many technologies might coexist in a social formation. Deleuze does elsewhere give significant—indeed undue, in my opinion—attention to a different concept of Foucault's, that of the *dispositif* of power, but Deleuze does not conceptualize these technologies as *dispositifs* either, which indeed they are not, being much broader phenomena (Deleuze 1997, 185–186; 2007).

Having misunderstood what type of thing Foucault's discipline is, Deleuze also misunderstands its specific nature, wrongly identifying it as essentially a matter of *enfermement*. In the two published English translations of the "Postscript," this notion is rendered variously as "enclosure" and "confinement." While the former translation is more literally correct, it has a specific historical meaning in English, whereas the latter is closer to the sense of the French word, which is most commonly used to refer to phenomena of imprisonment and internment, though it should be noted that *enfermement* can also refer to mental and social exclusions, such that no English word provides an entirely adequate translation. *Enfermement* is thus negative and spatial, as a matter of shutting people in, shutting them up, or shutting them out.

Such spatial effects are not those that Foucault's work on discipline in the early to mid-seventies focuses on, but rather is the terrain of Foucault's first major book, the *History of Madness*, written more than a decade before. The confinement that book focuses on occurred in the mid-seventeenth century, before the century, the eighteenth, in which Deleuze in the "Postscript" correctly has Foucault placing the emergence of discipline. The confinement of the seventeenth century was a precursor to discipline, but not itself disciplinary: it saw people being shut away en masse, implying neither the positive training of bodies nor the differentiation of individuals that are the hallmarks of discipline for Foucault, albeit creating the institutions that later could become bases of discipline. Thus, confinement will occur in disciplinary institutions, but it is not what makes them disciplinary. Foucault (1975, 174, 269) specifically notes this movement away from simple *enfermement* multiple times in *Discipline and Punish*, and pointedly avers that "the principle of 'enclosure' is neither constant, nor indispensable, nor sufficient in disciplinary machinery" (Foucault 1979, 143). Deleuze (1988, 42) himself makes this very point in his earlier book on Foucault, taking issue with Paul Virilio for identifying Foucault's primary problematic as one of confinement, arguing that for Foucault confinement is *always* secondary, even in the nineteenth century; however, earlier still, in 1972, Deleuze already misidentified discipline with confinement (Deleuze and Foucault 1977, 206).

Deleuze's eponymous thesis in his "Postscript" is that discipline has recently been superseded by something he calls "control." Such a claim is not without precedent: Jon Simons (1995, 40) points out that both Zygmunt Bauman and Jean Baudrillard accused Foucault's account of power of being largely obsolete even at the time he described it. Deleuze differs in avoiding disagreement with Foucault by arguing that Foucault's account of discipline had become outdated, palpably so at least, only after Foucault had propounded it in the early to mid-1970s. Indeed, Deleuze (1995, 178) enlists Foucault to his cause, saying, without specifying what he means, that "Foucault sees [control] as fast approaching." In an interview conducted the same year, Deleuze (1995, 174) similarly, again without specification, claims Foucault "was actually one of the first to say that we're moving away from disciplinary societies."

I will note in passing, that, though Deleuze is careful not to contradict Foucault, he does contradict his own earlier position during a 1972 conversation with Foucault that the contemporary situation was marked by "the reinforcement of all the structures of confinement" (Foucault and Deleuze 1977, 212). One could argue that this was true in the mid-1970s, but changed later, yet Deleuze's "Postscript" position is that that discipline/confinement has been in decline for much of the twentieth century. Foucault's response to Deleuze in the 1972 conversation is to raise the problem of power itself, suggesting that *Anti-Oedipus* moved in this direction vis-à-vis Marx and Freud (213). Deleuze's response, tellingly, is to redefine the problem in terms of desire instead (215).

There are several public comments of Foucault's that might seem to provide a basis for Deleuze's claims that Foucault saw there as being an incipient move away from discipline; although it is also possible that Deleuze may have been referring to unrecorded private comments of Foucault's, I will argue that there is nothing in the available record that confirms Deleuze's claim. In a 1975 interview, Foucault (1980, 58) identifies an important change, wherein, "starting in the 1960s, it began to be realized that a cumbersome form of power was no longer as indispensable as had been thought and that industrial societies could content themselves with a much looser form of power over the body." This form he relates to "formidable disciplinary regimes in the schools, hospitals, barracks, factories, cities, lodgings, families" (ibid.). Foucault links this change to the emergence of new forms of sexuality. Foucault is speaking here the year before the publication of the first volume of the *History of Sexuality*. In that work, while he acknowledges that there has been a decline in the overt restriction of bodily activities in relation to sex, he famously argues that overall the strategy of power has remained the same, because repression was never its essence, as many seem to think. For Foucault, the shift in forms of power from repression of bodies to a looser control occurs within essentially the same regime. Since Deleuze equates discipline with confinement, of course, Foucault's position here might seem to betoken a decline of discipline, but this is not Foucault's own understanding.

Another of Foucault's remarks that might seem to confirm Deleuze's claim is Foucault's (2000, 57) assertion that "This is the age of social control." However, he says this specifically about the nineteenth century, and about "a form of power, a type of society that I term 'disciplinary society'" (ibid.). Here, in a lecture that contains one of Foucault's first invocations of the notion of "biopolitics," he speaks in terms of "control of the population, continuous control of the behavior of individuals" (59). Thus "social control" for Foucault appears as a synonym for what he in the first volume of the *History of Sexuality* will call biopower, a combination of anatomopolitics of the human body that he designates as "discipline" with the biopolitics of the human population. He continues to use the phrase "control" in the same way in later years (Foucault 2007a, 10).

One might refer to Foucault's invocation of societies of "biopolitics" or "security" or "government" as coming after discipline, but these terms are largely synonymous for Foucault and do not betoken a shift away from disciplinary power, so much as a supplement to it. Their inception is also located by Foucault hundreds of years in the past, so cannot correspond to the new form identified by Deleuze. It is true that Foucault's analysis of discipline—unlike his analysis of biopolitics—primarily concerns itself with the nineteenth century and stops well before the present. Almost all of Foucault's work is like this, however, essentially historical rather than contemporary, and for Foucault such work comprises "histories of the present," examinations of historical materials to understand the contemporary situation. He is explicit both that "We should not see things as the replacement of a society of sovereignty by a society of discipline, and then of a society of discipline by a society, say, of government" (Foucault 2007a, 107), and that "We live in an era of governmentality discovered in the eighteenth century" (ibid. 109).

Deleuze misinterprets Foucault here too, as Thomas Nail (2016) has shown, understanding biopolitics in his 1986 lectures on Foucault as effectively synonymous with control and thus essentially as the successor to discipline rather than presupposing discipline as it does on Foucault's (2003, 242) own account. Minimally, we may understand Deleuze's position here in line with Michael Hardt and Antonio Negri's interpretation of it, that although biopolitics may have been around previously, "only the society of control is able to adopt the biopolitical context as its *exclusive* terrain of reference" (Hardt and Negri 2000, 40), but this still essentially misunderstands Foucault, for whom the point is that we get multiple technologies mixed together, for example, never surpassing sovereign power, which Foucault calls "thanatopolitics," biopolitics's antonym, but nevertheless its constant companion, as an inverse, dark side.

In *The Birth of Biopolitics*, a rare foray by Foucault into contemporary history, he does argue that our most recent governmentality, neoliberalism, feeds into the formulation of a "less . . . disciplinary" form of economic policy (Foucault 2008, 207). Less disciplinary it may be, but this does not make it non- or anti- or post-disciplinary (and I would suggest it is if anything less rather than more biopolitical to boot). Contemporary public policy does not bypass discipline, but utilizes it in different ways: in neoliberalism we are disciplined not so much through the direct intervention of the state, but the provision of incentives to drive human behavior characteristic of neoliberal governmentality nevertheless requires disciplining at the level of enterprises.

Still, since Foucault rarely if ever engages in any kind of prognostication about the future, it does not contradict him to suggest things changed after he made all of these comments. Deleuze is right that things have changed in recent decades. It is in the nature of things always to change. The question is to what extent they are changing, whether the changes are breaks in some respect, and if so, how. I will maintain that recent changes identified by Deleuze have been of intensity, and not of type, at least in relation to the technologies of power outlined by Foucault.

Disciplinary Institutions

Foucault does not anywhere define discipline succinctly, but he consistently characterizes it differently from Deleuze. He understands it, as distinct from the older sovereign power that operated by damaging bodies, as shaping and cultivating bodies. For this reason, he uses the phrase "anatomo-politics" (that is, "body politics") as a synonym for discipline (Foucault 1998a, 139). Discipline does not stop at the body, however: rather, he argues in *Discipline and Punish* that disciplinary power produces a "soul" on the basis of the body (Foucault 1979, 29). This means that there can be "consensual disciplines," in which those disciplined identify with and accept their disciplining (Foucault 1984, 380). He also argues that "at the heart of all disciplinary mechanisms functions a small penal mechanism" (Foucault 1978, 178), which is to say that punishment (which may or may not take the form of confinement) is always involved in discipline, and that discipline is "essentially non-egalitarian and asymmetrical" (ibid.), even though it may be consensual. Any suggestion, then, that there is a new form of power abroad because today we are in the grip of a soft rather than a hard control that works by subtly influencing our behavior rather than gruffly mandating it misses the point that such a transition occurring already centuries ago is at the heart of what Foucault calls "discipline."

Not only does Deleuze define discipline narrowly and inaccurately, his claims for the decline of discipline even on his definition are overblown. Deleuze (1995, 178) declares that "we're in the midst of a general breakdown of all sites of confinement—prisons, hospitals, factories, schools, the family." Not only was this not true in 1990, it is still not true today. Imprisonment in particular has increased to previously unseen heights since Deleuze wrote these words, particularly in the United States, which now incarcerates its populace at a rate unprecedented in human history. Prison itself has not changed, at least not in any relevant way: prisons still brutalize inmates and make them work for the profit of others; there are calls for reform, but Foucault showed that these have always been a constitutive element of the carceral system. Far from the decline of disciplinary punishment in favor of new forms of punishment, we have seen earlier forms of discipline reappear, such as the chain gang and execution in the United States during the 1990s. Though these have since largely disappeared once again, both are still advocated and practiced to an extent that they once were not. Whichever direction this takes going forward, however, it does not pose a threat to the validity of Foucault's historical analysis, since he does not propound a unidirectional, progressive view of history: discipline has always been incomplete and has wavered historically (cf. Foucault 1978, 14–16).

Deleuze (1995, 182) claims that the traditional confining prison is being replaced through the use of electronic tagging. Thus far, however, an increase in tagging has coincided with a general increase rather than a decrease in confinement. Moreover, even were tagging to displace the prison, it is not at all clear that this constitutes a decline of discipline, or even of confinement. Deleuze (181–182) mentions (his major collaborator) Félix Guattari's vision of a card-access city, as an example of "a control mechanism that can fix the position of any element at any moment." This does seem like an increasingly possible development: with contemporary GPS we can be tracked and fixed to a minute level. But this would simply extend panopticism beyond the prison, completing rather than superseding disciplinary power. We are certainly today under much more surveillance than previously, with CCTV and the monitoring of Internet content and mobile phone calls. We are all now in the position of the prisoners in Bentham's panopticon, having to presume we are being monitored all the time. Deleuze does not mention any of these connections, however: the Panopticon, arguably the key figure of Foucault's account of discipline, is missing from the "Postscript," as are even very general themes, such as the surveillance or punishment of *Discipline and Punish*'s original French title, *Surveiller et punir*.

Deleuze claims that debt has replaced confinement, which if true would be a major shift toward a neoliberalization of punishment. The two are hardly mutually exclusive, however, as debtors' prisons once attested, and these indeed seem poised to make a comeback with changes to bankruptcy law. And haven't people always been controlled by debt? David Graeber has recently argued prominently that we have, and it's no new argument—Marcel Mauss said something similar the best part of a century earlier: both argue that accruing debts is fundamental to exchange and hence both to the economy and society itself. But in any case, since the prison is so resilient as a form, it seems to be an empirically vacuous thesis that confinement is being replaced.

To date, discipline remains based in the same old cast of institutions—the prison, the hospital, the school—to a large extent. Discipline can indeed never be dead as long as the prison exists in something like its classic form: all discipline has long been underwritten by imprisonment, wielded as the ultimate threat to ensure obedience. But just as prisons are growing, so too are several other disciplinary institutions. Educational institutions continue to expand, and continue to be disciplinary. More and more people study to higher and higher levels. Schools threaten to expand to take in more of the students' day as the proportion of the population corralled in workplaces till five o'clock or later increases. Deleuze invokes continuous assessment as evidence of a signal change in schools. This is indeed, as he thinks, the same kind of effect as tagging of prisoners, which is to say, not a decline but an intensification of disciplinary control. He is clearly right to see universities as becoming businesses (Deleuze 1995, 182), but this is simply neoliberalism, a shift in the boundary between public and private sectors, which is not a shift in the boundary of discipline, since it always straddled both. The same can be said, for example, of the privatization of prisons.

Regarding factories, disciplinary workplaces have in recent decades massively expanded their intake. In the First World, this expansion has occurred primarily through the bringing of women en masse from the home into the formal workforce (from the discipline of the family to the discipline of the workplace). Offices have displaced factories as the preeminent form of disciplinary workplace in the West, and office discipline might be described as being looser than that which prevailed in the factory, but one might also suggest that the opposite is true, since the office involves new forms of surveillance, particularly in the open-plan design that has become predominant in recent years. White-collar workers' hours have tended to increase significantly, with work blurring via new communications devices into formerly private time, also representing an expansion rather than contraction of workplace discipline. In the Third World, moreover—and hence on a global average basis—factories now employ a greater mass of humanity than perhaps ever before, with new industrializations of formerly agrarian populaces (Deleuze [1995, 181] indeed notes this offshoring trend in the "Postscript"). The family itself does show some signs of decline or fragmentation, partly under the weight of the pressures of new patterns of work, but thirty years on from the "Postscript," remains entrenched, albeit via transformations, such as the widespread legal and social approval in the West of families centered on same-sex couples. This indeed may be said to have extended the nuclear family model into a zone that was once outside it. The only institution dealt with by Foucault that had unambiguously declined by Deleuze's time is one Deleuze does not mention in the "Postscript"—the mental asylum. But this institution had declined already during the period Foucault was writing, and didn't lead Foucault to revise his thesis about discipline—and indeed Foucault (1977, 229) seemed already to be aware of the possibility of this shift *before* his writings on discipline. This, I would suggest, is because its replacement, known in Britain as "care in the community," is also disciplinary, since it involves the tracking, monitoring, and modification of behavior, albeit with confinement now no longer the rule.

Deleuze claims that the divisions between institutions are breaking down, that schools and factories are blending into one another. Certainly one can find increasing attempts at vocationalization, and new corporate mantras of lifelong learning. But neither thing is novel, and certainly the distinction has not been abolished: schools are still easily distinguishable from other workplaces. On-the-job education is more rhetoric than reality, moreover: the casualization of employment means a decline in pedagogy in the workplace. In any case, the idea of a hybridization between disciplinary institutions does not threaten disciplinary power as such, only particular institutional manifestations of it. Foucault tells us how in earlier days of disciplinary technology all kinds of "utopias" were experimented with. He gives the example of the "prison factory," in which vast numbers of workers lived and slept shackled to their work stations (Foucault 2000, 75). These, however, "were found not to be viable or manageable by capitalism. The economic cost of these institutions immediately proved too heavy, and the rigid structure of these prison factories soon caused many of them to collapse" (76).

The factory is the particular institution that concerns Deleuze the most—this is indicative of his residual Marxist privileging of production, saying of control that "This technological development is more deeply rooted in a mutation of capitalism" (ibid. 180). The factory is unique among the plethora of examples that Deleuze provides in that it is widely argued today in relation to it that there has been a recent major shift. I believe Deleuze's "Postscript" is both primarily animated by and has been most influential through its interaction with claims about the changed character of labor.

Deleuze's position in the "Postscript" represents a cross-fertilization of his thought with Negri's Marxism, in particular—it is worth noting the extent to which the interview from the same year, 1990, with Negri that precedes it in Deleuze's *Negotiations* shares the Postscript's perspective. Negri, an Italian Marxist philosopher living in exile in Paris since 1983, had become a collaborator of Deleuze. Negri's perspective is representative of a broader tendency sometimes called "Autonomism," among other appellations. Of central importance to Negri's thought and that of associated Italian Marxists is a particular elaboration of the notion of "post-Fordism." Deleuze does not mention "post-Fordism" by name in the "Postscript," but it corresponds closely to his notion of "control."

Theories of post-Fordism start from the premise that the paradigm of early twentieth-century working practices were those typified by Henry Ford's car plant in Detroit: the production line, with tasks split up into minute, repetitive motions (involving Taylorist time-and-motion management), producing homogenous products. "Post-Fordism," by contrast, refers to a shift in working conditions in recent decades, from such old-style factory production to a new kind of work that is more flexible, creative, "affective," and ephemeral. Theorists of post-Fordism emphasize recent trends toward flextime, working from home, open-plan offices, hot-desking, and so on. It cannot be within the remit of this chapter properly to consider the post-Fordist paradigm, but I will make a number of points in relation to Deleuze's tendency to argue that such trends portend a shift at the level of social power itself as such.

Some aspects of post-Fordism are not genuinely novel, so much as a return to pre-Fordism. Recent growth in "precarity" is an example of this, constituting a return to earlier conditions of employment, a loss of security won by workers in twentieth-century political and labor struggles. It is undeniable that, as Deleuze notes, the average working practice in the First World has shifted from factory to office, and from inflexible to flexible. Does this entail a shift at the level of technologies of power itself?

Some aspects of the shift affect what may be called the relationship of subjectivity to production, rather than concerning power and control as such, such as increasingly immaterial and affective labor practices.

The innovation that Deleuze points to in this post-Fordist direction that seems most genuinely novel, and most political to boot, is the individualization of employment contracts. This is a break with the earlier industrial system, which always tended to treat ordinary workers as a mass rather than in such a highly individualized way. The question is what the implications of this difference are. I believe this difference can be characterized as the coincidence of post-Fordism with contemporary neoliberalism. Neoliberalism is different from post-Fordism in that the latter is a form of working conditions, and the former is characterized by Foucault precisely as a "governmentality," a logic of government. Neoliberal governmentality specifically involves the state orienting itself primarily to fostering markets. Neoliberalism has seen governments aggressively breaking up worker solidarities that are judged to interfere with the operation of market mechanisms—resulting in something similar to the status quo ante those solidarities, but with new mechanisms in place to inhibit them developing again. Neoliberalism can be identified also with the increasing individualization and marketization noted by Deleuze in his "Postscript." It is not, however, a new technology of power; rather, it implies a new relation of the state to the economy within disciplinary, biopolitical capitalism.

Deleuze seems to think it possible to deduce effects at the level of power from changes in working conditions. To the extent post-Fordism exists, whatever political and economic implications it has (and it may have many), it is not a form of power or government. Fordism and post-Fordism are both, from the point of view of power, examples of disciplinary power. Deleuze implicitly conflates Foucault's discipline with Fordist production, whereas these are distinct kinds of things—a technology of power versus a mode of production—with different chronologies, to produce a thesis precisely about a social essence. My point, then, is not to argue that our society remains essentially the same as it was in the nineteenth century, that there are no major differences, only that the array of technologies of power remain the same—and I insist on the Foucauldian point that we should not reduce society to these, any more than we should reduce it to a system of production, of either things or of desire.

Catalogue of Control

Much of the "Postscript" consists of a dense catalogue of phenomena that Deleuze presents as indicative of the new control society. It at points reads like a newspaper op-ed piece, complaining about modern life without coherence or factual accuracy. Some complaints are apparently about the intensification of capitalism, but do not convincingly indicate any major shift. He complains that art has been marketized; it's true that the art market blew up in the 1980s, but wasn't this just a tulip mania, the kind of sudden commodification that always accompanied capitalism, as an effect of a surfeit of investment capital? He complains that rate fixing has replaced cost-cutting, as if capitalism had not previously exhibited tendencies toward monopolization or cartels. He complains that "we are taught that corporations have a soul, which is the most terrifying news in the world"; this is supposed to indicate the depth of our corruption in the new age, and it is a great line, but who is really saying this? Corporations in the United States have long (since 1886) been considered to be legal persons, and this led to accusations that they were soulless persons, and then in short order, by the 1920s, to corporations attempting to cast themselves as having souls (Marchand 1998).

Deleuze suggests that the "new forces" of control assembled gradually, beginning before World War II, but "accelerating" after it. He thus reads Franz Kafka's *The Trial* as standing, in the early twentieth century, already at the junction of discipline and control, with the old system, supposedly one of decisive judgment, meeting a new "endless postponement." Thus, although the eponymous trial threatens to drag on indefinitely, it in fact ends decisively in execution; presumably were the novel written now, by Deleuze's lights it would be entirely without conclusion, a juridical *Waiting for Godot*. From the point of view of the early twenty-first century, *The Trial*, however, seems perhaps more prescient than ever, with secret charges and secret courts, and guilt presumed, leading to sentences passed. But of course such forms are not entirely new. Rather, they have always haunted the judicial system: the system has long been a nightmare to navigate, baffling, arbitrary, unfair. I would suggest that really this novel deals with what in Foucauldian terms is the replacement of older forms of law with the rule of the norm, by which everyone is endlessly investigable and always guilty of some abnormality, an effect associated with biopower going back to the end of the eighteenth century.

Deleuze is right that things are postponed more than they used to be: criminal trials are longer (though rarely endless), penal sentences are longer (and increasingly endless); we on average spend longer in education, wait longer to marry, to have children, to establish ourselves in our careers, and in all these areas people increasingly postpone things indefinitely. However, this is only a change in degree, not of kind, a drawing out of disciplinary power: postponement was always a hallmark of discipline, which introduced both prison sentences as an alternative to summary corporal justice and education to mediate between infancy and adulthood.

Deleuze alleges that we have moved from analogue to digital institutions (*analogique* to *numérique* in French).[3] While clearly several technologies have made this shift, I don't understand what this could refer to in terms of power, and am reminded of Sokal and Bricmont's (1998, 154) assessment of Deleuze's use of technical vocabulary. If anything, the opposite is true according to comments Deleuze then makes about the modulation of control: it is actually discipline in his schema that is digital and control that is analogue, since it is the former that involves discrete units, whereas the latter is continuous and without boundaries. Such a move from digital to analogue would tend again to correspond to the distinction that Foucault located much earlier in history from inflexible law to the ambiguous norm.

In a risible crescendo to his litany of complaint, Deleuze (1995, 180) inveighs that "*surfing* has taken over from all the old *sports*." The opposite is true, however: surfing has been codified into a sport, just as other countercultural activities, such as skateboarding, graffiti, and punk rock, have been professionalized and disciplinarized.

Deleuze's (1995, 179) most serious claims concern the way work has been reorganized. There has been a tendential shift away from an older pattern wherein workers at the same level in the same workplace were paid the same rate, to individualized contract negotiations. However, individualization is the very stuff of discipline. The individual himself is precisely an artefact of discipline on Foucault's account.

Now, Deleuze wants to argue that control has gone further than discipline in this regard, producing not individuals but *dividuals*. This concept, coined by Deleuze in this text, has been taken up widely since. However, it lacks any clear determination—unsurprisingly, given the brevity of the "Postscript." Deleuze does correlate "dividuality" to the various other aspects of control society that he enumerates, but then these are themselves confused. The clearest indication he gives in the "Postscript" of the way in which he believes individuality is heading, though he does not explicitly link this to the concept of the dividual, is to say that today individuals are "divided each within himself" (Deleuze 1995, 179–180). However, this seems to me to describe a generic fact of human existence: individuals have never been solid kernels; rather, individuality is a constitutive fiction masking considerable internal dehiscence. Discipline establishes individuality in a particularly monolithic way; by setting up individuality as absolute, it creates a particularly fragile subject, beset on all sides by disintegration, and hence leads us to feel peculiarly fragmented today when confronted with the fact of our inherent divisions. One might argue in a quasi-Marxist way that discipline thus undermines itself, causing its own workers to disintegrate at the level of their subjectivity, but if this is so it is a side-effect. We see little decline in any case in the insistence on the individual and his truth and self-presence in contemporary culture. The rampant individualism of online social networks is a case in point, and perhaps more than a mere case, but a bold new axis of confessional articulation. While new media clearly open up radical possibilities, they are prevalently used to cultivate individual identity to new heights.

What is odd about Deleuze's complaint about what we might call our "dividualization" is that he was critical of individuality to an even greater degree than Foucault himself: as Foucault (1983, xiv) describes Deleuze's position in his preface to *Anti-Oedipus*, "The individual is the product of power. What is needed is to "de-individualize" by means of multiplication and displacement, diverse combinations." The difference between this "de-individualization" and "dividualization" is clear already in this quotation, however: Deleuze proposes to break the individual through establishing linkages between persons that transcend individuality, while dividuals are not more linked to other people, but rather simply more divided; dividualization is hyper-individualization. Deleuze (1995, 179–80) claims that a hallmark of discipline is the absence of a contradiction between individual and mass, thus implying only in the era of control has individualism ceased to be at odds with group solidarity. However, it is surely not empirically the case that no one protested in the name of the individual against massification during the disciplinary period—quite the opposite. Rather, I would argue that dividualization is inseparable from individualization: the more our fictitious individuality is insisted upon, the more its fragility asserts itself, but this has continuously occurred throughout the process of disciplinary individualization.

Deleuze argues that the loss of solidarity individuals experience in recent times involves a replacement of collective "watchwords," shared maxims, with individual "passwords." From our contemporary perspective, with its profusion of passwords, this seems plausible, but is again an intensification of individualizing tendencies inherent in discipline.

Deleuze in Marxist fashion sees resistance as emerging out of the tendencies of contemporary capitalism. Oddly, he sees this in the fact that today young people boast of being motivated, throwing themselves willingly into unpaid internships (Deleuze 1995, 182). I would suggest that it is a mark of the success of discipline itself that people do willingly what they previously had to be cajoled into: it is a case of consensual discipline. Today's individual has an increased level of autonomy relative to her forebears: she does what is expected without having to be told. This was always the aim of disciplinary power, completely explicit in every disciplinary institution, even if success in this has varied. This is not to say that there is no resistance from such subjects, but there is no particular reason to expect more resistance from them than from others.

Deleuze (1995, 178) tells us that he gets the term "control" from William Burroughs. What Deleuze takes from Burroughs is the notion that power today is softening such that physical force is not needed. This accords, however, with precisely the sea change that Foucault (1975) identifies in relation to discipline, and which Deleuze thinks wrongly is characteristic of post-disciplinary control. He elsewhere suggests Burroughs was a significant influence on Foucault (Deleuze 1986). Burroughs's notion of control indeed seems rather closer to Foucault's (1998a) notion of power than Deleuze's concept of control, inasmuch as Burroughs's (1975) concept is transhistorical, and the softening of control for him is a recent, albeit repeated, transformation in social control that presages its possible overthrow.

Stakes

I have used a lot of words to criticize a minor, marginal publication of Deleuze's—my treatment is indeed significantly longer than the "Postscript" itself. My main motivation for doing this is that the "Postscript" has been enormously influential, for all that Deleuze probably didn't put much care into it. Probably the "Postscript" has been so influential because it is so much shorter and easier to read than Deleuze's big books. But there's something else about this text too: it strays directly into a kind of contemporary political commentary and analysis that isn't found in Deleuze's books, even in the more popular and political books he co-authored with Félix Guattari. Deleuze's stock in trade is something different: he's a philosopher in an ultimately conventional mould, more specifically, a metaphysician. The "Postscript" for our purposes stands as an example that differentiates metaphysical-theoretical takes on the world from Foucault's political thought.

Deleuze is a normative thinker. By Hallward's lights, his chief norm is that of "creation," and in political thought he really seems simply libertarian, albeit different to classical libertarians in that Deleuze demands the "liberation" not of individual humans, or even of a social class, but of multiplicities and flows. Deleuze's political philosophy is based in the assertion of a metaphysics in which forces try to free themselves from evil reconfigurations of them. Deleuze is not crass enough to use such obviously moral vocabulary, because he's deeply embedded in a context where overtly normative thinking is frowned upon, influenced greatly by Nietzsche and Marx. What we see with Deleuze, though, is a thoroughly retrograde step in relation to normativity and theoretization, taking anti-normative figures like Nietzsche and Foucault and re-theoretize and re-normativize them. Deleuze takes the insights that Foucault himself pushes—the end of the sovereign subject in particular—and elevates these into new norms for the grounding of a political theory. He does this through the paradoxical measure of elevating opposition to norms into a new norm itself, one written into the fabric of reality. What we see, then, in the "Postscript" is Deleuze in quasi-Marxian fashion diagnosing the breaking free of forces of creation in the midst of a form of power that has increasingly set them free.

Deleuze, in common with many Marxists, is too economically reductive about politics and places theory above analysis. This makes him "political" in the sense in which Foucault condemns politics: he takes up strident and polemical positions on the basis of a kind of normative-theoretical dogma. Deleuze's condemnation of the West German state as fascist to which Foucault refused to assent is a case in point: such shrill condemnations of one's enemies is a hallmark of a certain type of leftism, which sees the enemy as always the same, as always essentially fascist, rather than attending to the great diversity of political positions that exist in their own particularities. West Germany to be sure was closer to fascism than it liked to admit, its key personnel and institutions rooted in the Nazi era in a way that was concealed by silence, but it was also in many ways a very different state to the Nazi one, a constitutional liberal democracy which at its heart incorporated a rejection of key aspects of fascism.

Doubtless many of the individual problems I have identified in the "Postscript" are idiosyncratic to that text, but I believe there is an overall pattern of problems here that is generic to Deleuze's thought. Deleuze's tendency toward apriority, placing political line and theoretical norm above analysis, produces specific problems when Deleuze tries to extend Foucault's genealogy.

Deleuze's position in our history of antinormativity, then, is unique. Marx reaches for antinormativity, but is held back by Hegelianism. Lenin turns Marx's Hegelianism into the basis of a new form of governmentality. Althusser tries to rescue Marxism from Hegelianism, but can't quite do it. Deleuze is also famously anti-Hegelian, but his effort to rescue Marxism also fails, because it means falling back into a different kind of theory, namely metaphysical naturalism, which is itself normative. Apparently antinormative ideas are elevated in Deleuze into norms.

Deleuze makes innovation a value in its own right. As such, Deleuze provides an ideological support to the cult of innovation that exists in certain quarters of our accelerating society. It is important on this point to differentiate Deleuze from Foucault. While it might be said that for Foucault hope lies in radical breaks, there is simply no implication at all that breaks, change, multiplication, or differentiation are good in and of themselves, because in Foucault nothing is given a normative value. While Foucault seeks to destabilize, it is not because he thinks instability is better than stability. It is because there are things he doesn't like, and he seeks to destabilize these as the only possible way to change things. This is not because change is always good, since we don't know what will happen, nor do we have any basis to decide which situation is better. Foucault takes nothing more than an oppositional stance, not even propounding a hypothetical imperative. By contrast, in Deleuze there is a categorical imperative: we must change ceaselessly to coincide with reality's own structure once again.

5

Rorty

Relativizing Normativity

Thus far, I've criticized a series of more or less Marxist thinkers for not going far enough in evading normativity. I'm now going to look at quite a different case, Richard Rorty, who in a sense goes too far in his anti-Marxism. Rorty rejects any kind of transcendental grounding for morality, accepting the mantle of moral relativism. For him, this relativism does not diminish the force of norms, however, but rather means that we are all tied to the normative framework of our society. A similar, albeit less extreme, move is made in contemporary Frankfurt School Critical Theory, which I will deal with in the next chapter. This similarity is no coincidence, inasmuch as the seminal figure of contemporary Critical Theory, Jürgen Habermas, was, like Rorty, significantly influenced by American pragmatism. Sometimes described as America's only homegrown philosophical movement, pragmatism has for almost a century been overshadowed in American academic philosophy by the Anglo-American "analytical" tradition, in which Rorty himself was primarily educated, though he nevertheless in his lifetime came to be regarded as pragmatism's major contemporary standard-bearer. Pragmatism has tended to have a greater degree of communication with continental philosophy than mainstream Anglo-American philosophy, and Rorty was certainly much more sympathetic to his continental contemporaries than were most American philosophers of the time.

The case of Rorty is interesting in relation to the Foucauldian project of demolishing normative political thought primarily because Rorty is close to Foucault's position, but remains strongly committed to normativity. Rorty's position that we are incapable of thinking our way outside of the mores of our time and place is sometimes mistakenly imputed to Foucault, particularly to *The Order of Things*, though in fact what he says there about the rules of formation of knowledges explicitly concerns the human sciences specifically, not culture in general—much of human culture occurs outside of such restricted knowledges, excluded from a scientific status, but nonetheless popularly believed—and in any case his claim is not that we cannot think outside an *episteme* but that discourse outside of it will not be accorded the status of science within it. Foucault and Rorty certainly share a certain historical relativism about knowledge and morality, holding that these change over time and between different places. However, for Foucault, critical attention to this fact inevitably destabilizes epistemic and moral certainties in a way or to an extent that it does not for Rorty. While for Rorty politics is about self-consciously assuming and pursuing the values of our society, Foucault wants to criticize and undermine these.

Rorty in his later years frequently engaged with Foucault's thought. Rorty's attitude to Foucault is ambivalent. Rorty sees Foucault, and a number of his French philosophical contemporaries, as fellow-thinkers, inasmuch as they too reject transcendental accounts of truth and morality.[1] However, he also sees Foucault as a primary inspiration for a tendency in the American academy that he laments and wishes to attack, which he calls "Foucauldian leftism," though he does not identify whom he considers to be part of this tendency.

Rorty finds two main faults with Foucault, and this chapter will deal with them in turn. First, I will deal with Rorty's accusation that "Foucauldian leftists" in general wrongly conclude from their relativist insights that we no longer have a moral cause to pursue—effectively he sees them as demanding a transcendental reason to do things and, when it is not forthcoming, falling back into pessimistic inaction. Second, I will deal with Rorty's accusation that Foucault illegitimately bases his political thought on a personal agenda.

The End of History

For Rorty, normativity is a social fact, and is no less factual for our understanding that it is socially constructed rather than transcendent. While

Rorty allows that there may be diverse political ideas in a society, he argues that in ours there is no alternative to political liberalism.

Now, I think this claim has a substantial basis: we in the West today seem caught within the political horizons of democratic liberalism to the extent that there is almost no one who articulates a position that is not broadly liberal or democratic. Liberalism—understood literally to mean belief in government that guarantees certain freedoms and is based on a mandate from the people, and not the American usage of "liberal" as a synonym for the left—does seem to be embraced by almost everyone in Western society. Even the extreme right today clothe themselves for the most part in the rhetoric of liberalism and democracy, even while expressing admiration for fascists of the early twentieth century who openly declared that democracy and liberalism were degenerate. On the left fringe, while small Marxist-Leninist groups, for example, continue to exist in the West, and while some of their membership may genuinely defend Stalinism, most of their rhetoric is couched in liberal terms—in terms of calls for rights and justice and democracy—as are the beliefs of much of their membership; any defense of Stalinism in practice tends to overlook or deny rather than celebrate the extent to which Communist states trampled basic liberal freedoms. While there are fascists and Leninists who in private would say they are in favor of utterly illiberal genocides on the one hand, or liquidation of anyone who opposed the rule of the workers' party on the other, such views are thoroughly disallowed in public discourse, even though the prevailing interpretation of the First Amendment means that the expression of such views remains legal in the United States.

Rorty takes this hegemony of liberalism to mean that political thinkers must also operate within this paradigm, and that those who do not are at best terminally confused. By contrast, I take it (that the Foucauldian position is) that the realization of the existence of such a liberal horizon means we can critique it with a view to moving beyond it. Rorty, for his part, rules out such a possibility, on the basis that criticizing liberalism without posing an alternative vision amounts to a futile political stance, a holdover from the old Marxist critique of capitalism, shorn of its positive significance in the absence of any real alternative. This means that he believes that anti-liberal stances were formerly possible, but have today contingently ceased to make sense as a result of a global victory of liberalism. Rorty (1989, 63; 1995, 212) here explicitly endorses the narrative that liberal politics is the final phase of the evolution of politics on a conceptual level—that is, that it is, in Fukuyama's (1989) (in)famous neo-Hegelian formulation, the "end of history." Rorty (1997, 41) doesn't think we have reached the absolute end point yet, since he still advocates social reforms within our society, but he is hopeful of reaching it within the liberal-democratic paradigm.

It is difficult to see how Rorty can justify the assertion that there are no major social revolutions to come, no form of political society beyond ours, since he rejects Fukuyama's Hegelianism.[2] Rorty (1995, 211) inveighs that "I hope that the intellectuals will use the death of Leninism as an occasion to rid themselves of the idea that they know, or ought to know, something about deep, underlying, forces—forces that determine the fates of human communities." While I applaud Rorty's anti-theoreticism here, it seems to me that Rorty himself poses ultimately, if implicitly, as knowing of deep forces that direct our fate in the direction he prefers. Foucault (1972), for his part, sees history as fundamentally ruptural and discontinuous, as unpredictable, which ultimately means not that there is always a revolution to come, but that history is so discontinuous that revolution may disappear altogether as a form of change, hence we simply cannot know whether or not there will be further revolutions.

Rorty, across various texts, dismisses anti-capitalist discourse on the basis of a twofold argument that (1) liberal democracy is the best alternative open to us—a claim that is cashed out by him as meaning "that nobody who has experienced both would prefer" any given alternative (Rorty 1991b, 21) and (2) that there simply are no other viable alternatives in any case.

Rorty's argument that if no one has ever preferred a different system to liberal democracy having experienced it, then the alternatives can be disregarded has a certain prima facie plausibility, but I think it beggars belief to say that any alternative system fails by such a drastic margin that no one prefers it. Take the example of the former Soviet bloc, where there are certainly people who claim to have preferred the old order, particularly in Russia, where surveys over many years have shown that a majority actively preferred the Soviet model to what has come after. Now, I imagine many Western liberals would scoff at the idea that twenty-first-century Russia is really liberal, but to the extent this is true I would argue it is an effect of most Russians rejecting the neoliberal deregulation of 1990s in favor of something more centralized under Putin. One might argue that the appropriate test would be life in the Soviet Union versus life in authentically liberal-democratic America, but this test would be hopelessly confused by the greater wealth of the latter country. In any case, Rorty's claim is falsified if any one individual has preferred one system to the other, and it is hard to believe that absolutely no one could be found who had experienced both the USA and USSR and didn't express a preference for the USSR. An alternative argument might be to require a majority to prefer one system to another, but this would build liberal-democratic premises into one's argument for liberal democracy, and indeed even this would not be entirely clear-cut, given that majorities in Russia apparently preferred the Soviet Union in surveys.

Rorty (1995, 217) blurs the normative and factical in his reaction to the collapse of Soviet client states in Eastern Europe in 1989, concluding from this that "the Marxian suggestion now has to be dropped. The events of 1989 have convinced those who were still trying to hold on to Marxism that we need" to abandon Marxism. First, he makes a normative claim that everyone should stop being Marxist. Interestingly, this claim is historically indexed to the "now": he seems to allow that Marxism was permissible in its time, if always flawed. In this historical assessment of Marxism, he is basically on the same page as Foucault. Even the apparent normativity here is not necessarily incompatible with the Foucauldian perspective I am advocating, insofar as a meta-normative demand for the abolition of a normative political theory like Marxism may be invoked in accordance with my minimally normative anti-normative norm. Rorty's basis for his injunction is, however, not Foucauldian anti-normativism, but rather appears to be a claim that everyone had given up the cause of Marxism. However, this claim is clearly simply false: while certainly some Marxists did part company with Marxism in 1989, this was not a watershed moment in the history of Marxism as a theory, but rather only as a practice. In the West, few Marxists were by 1989 oriented toward the Soviet Union (let alone its satellite states that collapsed in 1989). Left-wing Marxists thought that the Soviet Union had parted company with Marxism decades before (and some never thought it had really been Marxist in the first place), and hence were untouched. To their right, mainstream "Eurocommunist" communist parties in the West had typically broken with the Soviet Union a decade or more before, though they were paradoxically more affected than those to their left who had still upheld the USSR, and some of these Eurocommunist parties folded (notably in Britain and Australia), while others, most notably in Italy, morphed into mainstream center-left parties—though this shift followed a trajectory they were already on. Marxist governments outside of Europe have continued to exist to this day. Doubtless, Rorty expected Marxism to fade away everywhere with the collapse of the Soviet empire, but it would have been a simple matter to check whether this was actually happening. In ignoring reality, he recapitulates in the opposite direction the arrogance of Marxists in ignoring facts that do not match their theory of history. Rorty's conclusion that 1989 constitutes some kind of practical refutation of Marxism is only possible given his independently held view that Marxism does not offer a better alternative, taking 1989 as a spectacular proof of this view.

Another basis Rorty (1995, 218) offers for his conclusion is Habermas's view that complex societies require market regulation. But this is not a lesson that can possibly be empirically inferred from the limited evidence of the collapses of 1989, given the diverse confounding variables; rather, it is a theoretical thesis, albeit one emanating from a form of systems theory, rather than classical philosophy. By my lights, and I think also by Rorty's, this form of reasoning should not be accepted. In any case, even if Habermas is correct, which I don't accept, it is possible to agree with him and remain an anti-capitalist: some who agree with him are market-socialist Marxists. Rorty apparently fails to understand that the market is not synonymous with capitalism: markets existed long before the rule of abstract capital and might therefore survive it.

Rorty rejects Marxism partly on the basis that it claims to know how history operates when it does not. However, Rorty himself in effect does the same thing—claims to know what he cannot—by not simply rejecting Marxism, but going further and rejecting all non-Marxist discourse that criticizes capitalism. Rorty says that we now know that we cannot exit capitalism, and hence must stop using even the term "capitalism," since it is redundant for him because he believes we now know there is literally no alternative.

The case of Foucault is quite distinct to that of Marxists and others who wish to commend alternatives to capitalism, since Foucault does not suggest any. For Rorty, Foucault's position here is a nonstarter, since Rorty holds it to be impossible to meaningfully criticize anything unless one posits an alternative against which to criticize it. Hence, for Rorty, Foucault and others of his ilk are futilely attached to a critique of capitalism that is outdated due to the death of Marxism, a death that in a certain sense Foucault agrees has occurred. Rorty (1995, 217–218) claims that terms like "bourgeoisie," "capitalism," and "working class"—all terms Foucault does use—are only meaningful within the framework of Marxism, with a world historical vision that indicates that our society may be superseded. This is a novel form of criticizing Foucault for not being normative, effectively inverting the criticism as made by Marxists. For Rorty, as for many Marxists, one cannot criticize if one does not have an alternative vision; Rorty (1991b, 220) criticizes Foucault, along with his French contemporaries more generally, for their "antiutopianism."

By contrast, Rorty (1995, 215) situates himself as taking a via media between the grand utopianism of the Marxists and radical antiutopianism, by supporting only small concrete, local, banal fantasies "that can stand on their own . . . about a future in which everybody can get work in which they take some satisfaction and for which they are decently paid." That is, Rorty, like Rawls, seems to favor what the latter calls a "realistic utopia," made up of modest and achievable goals, though I would aver that the utopia Rorty describes here is no more or less achievable as far as we know than full communism. That is to say, it seems very unlikely that capitalism can allow *everyone* to have work with decent pay and satisfaction, and that Marxists' claims that a revolution would be required to allow this are at least as plausible as the claim that we can reach these goals without a revolution. The Foucauldian will in any case no more endorse real existing alternatives than he will utopias, since Foucault's primarily complaint about utopianism is its capacity to support existing political systems. Rorty is right, then, that Foucault seeks an historical rupture more radical than anything Rorty advocates.

With Andrew Cutrofello (1993, 142), I fail to see why such an ambition requires one to have a mapped-out project for change.[3] Rorty (1995, 212) claims that we literally cannot deploy critical language without an alternative, but I would argue that it is meaningful to criticize capitalism because it has characteristics we dislike, and we know it to be a contingent formation, since it has not always existed. That is not to say that this is automatically a well-founded criticism: I am only delimiting the conditions of the possibility of criticism.

It might seem utterly incautious to take a leap in the dark away from what we know in the hope that there might be something better on the other side. Indeed, Foucault does not advocate any such thing. He rejects revolutionism, the idea that we always need a revolution (see Kelly 2013c). Rather, he recommends always attending to the power relations that obtain, criticizing these, even as change occurs. He is not on the side of any particular change, even though his critique might serve to catalyze it.

Rorty feels that Foucauldians have fallen into a post-Marxist cynicism, in which they continue with the total critique of capitalist culture, but without having any hope of improvement. This is inaccurate, inasmuch as hope continues, to paraphrase Marcuse (2002), to be the apriori of critique. Hope is not the same thing as arguing for a determinate alternative, so much as a belief that "another world is possible," even if we do not know how.

The Public–Private Distinction

Rorty's rejection of Foucault is far from total, however. Rather, Rorty distinguishes between two aspects of Foucault's thought, one that he endorses, and the other that he rejects. He makes this distinction based on his distinction between public and private spheres. He believes in a strict separation of public and private concerns and, rightly, thinks that Foucault does not respect this distinction.

Now, it might seem that there is something akin to this distinction in Foucault's thought from the way in which I have been insisting on distinguishing the personal motivations of political thinkers and the substance of their thought. However, this is not quite the public–private distinction. I do not argue, as Rorty does, that there should be a division between private preferences and actions taken in the public sphere. In fact, I argue more or less the opposite: that political action and critique are motivated by personal preferences. I therefore do not bracket biographical details of thinkers' lives from discussion of their thought, even though Foucault himself does tend to argue in that direction. What I argue for is the excision of normative stances from political thought as such; it does not matter to me, though, whether these normative stances have a "private" or "public" character—nor do I demand the separation of "private" normativity from the "public sphere" or vice versa.

Rorty wants to distinguish between political comments that arise from private motives and those that are appropriately public political statements. Foucault's critical analysis of the structures of our society belongs in the latter category, and Rorty embraces this "public" Foucault. Rorty doesn't agree with what he sees as Foucault's private preferences, but for him this is in itself utterly unimportant, as he sees no basis for reaching such agreements about private thoughts, nor any basis for desiring to. It is only when such inclinations carry over into the public sphere that Rorty might be affected, and hence when they by his lights become his concern.

Rorty alleges that Foucault's political thought is crypto-private, importing not so much normative stances as personal preferences, which then serve as the hidden bases for political claims. I am happy to acknowledge a personal motivation for Foucault's thought, but not that his canonical thought contains any claims per se based on this motivation. Rorty here misunderstands the thrust of Foucault's thought. Rorty (1991a, 195) thinks that aspects of Foucault's political thought emanate from a personal quest for "autonomy" from social norms. He thinks this autonomy "is not the sort of thing that *could* ever be embodied in social institutions. Autonomy is not something which all human beings have within them and which society can release by ceasing to repress them" (Rorty 1989, 65).

"Autonomy" as such is not a concept Foucault uses, nor does he invoke any equivalent concept. Rorty does not imply that he does, but only that it seems that Foucault demands a kind of total autonomy, which Rorty rightly thinks is impossible. But such an idea is utterly foreign to Foucault: indeed one implication of Foucault's analysis of power relations is precisely that there is no total freedom. Rorty (1991a, 196) alleges that Foucault is an anarchist, but this seriously misunderstands Foucault. Foucault does not hope for the abolition of power relations in general. It is, rather, only that he hopes for the abolition of the specific strategies of power he analyzes. In thinking Foucault is set on the total elimination of social norms, Rorty has inferred invalidly from Foucault's opposition to particular social norms to think he is opposed to any possible restriction of human liberty in general.[4]

Rorty is right, however, that Foucault does not honor the public–private distinction. This is because Foucault's reconception of power renders this distinction redundant insofar as strategies of power don't respect it and, indeed, must lead Foucault to understand such a distinction as imbricated in strategies of power. Although Foucault does not specifically discuss it, the notion of a strict distinction of public and private domains is part of the old way of thinking of power that Foucault condemns, which is to say, part of the concealing mask of sovereign power. Foucault's analyses are not a matter of an inappropriate mixing of public and private concerns so much as meant to undercut such a distinction.

Rorty (2000, 130) claims that the public–private dichotomy dates back to the "Babylonian scribes," and thus seems to cast it something of a transhistorical constant, with historical cultures playing out across and within these two spheres. While it cannot be within the scope of this chapter even to begin to discuss the genealogy of this distinction, it seems to me that while it might be the case that a public–private distinction can be traced to antiquity, philosophers or political thinkers were manifestly concerned with both statecraft and private morality throughout the history of Western thought, and the idea of a sharp distinction between the two is a recent development that must be associated with liberalism. There is in any case surely no other political ideology that has insisted so strongly on the public–private division, that there is a private realm in which people may do and think whatever they want so long as they do not harm anyone by doing so, and Rorty's insistence on this distinction is surely part and parcel of his liberalism.

Rorty indeed contends that liberal democratic capitalism makes possible the reconciliation of the interests of all agents and the maximization of freedom (or at least potentially does with the kind of economically redistributive egalitarian reforms Rorty recommends). Rorty's freedom is a negative freedom from interference with persons' private projects and eccentricities, from any kind of persecution and, more idiosyncratically, from any kind of suffering. Rorty posits these goals as tenets of politics that do not require any justification and cannot sensibly be questioned.

Such tenets are questioned by Foucault, however. For Rorty, this questioning is simply indicative of Foucault's inability to separate his private proclivities from what is a public good. Here Rorty (1993) is apparently influenced by James Miller's (1993) sensationalist biography of Foucault, which links Foucault's thought to marginal aspects of his lifestyle, particularly to experimental sex and drug use practiced by Foucault late in his life while visiting California. For example, Rorty (1989, 65) argues that as a practicing sado-masochist, Foucault did not "desire to avoid cruelty and pain." Rorty (1997, 44) even declares that it is precisely "sado-masochism" as such that liberalism seeks to minimize. However, the political conclusion that Rorty connects to Foucault's personal practice is not something one must be a practicing sado-masochist to reach. Foucault does not dream of a world of active erotic suffering: he is not Sade. Rather, he merely refrained from affirming a dream of a world without pain and suffering. Undoubtedly, this dream is implicit in much of our society, in our medical institutions in particular. For Foucault (1998a), this tendency comes under a critical category, "biopolitics." Rorty dreams the dream of minimizing suffering, whereas Foucault takes no position in this regard, while remaining wary of any such goal. To be sure, Foucault would by the same token be wary of any discourse that sought to justify or increase human suffering. But it is precisely to the extent that it appears that the reduction of suffering must be a goal of political action that Foucault is suspicious of this goal. Pain may be inherently unpleasant, just as pleasure may be inherently pleasant, but we do not have to want things always to be pleasant, or even predominantly to be pleasant, and there could conceivably be a point at which the insistence of society on pleasure becomes tyrannical and much resisted (even if Foucault [1998a] himself famously sided with pleasure for tactical reasons).

Rorty (1991a, 195) takes Foucault's refusal to commit to such guiding principles to be a step too far: "you would never guess, from Foucault's account of the changes in European social institutions during the last three hundred years, that during that period suffering had decreased considerably, nor that people's chances of choosing their own styles of life increased considerably." This is untrue, however. This information is certainly there in, say, *Discipline and Punish*; Foucault does not spare us any gore in his descriptions of the punitive methods of the *ancien regime* and acknowledges prominently that things have changed by the measures Rorty mentions. Foucault does not, however, put what Rorty would see as the appropriate normative gloss on these facts. Rather, Foucault casts such gains in terms of an increase in the intensity of power relations. Today's profusion of choice has allowed a massive profusion of power: we now have to define our sexuality, for example; a few haphazardly-if-brutally-enforced prohibitions on sexual conduct have been replaced with a highly graded field of acceptable and unacceptable acts, and a mass of incessant discourse concerning these, indeed to a large extent *constituting* them, within which we are encouraged to create ourselves as sexual beings (Foucault 1998a).

Rorty interprets this kind of criticism by Foucault as a failure to appreciate that anything good has happened. Foucault, however, doesn't assert that the change is morally ambiguous. Rather, he simply doesn't address this issue, since normative evaluation isn't part of his modus operandi. He only tries to critically understand how we have been made to relate to ourselves in different time periods. For Rorty, this private question of self-relation is not political, however. He sees politics and philosophy as independent spheres of their own, which have some necessary, but ultimately unimportant, interaction (Rorty 1997, 36–39). For him, Foucault only becomes truly political when he highlights correctable aspects of liberal democratic institutions that can be identified as nefarious by the norms of liberalism itself. Even in such cases, however, Rorty thinks that Foucault tends to "overphilosophize" politics. Rorty (1993) attempts to explain his differences from Foucault in terms of a difference between "French" and "American" culture, specifically in the fact that the French have much more exposure to philosophy, which leads them to attempt to find philosophical solutions to practical problems. I don't think this properly understands Foucault at all, who, notwithstanding perhaps his tendency toward a degree of French stylistic obscurantism (if much lesser than most of his peers—Searle 2012), is oriented away from philosophy toward practices. If Rorty is right about the difference between French and American attitudes, this might perhaps explain why Foucault's thought found a more enthusiastic reception in America than in France, and indeed why Foucault himself preferred America to France.

Rorty's position differs from Foucault's at base not because of a difference in the degree of philosophicality but because Rorty does not share Foucault's understanding of power relations. Rorty (1995, 195) thinks Foucault conflates two different kinds of power, one serious and political, one harmless and personal, as a result of an illegitimate desire to carry his personal problems over into the public sphere. However, Rorty's distinction here is actually based on normative presuppositions: power is power, whether it is of a child over a parent, or a dictator over millions. His distinction between the public and the private spheres divides up power into two types based on the norms of liberal society. Because Rorty thinks power is a public issue, he doesn't recognize that power exists in ways that do not relate explicitly to state power, even though all power relates to state power to some extent in more subtle ways. To constrain ourselves to commenting on instances of power in the public domain *strictu sensu* means neglecting to understand the social basis of much that occurs in that domain.

Vincent Colapietro (1998, 34) suggests that it is Foucault's direct experience as a homosexual that makes him unwilling to distinguish public and private; by contrast, one can certainly imagine that Rorty has no problem separating public and private in his own life, because he has adopted a conventional lifestyle that already accords with it. Rorty advocates freedom of private sexual behavior, but Foucault's analysis of sexuality aims to show the limits of such a negative liberation of sex, because the demands for the liberation of sexuality already invoke a conceptual vocabulary that belongs to what Foucault calls the "regime of sex," which is to say of a strategy of power that straddles the public–private distinction. That is to say, what we think in public and in private always bears the hallmarks of power, and hence all needs to be within the remit of critique. Rorty (1991b, 26) actually does make approving reference to Foucault on the inseparability of knowledge and power, but he does this by way of a traditional, limited understanding of power as being about a repressive apparatus.

Conclusion

Foucault's conception of power is fundamentally subversive in relation to liberal democracy, precisely because it undermines the attempt to separate private and public, undermining the discourse of this political system. Cutrofello (1993, 145–146) points out that Rorty ignores how his discourse may function to support the status quo. In contrast to Foucault's attempts to be self-consciously critical of discourse and its relations to power, at the heart of Rorty's politics is a deliberate refusal to do this beyond a certain point. Rorty attempts to justify this refusal, but fails: he implies that he has no choice but to go this ethnocentric liberal path, and that the only alternative is a kind of pessimistic withdrawal from politics. But this is not so. With Wojciech Małecki (2011, 121), we may demand that Rorty's reading of Foucault's position as symptomatic of his personal preferences be turned back on Rorty himself, to point out that Rorty's own desire to distinguish public and private is not unmotivated. Indeed, in the end, it is Rorty himself who does more or less what he accuses Foucault of, in the sense that he elevates his normative preferences to the status of inarguable political truths.

As Mark Lance and Todd May (1994, 297) point out, Rorty is much more enthusiastic in support of political liberalism that is warranted merely by being bound to advocate this position. He does not see his own opinions simply as a sociological fact, but rather searches for additional supports for them. In his defense, his ethnocentrism implies precisely that we are not only bound by the perspective of our time and place, but are believers in it. Here, though, I think Rorty is ensnared in a relativist paradox: he wants to eschew any transcendental frame for making arguments, yet the culture he finds himself in, and which he wants to uphold, that of the bourgeois Enlightenment, is based around transcendental claims, and so he in the end cannot help availing himself of transcendental arguments to defend his ethnocentrism.

Contra Rorty, we are not trapped in this way: realizing the relativity of a belief gives us a certain critical distance from it. Indeed, I think this is precisely Foucault's procedure: to contextualize and detach from one's prejudices through historical studies that show their contingency. This does not mean an immediate exit from, for example, liberalism, but does nonetheless allow us to say "no" to liberalism without having a clear alternative in mind.

6

Honneth

The Poverty of Critical Theory

In this chapter, I consider the thought of Axel Honneth in relation to Foucault. Honneth is a major representative of the main school of critical post-Marxist political thought today, the aptly named Critical Theory, which can with more precision be designated as Frankfurt School Critical Theory, to distinguish it from the theory of literary criticism.

Honneth's Case against Foucault

Foucault has a dual importance in Honneth's philosophical formation: positively, as an influence, and negatively, as someone against whose stance Honneth defines his own. Honneth (2007, 42) considers Foucault one of the two most important recent social philosophers, along with Habermas.

Honneth engages with Foucault primarily at the beginning of Honneth's own career, devoting fully half of his doctoral thesis to Foucault, a section that goes on to comprise the mainstay of his first sole-authored book, *The Critique of Power*. Despite the fact both that this work is supposed eponymously to be about power and that Foucault focuses on this theme more than the other thinkers discussed, and indeed perhaps to a greater extent than any other political thinker, neither thesis or book is in my estimation really about Foucault. Almost exactly equal portions of this book are devoted to each of three different moments: the first generation of Frankfurt School Critical Theory, represented principally by Max Horkheimer and Theodor Adorno; its second generation, represented by Habermas; and Foucault. The first two of these constitute the tradition that precedes Honneth himself qua the main figure of the Frankfurt School's third generation. Foucault, by contrast, represents a figure outside of this tradition, a foreigner both literally and intellectually. Yet, he appears sandwiched between Adorno and Habermas, and Honneth combines his treatments of Foucault and Habermas into a single subdivision of the book.

The sequence of thinkers in the *Critique of Power* is chronological, reflecting their ages. There is a deeper logic at play, however, for Honneth, a dialectical-teleological development of social knowledge, indicated in the subtitle of the book, *Reflective Stages in a Critical Social Theory*. In this, Foucault represents a stage in between Adorno and Habermas. Honneth thus posits a progression in social philosophy in the twentieth century leading up to his own reformulation of it. This implies in itself a critical attitude toward Foucault, as someone whose thought has been superseded both by Habermas and by Honneth himself. It also, I will argue, implies an extraordinary leveling of the differences between Foucault and the Frankfurt School Critical Theory tradition, which plays into Honneth's misreading of Foucault.

The key feature of this misreading is that Honneth repeatedly and throughout takes Foucault to be trying to give a totalizing account in each of his books, disregarding Foucault's own claims to the contrary. This amounts to reading Foucault as if he were a Frankfurt School Critical Theorist, even though he is not. It leads Honneth to read different phases of Foucault's work as profoundly different theoretical projects, since Foucault says very different things in different books: he reads Foucault's 1960s output as a failed experiment that Foucault's work of the 1970s superseded, before itself in turn ultimately failing. This again runs contrary to Foucault's own self-understanding of his work. As I have argued elsewhere, Foucault's work is a concatenating enterprise, a series of accumulating and largely mutually compatible insights (Kelly 2009).

The portion of the *Critique of Power* devoted to Foucault comprises three chapters. The first of these deals with two of Foucault's books, *The Order of Things* and *The Archaeology of Knowledge*, the second focuses on the first volume of his *History of Sexuality*, and the third is about *Discipline and Punish*. In his first chapter on Foucault, Honneth interprets Foucault's "archaeological" works of the 1960s as reducing society to signification. Here Honneth considers only *The Order of Things* and *The Archaeology of Knowledge*, Foucault's last two books of the 1960s, and not his earlier archaeologies, *The History of Madness* and *Birth of the Clinic* (which Honneth mentions only in passing), about which such a claim would look much less plausible, since they treat a range of things, including political and institutional phenomena, that clearly are not understood as merely discursive. *The Order of Things* and *The Archaeology of Knowledge* are, by contrast, indeed exclusively concerned with discourses and their transformations, but Foucault is nonetheless clear that in each case the book represents only a single possible approach to a particular problem, saying in the conclusion of *The Archaeology of Knowledge* that the methodology of "archaeology" "designates only one of the lines of attack for the analysis of verbal performances" (Foucault 1969, 269).[1] Similarly, in his foreword to the English edition of the *Order of Things*—which also served as the foreword for the German edition—he inveighs that "I should not like the effort I have made in one direction to be taken as a rejection of any other possible approach" (Foucault 1970, xv).[2]

Honneth goes on in the next two chapters to read each of Foucault's two canonical genealogies, *Discipline and Punish* and the first volume of the *History of Sexuality*, as reducing society to power. Honneth contends correctly that trying to understand the entirety of social life as a matter of power would mean neglecting important aspects. However, Foucault engages in no such reduction. He aims rather to do something much more modest, namely, to emphasize the relation he called "power" as something that he argued had previously been almost completely neglected in political thought, much as his archaeologies had been attempts to cast a different light on the history of discourses through applying novel methods. Foucault's thought appears reductive from the methodological perspective of philosophical anthropology adopted by Honneth himself, according to which Critical Theory is about trying to provide a holistic account of human life. By contrast, Foucault's work comprises an interrelated series of targeted, tendentious interventions in the field of discourses that engage in no such attempt to produce a unified account. Honneth, in effect, takes Foucault to be implicitly dismissing the significance of anything not included in any given account, but actually the opposite is often the case—that is, that Foucault does not bother repeating what is already well known, in particular well-trodden questions of the importance of economics and law to society, and explicitly acknowledges as much.

This basic misunderstanding of Foucault's intentions leads to some important specific errors, in particular in Honneth's reading of Foucault's

1970s output. Like Habermas, Honneth categorizes Foucault as a "functionalist," meaning that Foucault holds that social institutions and practices can be reduced to the "functions" they play within a social machine. It is unclear which of the two Germans is echoing the other here, or whether it is a case of coincidence or mutual incitement, given the near-simultaneity of their critiques. Honneth's evidence for the allegation is, like Habermas's, unconvincing—I will consider only Honneth's case here, since Habermas's has been dealt with extensively by myself and others elsewhere (Kelly 2009).

One reason Honneth deems Foucault a functionalist is that he thinks Foucault believes power inevitably intensifies over time, and hence that power relations have their own historical logic (Honneth 1991, 183–84). Honneth is right that Foucault posits an intensification of power relations in late modernity, but he is wrong that Foucault thinks this as inevitable (201). Foucault simply makes no such assertion, and it would be profoundly at odds with his more general historical relativism, which Honneth otherwise acknowledges, criticizing Foucault's anti-Hegelianism (118), but then reading Foucault as having a progressive view of history.

One piece of evidence in favor of the allegation of functionalism is that Foucault does use the word "function" in relation to social institutions, but this is, so to speak, circumstantial: I would suggest this is a loose way of talking, not intended to imply functionalism in a strict sense, but rather only that social entities play particular roles as an aspect of their complex interplay.

The best evidence Honneth (1991, 181) adduces for the allegation of functionalism is Foucault's interpretation of prison reformers as constituting a component of the carceral system. This is not functionalism, however, insofar as Foucault's position is not that this happened inevitably, as a matter of an ineluctable functional coherence of social systems, but rather contingently: he claims that prison reform discourse happens to have had this effect, not that any and all forms of resistance are co-opted in advance. He indeed is at pains to stress that they are not (Foucault 1998a, 95).

In addition to "functionalist," Honneth (1991, 195) applies two related categorizations to Foucault, misidentifying him as a "behaviorist," as reducing human beings to effects of structures, and as a systems theorist.

Honneth's allegation of behaviorism derives from extraordinary missteps in his reading of Foucault. He first focuses exclusively on the relatively brief section of *The History of Sexuality* in which Foucault outlines his views concerning power, referring to no other part of the book. He moves on to consider Foucault's views on subjectivity, here mining Focuault's *Discipline and Punish*, a book that Foucault wrote more than a year before volume I of *The History of Sexuality*, and wherein Foucault's account of subjectivity is unsurprisingly less developed than in the later book. Indeed, when considering Foucault's attitude toward subjectivity, Honneth avoids, both in his *Critique of Power* and also in his roughly contemporaneous and thematically overlapping article, "Foucault and Adorno: Two Forms of the Critique of Modernity," engaging with any of Foucault's copious writings on this topic after *Discipline and Punish*. Honneth cannot of course be blamed for not knowing Foucault's copious writings on subjectivity published posthumously, but Honneth neglects even most of the contemporaneously extant material. He also misinterprets the one source he does attend to, Foucault's treatment of the "soul" in *Discipline and Punish*, since he takes it to represent a kind of final, total view of subjectivity, rather than as what it is, namely, simply a remark about a particular subjective effect of a regime of psychologizing discipline. Thus, Honneth takes Foucault to be saying that all human subjectivity is an effect of power, when Foucault actually only notes the extent to which human subjectivity is affected by power. Far from seeing subjectivity as formed by "violent strategies of domination," as Honneth (1995, 131) alleges, Foucault shows how subjectivity became a target of power, in a modern shift away from violence in controlling people.

Honneth (1995, 129–130) contends that Foucault is "attacking" "the idea of human subjectivity itself": "According to [Foucault] the modern subject is finally nothing but the fictive unity generated either by the anonymous rules of discourse or produced by violent strategies of domination" (ibid. 131). Honneth conflates Foucault's position with Nietzsche's in claiming that Foucault sees the subject as a "fictive unity." It is worth noting, perhaps, that Honneth offers no citations for these specific claims about Foucault. In surrounding sentences, he cites only secondary texts, and then only as general "cf." or "see" references. Foucault nowhere in his output directly attacks the idea of human subjectivity as such. Rather, he attacks certain ways of conceptualizing human subjectivity, as invariant, sovereign, etcetera. Foucault brackets subjectivity out of consideration in his high archaeological writings as a way of rejecting its conventional methodological centrality in the human sciences. In his genealogical works, he does include subjectivity, but again denies its centrality. Later, in his last years, he tries to articulate something like his own account of the nature of subjectivity (which I have tried to summarize in Kelly 2013a), albeit one that, like all of Foucault's accounts, is not meant to be definitive.

Foucault's treatment of subjectivity in his genealogical period more frequently refers to the body than to the subject. Honneth (1995, 127) reads Foucault as positing the body as a "repressed" substrate beneath power and subjectivity. This is in line with criticism made by others against the first volume of the *History of Sexuality* that Foucault simply displaces the allegation of repression to a different level, from the repression of sexuality to the repression of bodies and pleasures. This reading would seriously undermine Foucault's critique if it were correct, but it is not. He does not see bodies or pleasures as repressed, but rather merely as modified. He does posit them as a *point d'appui* for resistance to sexuality (Foucault 1976, 208),[3] but this is precisely because they may be constituted otherwise, not because they have a naïve natural form to be liberated. Nor does Foucault (2011, 159) reduce subjectivity to bodily behavior: he will later (in a lecture series published only recently) explicitly understand the concept of subjectivity as one of "a reality ontologically distinct from the body."

Honneth's description of Foucault as a systems theorist relates to the claim that Foucault is radically anti-subjectivist, since systems theory completely excludes the subject. This depiction implies that Foucault is committed to describing society as a system composed of subsystems. Honneth (1991, 201) rightly argues that systems theory is incompatible with an account of society based in struggle, which he rightly takes to be Foucault's position. Honneth argues that social power in a context of struggle implies the existence of contesting groups and normative principles. For Honneth, Foucault's failure to posit such groups or principles is what makes him a systems theorist in spite of himself. In point of fact, however, Foucault does posit groups—he mentions "the bourgeoisie" even in passages directly quoted by Honneth himself (197). It is true that Foucault does not talk about normative principles as such, but this does not stem from a systems-theoretic exclusion of them so much as a methodological exclusion for quite different reasons, which I have earlier explained in the introduction and will explain further below.

Even casting Foucault as having a "theory of power," as Honneth (1991, xi) does, ignores Foucault's consistent denials that he is propounding any such thing. Foucault (1998a, 154) proclaims in the first volume of *The History of Sexuality* that he is less interested in producing a theory of power than in simply analyzing it, and reserves the word "theory" for positions he is attacking. The best explanation of this distinction is found in his later rumination, "The Subject and Power," published only in 1982 and seemingly not read by Honneth, where he says that "a theory assumes a prior objectification," and hence a theory "cannot be asserted as a basis for analytical work"; by contrast, Foucault (2000, 327) proposes only the "ongoing conceptualization," a methodological distinction that I would argue applies not only to power but to everything Foucault does.

Of course, one might argue that this is an impossible compromise and in practice no different from developing a theory, since theories are always tentative and defeasible. The difference, I would suggest, lies in the intention of the operation: theorists, such as Honneth, are trying, if perhaps asymptotically, to produce a final version; Foucault is not even attempting this, but rather engaging with concepts as part of a concrete operation. Foucault's intention, throughout his career, is to introduce into systems of thought the disruptive effect of an outside that they cannot account for by studying the history of their formation, not to propound new systems. Foucault (1994b, 523) saw his genealogies as "toolboxes" and saw two potential fates for them: they encounter readers who readily recognize the structures described in them, find grist and practical help for their resistance, or they fall on deaf ears, in which case nothing is lost.

Honneth treats Foucault as if the Frenchman were a deliberate contributor to Frankfurt School Critical Theory, when it should be obvious both biographically and intellectually that this is not so. We may conclude that Honneth decides to read Foucault in this way intentionally because he is interested only in thinkers outside his own school for the purposes of enriching it, and not in considering the merits of fundamentally different perspectives. While Danielle Petherbridge (2013, 2) may be right to suggest that Honneth allows much more of the thinkers he engages with into his theory than does Habermas, their fundamental orientation remains the same.

Recognition or Resistance?

The great thing that Honneth does adopt from Foucault is an emphasis on struggle, although we should acknowledge the extent to which this element has disappeared from Honneth's later work (Honneth 2011, 410; Petherbridge 2013, 37), and the extent to which—as Honneth points out—the notion of struggle is already found in Marx and Hegel, seminal references for Frankfurt School Critical Theory. Foucault's foreignness from Critical Theory is in this regard far from total: like all French thinkers of his generation, he was influenced by many of the same nineteenth-century German thinkers who were seminal to the Frankfurt School. There is nonetheless a disagreement between Foucault and Honneth regarding what drives social struggle. Honneth's answer, the signature move of his thought, derived primarily from Hegel, is that the mainspring of social struggle is the demand for recognition.

Honneth, after Hegel, argues that recognition is a basic intersubjective relationship by which humans relate to one another. Though Foucault posits no such relation, I do not believe this means that Foucauldians cannot accept that all political and social questions may indeed have a recognitive dimension, precisely because Foucault's genealogy is not meant to be a total analysis. Honneth's position, however, is not just that recognition is a ubiquitous and irreducibly fundamental social factor, but that it is in some sense the primary dimension of the sociopolitical. Here, we can schematically distinguish Honneth from Marx, who takes the economic to be the primary social relation, and Habermas, for whom it is communication that is primary. From a Foucauldian perspective, economics and communication are of course very important. Foucault's gesture against all these perspectives, however, is to declare that politics has its own specific dynamic, that of power, which is not mutually exclusive of any of the other dimensions—hence, his approach is not reductive. Despite how obvious this insight may seem, it constitutes a revolution in political thought. Earlier attempts to explain it before Foucault's, like Machiavelli's or Hobbes's, reduced power to a calculus of interests, rather than positing the specificity of power relations.

Jean-Philippe Deranty and Emmanuel Renault (2007, 99) declare, after Honneth, that "It is only when individuals and groups are fighting against the denial of recognition produced by the institutions of social life that their struggle is political and that it really involves political normativity," but if this is so it is only because recognition is a ubiquitous dimension of the social, not because it distinctively marks struggles as political. As they note, not all struggles for recognition are political: recognition is a necessary but not sufficient feature of political struggles.

Foucault is unconcerned with the question of what the ultimate motivation for the social struggle that begets power might be (in the unlikely event that there is any single thing so characterizable). Honneth finds this absence in Foucault unsatisfyingly "systems-theoretic": recognition for Honneth provides a normative motor of history, and he finds no equivalent in Foucault. Honneth (1991, xvii) casts history as a struggle for recognition by which we tend, if not inevitably or consistently, to approach an asymptotic universal mutual recognition. By contrast, when assessing how history is supposed to work for Foucault, Honneth (1991, 177) quotes Foucault's (1977, 151) essay on Nietzsche, which casts history as driven by a ceaseless combat, proceeding "from domination to domination."

Once again, I think Honneth here conflates Foucault and Nietzsche, this time by confusing Foucault's exegesis of Nietzsche's thought for Foucault's own. The key thing for Foucault is not power, as it is for Nietzsche, but resistance to power. As Foucault (1997b, 167) has it, "resistance comes first."

It is conspicuous that Honneth does not talk about resistance as such at all in relation to Foucault, even though he mentions it multiple times in relation to Adorno. Where Nietzsche sees life in terms of a struggle for power, Foucault is more apt to see things in terms of a struggle against power, and not for anything particular, even if power is the inevitable result. For Foucault, unlike Nietzsche, it is possible in principle to tear down dominations without erecting new ones. This is not to say that Foucault believes, like Marx, that history is the inexorable-if-dialectical movement of liberation, because, even if new dominations are not automatic, we also cannot guarantee anything like a regular progress, or that new dominations will not emerge that are greater than those that came before. We can also for Foucault presume that power will continue to exist, but for him power is not synonymous with domination, but rather can take forms in which no one is "dominated" per se. There is for him no extracontextual frame from which to evaluate success or progress in any case.

Thus, from a Foucauldian perspective hope lies in the unknown: the only thing we can ultimately be sure of is the errancy of our own knowledge, which means irruptions of opposition will occur that we cannot predict. Resistance might be characterized as always proceeding from needs and demands of some type, but it does not seem to me that we can presuppose it always comes generically from any particular kind. It could be motivated by a recognitive deficit, but could be motivated by something else: anything that causes us to chafe against power relations can lead us to political resistance. All real cases may be presumed to have a recognitive dimension, but this may also be presumed never to constitute the entire motive force of social struggle.

To give Honneth his due, "recognition" identifies an important question of intersubjective motivation at the heart of human activity, which is a lacuna in Foucault's thought. I see no reason why Foucault could not accept that the struggle for recognition is a major motivator for social action; he does acknowledge, albeit very peripherally, that the self is constituted intersubjectively.

Critique

Still, as I have suggested above, there are major methodological differences between the two thinkers: Honneth qua Critical Theorist wants to provide a holistic social theory, whereas Foucault has no such ambition. Honneth aims to produce a theory of society that can serve as a motor for social change; Foucault engages in historical criticism and analysis of particular aspects of society to provide a tool for those trying to produce social change. Desire for social change is undoubtedly a commonality, marking both Honneth and Foucault as "radical," "left-wing," "progressive" thinkers. The relation of theory to praxis implied in the two methodologies is quite different, however. Honneth stands in a classical Enlightenment tradition seeing truth as on the side of counter-power, seeking social progress via the advancement of social knowledge. In this much, Honneth is Hegelian, even idealist. In common with earlier Frankfurt Theorists, Honneth recognizes the possibility of perverse uses of Enlightenment values, and the extent to which knowledge is always generated as part of a social situation, but sees no way out of this trap other than cleaving to the Enlightenment project. Foucault (1997a, 314), for his part, also seeks to continue the Enlightenment project, but more minimally, abandoning all but the critical component of Enlightenment reason, reducing it to critique. The key difference between Honneth and Foucault here is that where Honneth takes it as axiomatic that one must deploy existing values in critique, Foucault refuses to leverage such values, since it would constitute a limitation on the potential scope of his critique, and does not see any need to do so, since genealogy can achieve its critical aim on the basis of description alone, as I will now argue.

In later reflections on Foucault, first published in 1994, Honneth (2007, 39) describes "Foucault's methodological justification for his critique of the disciplinary society" as "impenetrable." Indeed, it is impossible to penetrate, because there is nothing beneath the surface: there may be some personal motivation for Foucault to critique discipline, but there is no methodological justification, because Foucault's methodology neither requires nor allows for justification. Honneth declares that "Foucault's normative criteria remain . . . obscure" (40), but I would argue that they are not obscure so much as nonexistent, or at least irrelevant. Clearly, Honneth, in common with many others, including analytical political philosophers, does not recognize non-normative political thought as a possibility. Hence, while Honneth in almost the same breath recognizes Foucault as having started a "movement" in philosophy around "the thesis that every context-transcending norm . . . merely conceals a power-related construction," he appears only to be able to conceive of Foucault as a pragmatist (though he uses the descriptor "perspectivist," since he is trying to connect Foucault to Nietzsche), seeing norms as entirely context-bound. Here, Honneth conflates the positions of Foucault and Nietzsche with another figure he mentions, Richard Rorty (40).

Vis-à-vis Honneth, such a pragmatist position toward norms would leave Foucault capable of immanent critique, but incapable of the philosophical anthropology Honneth wants to show the universal principles behind the operation of immanent critique. Honneth (2007, 42) argues though that Foucault's thought is still compatible with a project of historically relative "weak" philosophical anthropology outlined by Charles Taylor. I have argued above, however, that Foucault does not even accept using norms immanently. For him, indeed, it is not only "context-transcending norms" that are suspicious due to their imbrication in strategies of power: it is all norms per se.

Taylor is, like Honneth, a commentator who has tried to square Foucault with Critical Theory. Others have gone further in trying to incorporate Foucauldian insights into Critical Theory. Amy Allen's work is one example, taking much more from Foucault than Honneth does, while retaining a commitment to normative Critical Theory, which requires her to read Foucault as—albeit quite minimally—normative. One may refer also to Beatrice Hanssen's attempts to eponymously situate herself *Between Poststructuralism and Critical Theory* or Colin Koopman's recent attempt to bring Foucault into communication with Critical Theory.

Petherbridge (2013, 37) has specifically argued that Honneth's own Critical Theory can be improved by taking up the theory of power from Foucault properly. Like Honneth himself, Petherbridge proposes to read Foucault as offering a form of philosophical anthropology, but thinks this anthropology is richer than Honneth allows (97). She argues that, despite Foucault's claim in "Nietzsche, Genealogy, History" that there are no transhistorical constants, he in fact posits several, including bodies and power (68).

Though his ontological stance in relation to these notions (or any others) is far from explicit, in his invocation of bodies and power, a distinction can be drawn between phenomena and concepts: the concepts by which these are identified are not historically constant, even though their referents may be said to exist transhistorically (that is, throughout human history, though perhaps not independently of it). In keeping with the way I have interpreted Foucault above as staging a limited and relative move to the outside of our current discursive frame, the use of concepts that appear to refer transhistorically I would suggest refers us precisely to the external conditions which bear on discourse from outside, even if that puts us in the paradoxical situation of representing this outside in discourse.

This critical orientation toward discourse itself is what makes Foucault's position possibly irreconcilable with Critical Theory per se, although there is a critical kernel of Critical Theory with which I believe Foucault may yet be compatible—even if I won't attempt to explore this prospect in the current chapter. This kernel is most developed as what Adorno calls "negative dialectics," a phrase that only occurs in Honneth's treatment of Adorno in *Critique of Power* in the very few mentions of the title of Adorno's work of that name. That is, despite Honneth's moves in a Foucauldian direction vis-à-vis the previous direction of the Frankfurt School represented by Habermas, I suspect he remains further from Foucault philosophically than the first generation had been.

"Critical theory" is not quite an oxymoron, but it does imply two aspects that are in tension. This is not what critical theorists think, it seems to me: they think rather that you need a theory to be effectively critical. But by my Foucauldian lights, articulating a theory dulls your critical edge, and it cannot be otherwise. This is not quite to say I want an absolute abandonment of any kind of organized thought in favor of a cynical purity of critique—I essentially agree with Critical Theorists that there needs to be a compromise between critical purity and organization of knowledge—it's just that I think that the level of organization required does not approach full-scale theoretization, since the goal of Foucauldian critique is only to undermine, not to build.

Honneth draws comfort when reconsidering *The Critique of Power* on the occasion of its second edition in 1988 from the fact that most commentators in the intervening period have rejected a radically non-normative reading of Foucault. Honneth (1991, xxv) suggests that were such readings of Foucault "completely unopposed, my own interpretation would be rendered problematic." This argument strikes me as implying the pragmatist view of truth, by which truth is determined by social acceptance—that is, exactly the view Honneth attacks when he imputes it to Foucault (40). By contrast, the Foucauldian position I wish to defend is one that sees breaking with received opinion as part of the core critical task of philosophy—hence, I am, if anything, encouraged by the idea that my position is not widely accepted.

Normativity

Honneth takes the position that social movements require a normative basis. I do not believe it is safe, however, to assert that we can know that social movements definitely require a shared normative framework: it is conceivable, I think, that social change can be wrought for example by a coalition of groups without a shared normative framework, agreeing to unite in opposition to the status quo. Honneth argues that we must develop a common sense of the nature of our grievance, but this can be provided by the strategic diagnosis of the danger we face, as a unifying target or enemy. A common normative framework might unify us more strongly, but there is no need for one. Indeed, it seems to me that in a pluralist society lifeworld, elements such as norms may not be appropriate to use to unify resistance organizations, and indeed that the attempt to unite around a shared morality may end up being reactionary. Widely accepted contemporary political values such as democracy and liberty might not seem to be dangerous values, but, as Foucault says, everything is dangerous, and the fact that something does not seem dangerous may make it all the more insidious. But in any case, it is neither my position nor Foucault's that social movements *must* do without norms: it is critique that we are trying to do non-normatively, not politics as such. It might be a problem for my perspective if social movements *had* to be normatively based, but I don't accept that this is so.

Honneth's position is that shared norms emerge automatically as it were out of shared experience of suffering (Deranty 2004, 313). However, this too seems to me to go too far in positing a universal pattern for politics. Much as Honneth's focus on recognition is a misidentification of the essence of politics, his focus on suffering is a misidentification of the wellspring of resistance: not all resistance requires us to *suffer*, only to chafe against power (though, like the demand for recognition, suffering is *a fortiori* ubiquitous to social life, such that one is not likely to find an instance of resistance where there is no suffering).

Honneth believes it is helpful to leverage normative demands in critique because he thinks normative demands are integral to our society anyway, and that social progress necessary flows through these. This being the case, Honneth's thought is intended as an intervention in favor of these demands against the "paradoxes" and "pathologies" that he believes are stymying their progress. He thus seeks to make the available political rallying points explicit, performing a positive tactical service, comparable in the opposite direction to Foucault's negative analysis of strategies of power. From a Foucauldian point of view, however, any such positive operation is suspicious, because it is no longer merely an aid to resistance, but rather provides a hook for power. By remaining resolutely critical Foucault hopes to avoid serving any particular positive agenda. While social change is never total, Foucault does not try to prescribe in advance what elements of the current order we should aim to retain. Honneth, by contrast, deliberately puts his thought at the disposal of social democracy, seeing this as the best hope of producing progress.

Honneth's valorization of social democracy is naïve about the profuse and perverse effects of social democracy as it has really existed. When the normative potential he identified in earlier work—in particular in *The Struggle for Recognition*—did not play out as he thought it should, he was forced later to claim that "paradoxically" the normativity of the struggle for recognition had been redirected against itself (Hartmann and Honneth 2006). Plausible though it is to suggest that capitalism has misled people as to what it offers, with neoliberalism posing as a bringer of individuality and freedom while it really harms these things, it is less plausible to suggest that this is a distortion of a set of otherwise innocent norms. In complex social formations, such effects are not unusual, but are rather the one thing that we should expect, viz. the unexpected. Social democracy has always been problematic and Janus-faced, just like every other political order. Foucault's analysis of disciplinary power and biopolitics in fact indicates exactly how apparently benevolent power that cares for our health and well-being remains a form of strategic power based on the constitution of docile subjects and racist exclusion. The Honnethian position can allow this is true, on the basis that the aspects of this situation we deem good can be mobilized against the bad ones. The Focuauldian-Nietzschean-genealogical point against this is that this normative distinction is a constitutive feature of this political arrangement, that is, the apparently positive values that appear good within this situation do not have their dark side as an eliminable side effect but as a component. What Honneth calls "paradoxes" are from a Foucauldian point of view a matter of the tactical polyvalence of discourses, which means that one cannot discern how discourses relate to strategies of power, or more generally what these discourses do, simply by looking at what these discourses say they want. Honneth presumes that political discourses naturally tend to bring about the effects they advocate, and regards their failure to tend in this direction as a perversion requiring an additional explanation.

Honneth thus naïvely believes that calling for the restoration of social democracy will actually regularly tend to bring that restoration about. On the contrary, it is conceivable that it will lead to these ideas being labeled abstruse, or unrealistic. Honneth inherits Habermas's faith in communicative rationality. We do not know what the sociopolitical effects of any discourse will be, because of social complexity, a fact grasped by Foucault, if not in as many words, and expressed neatly in the dictum attributed the Foucault: we know what we do, but we don't know what we do does (Dreyfus and Rabinow 1982, 187).

Foucault's account of power is not functionalist or systems theoretic, nor reductive; it is, rather, if anything, complexity theoretic. Power's strategies are for Foucault thus an emergent phenomenon, unpredictable through the prior observation of the components of the social situation, but rather analyzable only as effects. The effects of political thought are therefore always diverse and unpredictable. What this means is that one cannot then engage in it with a deliberate purpose in mind, since there is no guarantee that advocating something will help rather than hinder its actual production, nor even a basis for asserting that it will probably have one or other effect. If Honneth is right and history is already driven by a struggle for recognition, then it perhaps makes sense to hope to intervene in the current of history by analyzing the evils that have pushed this current off course, since there is a need then for only a limited intervention to liberate existing normative tendencies. However, I do not think there is a secure basis for such conclusions.

In addition to asserting what we cannot know, such schemata serve as potential anchors for power, for control and enforcement, for domination, and thereby threaten the negative movement of liberation. Anything that does appear to threaten the progress of one's designated path is apt to be cast as aberrant and dangerous and indeed even suppressed. A moral prescription is always potentially an embryonic conservatism. For Foucault, resistance springs eternal in relation to any power structure, no matter how well intentioned.

One might think that my ostensibly anti-normative Foucauldian agenda is guided by the fundamental normative assessment of resistance as good in contrast to power's bad. But neither Foucault nor I argue for a valorization of resistance per se. Resistance and power are ubiquitous and normatively ambivalent and instances of them may be adjudged variably good or bad from any given normative perspective, including that of Honneth. Foucault sides only with particular resistances in the critical targets he takes, not with resistance in general. He does not do this either from a valorization of resistance itself, or for some underlying normative reason particular to this struggle. Rather, it is a manifestation of Foucault's own specific resistance to power.

Now, for resistance to succeed in practice, it must coalesce into some kind of movement, that itself has power, specifically counter-power, power opposed to other power, and which therefore itself encounters resistance. Hence, if social movements do require norms, this may be said to be required to the extent that they have power relations within them, and are not purely resistant.

Resistance is no panacea. The case of insane asylums illustrates what can happen when resistance is successful. The asylum is a constraining institution. Resistance is ubiquitous inside it. There is also resistance from persons outside, from families of the committed, etcetera. Foucault himself wanted to resist the mental health apparatus, having encountered it as a young man. The anti-psychiatry movement, to which he had effectively been enlisted, after a decade or so enjoyed some success: the asylums began to close. Now, this wasn't the sole aim either of Foucault or the anti-psychiatry movement. Both had wider aims around changing attitudes to mental illness. But they certainly did criticize these institutions. And their closure was gratifying, but it led to new problems (see Foucault 1982a, 232). From a Honnethian point of view, this is a "paradox," by which an apparent increase in freedom in fact led to its opposite. From a Foucauldian point of view, this is not a normatively aligned event, but rather simply a success for a specific form of resistance, the appropriate response to the vicissitudes of which is not to call either for new institutions or for the restitution of old ones. Some will do this, but it is not for intellectuals to do. We can only continue to analyze, criticize, and resist.

7

Geuss

The Paradox of Realism

I. Geuss

In this chapter, I look at the recent political thought of the philosopher Raymond Geuss. His name might seem out of place among the august signifiers under which the chapters have been presented thus far, insofar as Geuss is not generally considered to be a major philosopher. Indeed, I don't claim that Geuss, whose work I nonetheless admire enormously, is as significant or original a thinker as the others I have focused on up to this point. However, Geuss's name does not stand in isolation, but rather at least in part stands in for a raft of recent Anglophone political philosophers who have moved very close to continental positions but, I want to argue, remain sub-Foucauldian in the radicality of their break with contemporary political theory. I esteem Geuss as perhaps the most radical of these thinkers, which is to say, the closest to Foucault's position.

In his *Philosophy and Real Politics*, Geuss sets out a project he calls "realism" in political philosophy. Now, the meaning of political "realism" is ambiguous and apparently uncontroversial: as Geuss (2008, 59) himself points out, hardly anyone would not declare fidelity to reality. The point of his claim to adhere to the real is, then, of course, to claim that he has succeeded in this where others have failed; Geuss considers orthodox political philosophy under the heading "Failures of Realism." I agree with him that conventional political philosophy fails, but I will argue that Geuss himself fails to carry through his realist project fully, and (of course) will argue that Foucault is the one who does. Foucault has been described as a realist, including by me, but it seems to me now that this designation unfortunately implies an attempt fully to symbolize the real, which Foucault does not engage in.[1]

It would seem likely that Geuss adopted the term from his sometime colleague Bernard Williams's sole political work, *In the Beginning Was the Deed: Realism and Moralism in Political Argument*, which appeared in 2005, following Williams's death in 2003, although Geuss does not explicitly acknowledge as much. William Galston (2010, 385–386) has situated Geuss and Williams as part of a much larger realist "countermovement" against the reigning orthodoxy in political philosophy, though these two men are the only *soi-disant* "realists" within it (Sleat 2010, 489). What unifies this current for Galston (2010, 386) is a rejection of liberal idealism's focus on law and ethics. Galston names twenty representatives of this tendency,[2] as well as multiple groups of scholars within it of which he does not list the individual members. All those he names work in the United States or England; a plurality of the figures named by Galston, eight in all including both Geuss and Williams, share a connection to Cambridge University.[3] Galston's "countermovement" can thus be identified as one within Anglo-American analytical "political philosophy," though some of the figures he names are more influenced by continental than analytic philosophy: Chantal Mouffe is perhaps the most extreme example, not least because she actually comes from continental Europe, and Iris Marion Young and Bonnie Honig are also more influenced by continental than analytical philosophy, as is Geuss himself. However, it seems to me that all are, due to their geographical and institutional situation, drawn into the discourse of political philosophy defined by the dominance of Rawlsian thought. Even if, like Geuss, they seek prominently to oppose that model, I will argue that they are inhibited by their imbrication within the subdiscipline political philosophy as such. An example of this influence is Iris Marion Young's phrasing of her entire problematic in terms of justice, Rawls's key term, even if she defines the term very different from the way Rawls did, in which she applies the thought of Marx and Foucault, thinkers who overtly rejected the notion of justice (while quoting Foucault misleadingly to imply he supports her agenda—Young 1990, 96).[4]

Distinctions between continental and analytical philosophy are today more blurred than ever, and correspond less to geography than ever: there is more aggregate interest in continental philosophy in English-speaking countries today than in France and Germany put together, and philosophy departments on the continent of Europe are increasingly staffed by scholars in the analytical tradition. The emergence of the realist countercurrent in political philosophy in recent years in the Anglosphere is testament to this blurring. Still, for all its heterodoxy it remains distinctly Anglospheric insofar as it is still precisely within *political* philosophy. Anglo-American philosophy is conventionally subdivided into specialisms, of which "political philosophy" is one, whereas continental philosophy is not: any given continental thinker typically has views running the gamut between epistemology and politics. Some continental thinkers are more political than others, but continental philosophy does not segregate political or literary concerns from the main business of philosophy. This is at least partly because of the influence of Marx's eleventh thesis in convincing continental thinkers that all philosophy is ineluctably political. By contrast, analytical philosophers typically do not take up politics as an area of philosophical concern at all, such that political philosophy is a marginal area of philosophy, subordinated to ethics, which is itself in turn marginal relative to the prestigious core of metaphysical and epistemological research.

Geuss versus Rawls

Geuss argues that contemporary political philosophy is crucially disconnected from the reality of politics, and proposes to reconnect the two. The dominant position in political philosophy against which he defines himself is the one that I dealt with in Chapter 1 in its Marxist incarnation. Characterized by Geuss as "ethics-first," this is a form of political idealism descended from Kant that sees politics as a matter of the application of principles derived from reflection. Rawls, the pre-eminent political philosopher of recent times, provides its touchstone.

Geuss engages in a comprehensive denunciatory critique of Rawls in *Philosophy and Real Politics*. All Geuss's criticisms are at least similar to ones already found within the critical literature on Rawls: he criticizes Rawls's device of a "veil of ignorance" on the basis that ignorance does not lead to good—let alone binding—political judgments (Geuss 2008, 72), suggests that it is far from obvious that Rawls's "difference principle" is what people would choose under a veil of ignorance in any case (87), criticizes Rawls for failing to deal with the question of power (90), and points out that Rawls's intuition that justice is the main concern of political philosophy is limited to our historical period, and even then not universally shared (72). Rawls's defenders can relatively easily answer, or more likely simply dismiss, Geuss's critique on the basis of nuances of Rawls's position that Geuss fails to account for. For example, Geuss takes Rawls to be advocating a universal perspective, when Rawls understood (albeit not explicitly in his *loci classici*) his tentative thought-experiment to be specific to his historical and geographical location, viz. late twentieth-century America.

Geuss does produce more interesting criticisms of Rawls, however, in earlier essays entitled "Neither History nor Praxis" and "Liberalism and Its Discontents." Geuss's invective here is at a level of generality that deals not only with Rawls's thought but with orthodox political philosophy in general. For reasons I will explain, I think Geuss's specific presentation of these criticisms misfires, but their critical kernel, which I will now reconstruct, constitutes his major specific challenge to Rawlsianism.

Despite the fact that these pieces were written before Geuss announced his *soi-disant* "realism," the critique found in them is more germane to the connection between "philosophy and real politics" than the one found in the book of that title. Geuss (2005, 22) in the earlier essays criticizes Rawls for not thinking about how to apply his ideas in practice. Rawls's defenders might here point to his "nonideal theory," which deals with how societies might move from an unjust situation to a just one, relatively marginal though that may be within his work, as evidence that he does not ignore this problem. Indeed, he does not completely neglect the problem of implementation. His thinking about the relationship of theory to implementation is nonetheless entirely inadequate, in two ways. First, his conception of implementation is simplistic, naïvely ignoring the enormous complexities of politics and society that I will argue make thinking in terms of "implementing" political theories in itself inadequate, no matter how sophisticatedly. Second, he considers only the question of how to implement his position given the existence of the political will to do so, not the more immediate political problem of how to generate such a will in the first place.

It is reflection on the constitution of the political will that marks the crucial lacuna in thinking about the relation of theory to praxis in contemporary conventional political philosophy, in marked contrast to, say, twentieth-century Marxist and post-Marxist approaches in (continental) political theory. Rawls, like other contemporary orthodox political philosophers, does not reflect as to the process that might connect his statements to their realization, that is, does not consider the relation of political ideas to reality beyond thinking of the "application" of ideas. He does consider the importance of ideas within the utopian situation he imagines inasmuch as he considers widespread explicit assent to some variant of his theory of justice to be necessary to the establishment of justice in practice (Rawls 1971). He doesn't, however, tell us how this can come to be widely agreed upon in the first place. This is a serious failing given that the intrinsic purpose of Rawls's theory, like most political theories, is to realize the utopia it envisions: if we can't bring the theory into practice, it would seem at best to be little more than an idle fantasy (though Geuss argues it is actually more insidious than that). This failing is inherited at least to some extent by almost all (post-)Rawlsian political philosophy.

Though this is not an explanation that Geuss considers, I think it has been possible for political philosophers to ignore the question of the practical role that political philosophy plays because they naïvely assume, as a suppressed premise, that ideas have a particular fundamental connection to "real politics," namely, that philosophical arguments are compelling for individual actors via an appeal to reason, with the concatenation of this effect of compelling argument producing the desired political outcome over time. Such an understanding of politics or human behavior may accurately be called "idealist."

Geuss (2005, 34), for his part, notes that Rawls's theory came to enjoy immense popularity during a period in which there has been a considerable growth in inequality. Geuss commits a misstep here by implying that the recent growth of inequality is incongruous with Rawls's theory, when, as Geuss will himself go on to note, Rawls's theory is not actually egalitarian. Strictly speaking, what is incongruous is not the growth in inequality per se, but actually only the extent to which the well-being of the poorest has declined, which is what would be unjust by Rawls's lights. Still, Geuss's basic point that Rawls's stock has risen while we move further away from realizing his utopia stands. This is a problem for Rawlsians because the spread of Rawlsian ideas ought to lead in the direction of realizing them. There is admittedly, however, no necessary correlation between the hegemony of ideas in academic discourse and government policy. It seems, on the contrary, to be quite possible for philosophers to believe any number of things without it affecting political reality, since philosophy obviously has a quite marginal position in relation to our political system. While this offers an avenue for Rawlsians to excuse their lack of practical success, it would then open the questions of what it is they think the point of their activity is if they are really powerless to affect real politics, or how they might propose to affect real politics.

James Gledhill (2012, 68), defending Rawls against realist criticism, including Geuss's, conceives of Rawls as seeing the relation of his ideas to practice as a matter of "muddling through towards" his ideal. This precise phrase actually comes from Thomas Pogge, who uses it to say this is *not* how Rawls thinks of things, but Gledhill disagrees; Pogge (1989, 136) indeed does not offer an alternative conception of Rawls's positive method other than exploring Rawls's nonideal theory. Pogge has in fact written an entire book entitled *Realizing Rawls* that does not explain how to realize Rawls's ideas. For his part, Gledhill attempts to imagine what method Rawls envisaged in the absence of any positive indications in Rawls's writings, concluding that Rawlsians simply have to "muddle through" the practical exigencies they face.

A difficulty here for Rawlsians, noted by Geuss, which I believe is intractable, is that Rawls's difference principle is thoroughly ambiguous in practice, a principle adopted for purely theoretical reasons, without concern for the difficulties of applying it. Geuss (2005, 22) compares Rawls unfavorably to simple egalitarianism here: though Geuss (2008) himself rejects egalitarianism on Marxian grounds, he notes that, as a measure by which to judge reality, egalitarianism has the virtue that it is relatively clear how to discern how well reality accords with it, whereas the application of Rawls's theory is basically impossible to verify, since it is based on an untestable counterfactual, viz. that the least well off representative person is better off in a just society than they would be in an unjust one. Even if we were to concretize this by identifying a real person as this representative, we could never be sure whether any particular policy would actually make this person better or worse off than they otherwise would be when one allows for the complex interaction of economic circumstances and of different policies and institutions, because we can't model things well enough to be sure what would be the case otherwise without actually implementing measures, and even then the interference of other variables between any two actual historical situations is such that we can't be sure which factors are actually helping or hindering in any concrete instance. Even though neoliberalism has seen the poorest people in society qua poorest people in society worse off than they were previously, it is at least conceivable that not implementing such policies would have led to an even greater decline in living standards, hence an orthodox Rawlsian defense of neoliberal policies can still be mounted. In effect, politicians of all persuasions can and sometimes do claim to be honoring the difference principle, since the claim is impossible to falsify.

Geuss (2005, 34) suggests that Rawls's thought thus operates not as a guide to action but as "a compensatory fantasy," a dream people enjoy thinking about that distracts them from the problems of the real world. Geuss (2005, 38) further alleges that, because it endorses a society that fundamentally resembles American liberal democracy, "the structure and ethos" of Rawls's theory serves to assure Americans that their existing political arrangements are essentially the correct ones. Indeed, he even sees it as a major contributor to the rise of neoliberalism (Geuss 2016, 82–83).

Geuss's critique of Rawls's insouciance to the practical effect of his own theory is reminiscent of the challenge of Marx's famous eleventh thesis: "Philosophers have only interpreted the world, the point is to change it." While post-Rawlsian political philosophers are seemingly doing more than merely interpreting—namely, prescribing—they are nonetheless not actually changing the world. And indeed they end up doing rather less than interpreting it, and their contribution may be in practice the reverse of what they intend.

Geuss's Realism

The alternative, realist mode of political philosophy that Geuss sketches in *Philosophy and Real Politics* begins with observing the way politics actually works, rather than thinking about how it ought to work. For the realist, normative views are accounted for as contingent, empirical actualities one encounters in politics rather than as transcendent and universal bases for political thinking (Geuss 2008, 74). Geuss thus stands political philosophy on its head, subordinating ideas to political practice. His realism is then the very opposite of "moral realism" as it is usually construed, namely, as meaning that morality has a transcendent reality. For Geuss, beliefs are significant politically only insofar as they affect the actions that agents take, and the relation of beliefs to actions is quite variable (11). Nevertheless, beliefs, no matter how false they might be, do affect actions and thus should figure qua beliefs in political calculations (11).

Geuss's realism can also be usefully distinguished from "realism" in international relations theory. While Geuss (2008, 22), like international relations realists, wants to lay claim to some of the heritage of Thomas Hobbes, he doesn't conceive of agents as essentially self-interested, because reality does not bear out this conception (ibid. 7). Geuss (2010, 39) rather explicitly attacks such "hard-edged" realism, because he acknowledges that moral motivation is a real force, rather than just a screen for the pursuit of self-interest. Moreover, he does not oppose normative motives in political action: "Nothing in this book should be taken to imply that no one should ever allow normative considerations of any kind to play any role whatever in deciding how to act politically" (Geuss 2008, 99). He does not wish to reduce politics to a calculus, or for that matter to a blind process. Rather, for him politics is "a craft or art," rather than a matter either of a calculus of interests, or the application of theory in practice as on the Rawlsian model (ibid. 15). This specificity of political practice is, it seems to me, the kind of thing Foucault tries to capture with his notion of "governmentality." Just as the institutional and cognitive context of politics changes radically over time, so too does the art that the exercise of political power consists in. Correlatively, political philosophy is itself conceived by Geuss as a historically situated, historically variable inquiry, which must take account of both its own history and the history of what it studies (ibid. 14).

Given this variability, there is no transhistorically appropriate style for the study of politics, according to Geuss (2008, 17). However, he does list three quite general questions that he thinks are distinctive of the realist approach, with the answers varying historically. These are: Who does what to whom for what purpose? What do we want? and Why do we act? The first question, Geuss associates with Lenin (though this is not an aspect of Lenin's thought examined in my chapter on him above). It calls for analysis of the political sphere. This is not part of contemporary conventional political philosophy, which is concerned more with how things should be than with how they actually are. Since Geuss's realist position is that any philosophical conclusions about politics can come only from close study of political reality, this question is for him the *sine qua non* of political philosophy. This question is relatively Foucauldian, though the focus on agency ("who") means it is not framed in a very Foucauldian way. The second question for Geuss calls for the evaluation of alternatives, and is part of political philosophy as ordinarily conceived. This, I have argued, is not a question Foucault endorses asking. Geuss associates this question with Nietzsche, though I think this is an eccentric association and ultimately misguided, insofar as Nietzsche doesn't actually ever weigh the merits of alternative competing political systems. The last of the three questions is for Geuss an inquiry into legitimation in Max

Weber's sense. This is realist inasmuch as it implies simply the analysis of how legitimation works in real politics.

Williams

On this point of legitimation, before going on to consider Geuss's second question, we may usefully distinguish Geuss from one last version of realism, that to which he is closest, biographically and theoretically: Williams's (2005). This case is instructive inasmuch as it is a case of the failure of realism, where normative claims are allowed to creep back in through tendentious description of reality. Williams, as the subtitle of his book on politics indicates, like Geuss, takes realism to involve the rejection of moralism in political philosophy. However, Williams's realism features a much stronger notion of legitimation than Geuss's: Geuss only wants to allow that Weber's descriptive typology of legitimation is the kind of thing a realist political philosopher might produce, whereas Williams produces a normative theory of how legitimation works. As Matt Sleat (2010, 489) has argued, Williams in this respect remains somewhat idealist. Both Williams and Geuss are influenced by Weber, though only in Geuss's case is he clear that his remarks on legitimation relate to Weber.

The traditional attitude to legitimacy in liberal political philosophy is to define formally and universally what counts as legitimate government and then demand that real instances conform to this ideal (Sleat 2010, 491). By contrast, Geuss (2008, 34–36) holds that legitimation is a real process that occurs in political society, in a historically variable way, working differently in different societies. Williams, for his part, similarly sees legitimation as variable, but holds that politics in any given society always refers to what he calls a "basic legitimation demand" (a notion rather reminiscent of Hans Kelsen's theory of basic legal norms, though Williams does not refer to Kelsen). Williams casts this demand in realist terms: he claims that all states must engage in some form of legitimation in order to exist. If basic legitimation doesn't happen, he argues, there is no politics, but rather either tyranny or warfare (Sleat 2010, 493).

Sleat (2010, 494) points out that this dichotomy between tyranny and war on the one side and politics on the other is traditional to liberalism. The reality, I would suggest, is less clear-cut: all real states combine the use of force against those who don't consent with legitimating discourse. Even the most consensual liberal democracy has dissenters it represses and, conversely, no tyrant rules without offering some ideological justification; even simply averring that they are justified because might is right is a juridical argument, appealing to a right of conquest as a form of legitimation.[5]

Williams tries to infer an ought from an is in claiming we can make normative judgments as to whether states are legitimate or not based on a study of their actual legitimation conditions. The great flaw of Williams's procedure here is that when people do not obey what he sees as the basic criteria of legitimacy, rather than seeing this as a counterexample that falsifies his inference, he can cast these as ipso facto illegitimate instances to be opposed. Inside any state that Williams would regard as legitimate, those who disagree with Williams's principle of legitimacy and regard the state as illegitimate, must be then categorized as insane, or themselves tyrannical, as terrorists, fascists, et cetera (which some may in fact be, but not *eo ipso*). Moreover, any political system that functions without what he regards as the requisite degree of legitimation will be seen not as falsifying his claim that political societies need a basic legitimation principle, but can rather be doxastically declared not to be political at all, to be failed states, rogue states, et cetera.

Sleat (2010, 496) furthermore points out that Williams's understanding of legitimation implies a universal endorsement of the liberal principle of equality of moral agency between all humans, where most historical societies took inequality between persons as a given, and indeed the appropriate observance of inequality to be a mark of legitimacy. One can of course define such earlier societies as tyrannical, but this is a normative judgment not derivable from "reality." One could generously interpret Williams as saying that, de facto, a state requires the majority of the population to accept it as legitimate in order to function, but that would be false: as I argued in Chapter 2, all that most people have to do for the state to operate is not actively to oppose it, even though they might prefer other arrangements.

II. Against Geuss

Having distinguished Geuss's position from various failures of realism, I will now lay out the deficiencies that I believe still lurk in it. I make three accusations against Geuss, to distinguish the Foucauldian perspective from his, each corresponding to one of the three dimensions of attack in this book, normativity, theory, and politics. The first is the extent to which

Geuss wants to allow an aspect of normativity to remain in political philosophy: he explicitly allows that political thought can be non-normative, but still considers a certain degree of normativity acceptable, which I do not. The second is the extent to which Geuss's conception of political philosophy is still imbricated in an indefensible disciplinary division of knowledge. The third is Geuss's continuing vision of political philosophy as informing public policy.

Normativity

Geuss argues that we cannot reach a universal morality via an examination of reality. This means that realists have no objective basis for evaluative judgments that are normative, rather than merely descriptive. We can evaluate factual claims by reference to reality, but evaluation in terms of "good" or "bad" implies the imposition of an extrinsic norm or purpose not found in the thing itself.

Geuss still sees a role for evaluation in realism, however, making the Nietzschean point that human beings are evaluating animals. Geuss (2008, 39) concludes from this, with Nietzsche, that we ought to make our evaluative claims plainly. For Geuss (2010, 30), "Realism in politics does not mean trying to engage in the utterly incoherent task of thinking about practical politics while abstaining completely from making value judgments."

Now, this is a point on which Foucault, despite his proclaimed Nietzscheanism (Foucault 1998a, 251), parts company with Nietzsche. Nietzsche engages in florid invective against positions he dislikes, whereas Foucault's prose is for the most part exceptionally dry. Moreover, Nietzsche is sometimes held to propound some kind of normative morality, not merely implicitly as Foucault sometimes is held to do, but explicitly in depictions of a "higher man." I am bracketing Nietzsche's thought from consideration in this book, so won't consider whether Nietzsche should be considered a normative thinker. I do however contend that it is *possible* for evaluation to be non-normative. Expressing a preference, be it about the taste of food, art, or indeed human behavior, can be evaluative without being prescriptive. This form of evaluation may indeed be an ineluctable element of human existence (though I do not think one can state as much with certainty). But, regardless, I do not believe it is necessary to express such opinions in political thought. One might say that these evaluations color our political judgment, but the version of political thought I advocate, after Foucault, is one of rigorous critique that is substantively about pointing out objective problems and patterns in discourses and power relations, which stand regardless of evaluations. Geuss's position, that since we have evaluative orientations, and since these color our political judgment, we ought to state them openly in political thought, is to my mind a non sequitur. The point, from the Foucauldian point of view, is to minimize rather than maximize the coloring of analysis by prejudice. "Realism" could break either way here: one could argue that a "full disclosure" requires us to include our motivation in our inquiry; or one could bracket it in favor of an inquiry that tries to be rigorously realist by setting aside the motivational question. Since I am unconcerned with being "realist," this is not a consideration of mine (or of Foucault's), however. Stating our tastes I think serves in the context of political thought only to alienate readers who do not share these feelings. If we bring evaluative claims into political thought, we are then required to convince readers of the correctness of these claims—which I do not believe can be done, since I see no evidence that arguments in favor of any framework of evaluation can be generally persuasive. One might argue that being open about our motives can serve to humanize the author, to make a dry text more relatable, and can thus engage readers, particularly those who share the prejudices of the author. However, it focuses attention on whether motives are shared by the reader, rather on the facts. While we may have idiosyncratic grounds for engaging in speech, discourse can find a purchase in others who to be sure share some framework of understanding with us, but perhaps not all our presuppositions and inclinations: the rule of thumb in effect should be to minimize possible points of disagreement when we write.

This does not imply a criticism of Nietzsche's thought, insofar as his work belongs to a different genre: however we categorize it, it is not straightforwardly a form of political thought, but rather a scathing polemic against various cultural and philosophical tendencies. While Geuss wants to allow that Nietzsche does something that a realist political philosopher might do, Nietzsche is no realist political philosopher.

Geuss (2005, 153–160) himself deals with Foucault and Nietzsche's method in an essay entitled "Genealogy as Critique," but he misunderstands Foucault here. Geuss's starting point here is to define critique as necessitating both a negative evaluation and an analysis. This is a perfectly good account of how the term "critique" is ordinarily understood, but belies its etymology—as Geuss (2005, 153; 2014, 70) himself repeatedly notes, the Greek root implies only analysis—and does not accord with Foucault's activity, at least insofar as Geuss understands critique to include giving reasons for condemning something. Although Foucault does not explicitly engage in the form of evaluation Geuss imputes to him, Geuss reasons that, since evaluation is ineluctable to critique, and since Foucault clearly engages in critique, he must be engaging in evaluation. Here, Geuss's reading of Foucault as evaluative is a lesser echo of the common Anglo-American and German reading of Foucault as normative (Taylor 1984; Habermas 1987; Honneth 1991; Fraser 1995).

Geuss (2014, 70) apparently resiles this view in more recent work in which he provides an updated schema for "criticism" as comprising four distinct "elements," one of which he calls "critique," which he now understands to mean simply analysis; the other elements are evaluation, "argumentative connectivity," and "performativity." He now argues that "analysis will never be strictly value-free, but it will also not be the case that by virtue of engaging in 'criticism' of this kind I am in any way presupposing or expressing a *negative* attitude or judgement towards the object of criticism. 'Critique' in this sense is self-evidently an activity of virtually universal application in all fields of human endeavour" (70). He goes on to consider the meaning of this phrase "negative attitude" at some length, albeit inconclusively (72). I take it that the meaning here, though, is that there is a negativity inherent in analysis, which I would allow. Geuss's overall argument here is indeed that there is no need for criticism to be "constructive" (77ff.). This then seems to allow for the kind of political thought I am advocating, though Geuss certainly still wants to allow for more "constructive" forms of political thought that I wish to disallow: "in the political realm appeals to the need for 'constructive' criticism can *in principle* represent a (generally laudable) attempt to remind those involved in some evaluation of human action of the need to remain aware of a kind of internal demand under which such criticism operates, namely of the need to keep the question 'What is to be *done?*' firmly in mind; *in fact*, however, the demand for 'constructive criticism' in general functions as a repressive attempt to shift the *onus probandi* and divert attention from the possibility of radical criticism" (90). Here Geuss suggests that the demand for constructive criticism is rather better in theory than practice. Allowing it in principle while condemning its practice strikes me as a failure of realism for Geuss, insofar as practice ought to be the test of the principle. In any case, it seems to me that there is no compelling reason to accept that constructive criticism is an appropriate mode for political thought.

Realism and Analytical Philosophy

While Geuss analyzes the political functions Rawls's political philosophy performs in practice, the same question can be posed from a realist perspective in relation to philosophy in general of how it operates to motivate actions or inaction in the real world. Such critical questions have a long history in continental philosophy, and are at the heart of Marx's and Nietzsche's metaphilosophy in particular. This is not to imply that we have to reduce philosophy to politics, but Geussian realism surely should imply being aware of the effect of ostensibly nonpolitical philosophy on politics and vice versa.

Geuss (2014, 231–232) condemns most of the business of contemporary professional philosophy—which, in Geuss's Cambridge context, can be understood in some of its details to be aimed at analytical philosophy in particular, though one might reasonably ask how innocent much contemporary continental philosophy is of the same sins. Indeed, I think contemporary continental philosophy is in general not much better in practice, though the question of the political and social function of philosophy are much more prominently raised within it.

Geuss (2010, 175) describes analytical philosophy, alongside rationalism, pragmatism, utilitarianism, and German idealism, as having certain features that might characterize "bourgeois philosophy." Geuss (172) condemns "bourgeois philosophy" as a form of thought that "starts from the claim that the world is basically or fundamentally in order."

The implication here is that any philosophy in a capitalist society that assures us that things are the same throughout history is bourgeois, whether its claims are metaphysical or aesthetic, because it assures us that our way of interpreting the world, proper to our historical setting, is in fact the only true description of reality. I would go further and invoke the principle that Foucault calls "the tactical polyvalence of discourses" (1998a, 100). Geuss (2010, 175) shows a sensitivity to this principle in his essay on bourgeois philosophy, noting that the clarity of analytical philosophy currently serves bourgeois political purposes, whereas at other times it might serve others. I would suggest tentatively that contemporary mainstream analytical philosophy has the practical effect of depoliticization, by propagating the impression that fundamental questions are unaffected by history and politics. Its intradisciplinary subordination and quarantining of political questions is part and parcel of its essential conservatism. It thus performs the function that Geuss (2008), after Marx, designates as "ideological." Of course, a depoliticized philosophy remains by its very nature compatible with a number of political orientations on the part of its proponents—as we have seen, some analytical philosophers are Marxists—but it nonetheless performs a social function of evacuating most philosophy of politics.

Geuss (2016, 24) does seem more latterly in this final line of a recent essay to condemn analytic philosophy as such: "Whatever its potential liberating effect might have been in the 1930s, analytic philosophy has become dystopian in its effects in that it now encourages us to make ourselves at home in our social world, imagining ourselves to be secure in the knowledge that analysis and "empirical evaluation" are sufficient forms of criticism." However, in context, his argument is concerned clearly only with analytical political philosophy. In any case, even to the extent that Geuss advocates the overthrow of the analytical method more generally here, there is no indication he wishes to move beyond disciplinary subdivisions. He doesn't here say that he *doesn't* want to do that, either, but I think it needs to be declared affirmatively.

The problem with treating metaphysics and epistemology as independent of history and politics is not that it treats the real referents of metaphysics as ahistorical so much as that it fails to take philosophy itself to be a real thing that varies in relation to other real things.

In the subdisciplinary division of contemporary philosophy, political philosophy and its close cohort ethics alone are supposed to be about changing the world, whereas other areas are not. While Geuss clearly has little sympathy with analytical philosophy in general, his realist critique is focused solely on analytical political philosophy. He leverages continental philosophy to argue for a political philosophy "outside ethics," on the basis that the fundamental question of analytical ethics—"what ought I to do?"—is absent from the "main stream of Central European philosophy" (Geuss 2010, 60), but fails to apply this line of argument to contest other aspects of analytical philosophy vis-à-vis the continental tradition. A similar point about Geuss has been made by Cristoph Menke (2010), who concludes his review of Geuss's *Philosophy and Real Politics* with the specific criticism that Geuss fails to accede to the level of Adorno, one of Geuss's major influences, in producing something as philosophically rich and broad as Critical Theory, and that Geuss's realism is, by contrast, thin and narrow.

A broader criticism can indeed be made here, namely, that disciplinary distinctions between philosophy, literature, sociology, etcetera are ultimately untenable. Again, in much twentieth-century continental philosophy these distinctions have been elided, most obviously in the Frankfurt School, but also in other Western Marxism and neo-Marxism, and in some recent French philosophy: in France in the late twentieth century, academics like Foucault typically trained in classical philosophy before going on to do applied work in psychology, anthropology, or sociology. Like the subdisciplinary distinctions within philosophy, the distinction of philosophy from other disciplines is relatively recent.

One might argue that Geuss is being tactful or tactical in refraining from trying to storm the ramparts of analytic philosophy. To reject analytical philosophy is to risk being cast as a continental philosopher. Continental philosophy exists within contemporary philosophy as a corralled subdiscipline in its own right, within which it is free to be holistic, segregated from the mainstream of philosophical debate. One might thus argue that, by limiting his critique to political philosophy, Geuss might be able to gain some traction within the subdiscipline of political philosophy, escaping continental marginalization. However, there is no evidence that this is a deliberate tactical choice of Geuss's, nor any that such a tactic would be successful, either as a way of avoiding the "continental" label, or more generally in influencing political philosophy. Indeed one might, for Kuhnian reasons, for example, argue that piecemeal change will prove impossible and only a frontal assault aiming at revolutionary change has any prospect (albeit not much) of succeeding.

In the absence of a tactical rationale to constrain oneself to the critique of political philosophy as such, I would say one must go further, and reject analytical philosophy *holus bolus*.

Complexity

Geuss (2005, 39) calls for political philosophy to engage with public policy by "answering responsibly" questions such as "Is the actual regime of penal servitude, the family structure, or the system of compulsory school a good thing or a bad thing?" Geuss (ibid.) draws his notion of responsibility from Weber, to mean "thinking about [such questions] in a space organized around possible alternatives to the present existing state of affairs." Geuss (2008, 95; 2014, 68ff.) allows that we do not have to have an alternative in mind in order to criticize, a point made in almost the same terms by Foucault (2000, 236). Still, he seems to think that the evaluation of alternative courses of action is an appropriate task for political philosophy.

Here, Geuss enjoins political philosophers to "do politics" in Foucault's sense. Geuss seems to think this is unproblematic, and wants to put political thinkers at the disposal of public policy. There's a very specific problem with this, however, namely, that it is not possible to adjudicate between public policy alternatives until all available options have been implemented and studied in similar situations to the one in which they are being proposed. Geuss (2005, 39) acknowledges that "we have an inherently weak grasp on what is 'possible' and most societies are not set up so as naturally to improve this, or actively to make us aware of possibilities we may have ignored or taken with insufficient seriousness." He argues that the study of history can provide a guide, though then acknowledges that this can lead to illusions that things that used to be possible are still possible, but argues that further historical study may clear away this problem, in effect arguing for a hermeneutics.

I think, however, that there are serious limitations to what history can tell us about the political possibilities for today. One overarching problem for such a use of history is the extent to which the contemporary conjuncture is unlike any previously existing situation—most obviously because of our continual technological innovation, which means that the social situation today is radically different to that which obtained even a few years before. Another issue is that history can tell us very little about the potential for radically new political measures, hence the use of history as a guide would, in any case, tend to augur for conservative policies.

An alternative method for discerning new possibilities would be to use the imagination as our guide, but Geuss (2008, 49) rightly criticizes this. The fact that I can or cannot imagine something happening in politics has no a priori relation to whether it can or cannot occur in reality, since my imagination has a very limited capacity for modeling social reality. History thus seems a better guide, inasmuch as things that have happened once could, in principle at least, happen again. However, any specific occurrence in the past may have only been possible because of a configuration of circumstances that no longer obtains. Moreover, we cannot claim to know the exact coordinates of these circumstances, either the past or current ones, let alone those in the future: we know some facts about the present and past, but not all the details of every variable relevant to the operation of social policy.

George Santanyana's now-hackneyed dictum that "Those who cannot remember the past are condemned to repeat it" implies that by studying the past we can see where problems have occurred and thus avoid their recurrence. This does not, however, logically imply that if we do remember the past, we will know what positive things to do. There is an asymmetry in practice here ascribable to the precautionary principle: it is responsible, let's say, to argue that we know from the evidence that x can go wrong, therefore we should not do it; conversely, to say that because we know x has worked in the past we should do it now is, by contrast, irresponsible.

What stymies any attempt to adjudicate between alternatives by using historical evidence is, in a word, complexity. Society is much too complex for anyone to adjudicate between various courses of political action, because we can't possibly foresee the emergent effects that these courses of action will put in train. It is impossible to produce an entirely adequate elaboration or simulation of a system to be articulated within that same system, since it would have to have a complexity approaching that of the system itself. Moreover, William Connolly (2011) points out not only the complexity inherent in political systems (to the extent that these may be posited as independent "systems"), but also the extent to which political effects involve the complexities of other domains that interact with politics: climate, physics, biology, etcetera. It is thus impossible to evaluate an alternative scheme for social organization properly. It is inevitable that any attempt to realize any political scheme will have emergent consequences in excess of those intended by that scheme, and potentially opposite to it. This means that attempts to engineer society is futile, and hence I argue that intellectuals should confine their efforts to criticizing, revealing the relations between utopian visions and emergent social effects, rather than trying to produce new emergent effects without knowing what they will be.

The case here has been ably put by Ian Sanderson (2009) in relation to "evidence-based policy making," which attempts to put public policy on a "realistic" basis. Since the consequences of any policy are even in the short-term radically unforeseeable, evidence simply cannot provide an adequate basis for making public policy decisions. Rather, Sanderson (2009, 700) suggests that public policymaking "reflects the attractions of instrumental rationality as a response to the growing challenge of social complexity." That is, this form of "realism" occurs because people cannot think how else to proceed in politics in the face of complexity. Sanderson's solution is to engage in policymaking always tentatively, reflexively, and by continually adapting to emerging trends.[6]

Adrian Little (2012) responds to Sanderson's position, referring to Foucault, that the failure of public policy to have its expected outcomes is a consistent element of our political system. Political decision makers are not keen to acknowledge the extent to which failure is a standard feature of decision making, and indeed the criteria for policy success are generally ambiguous enough in any given area that it can be claimed regardless of the outcome (11). Little's conclusion is that we should see ourselves as "freed from the constraints always to succeed" to deal with political problems "unshackled by . . . epistemological certainties." Interestingly, he ends this sentence with a lone reference to Geuss's *Philosophy and Real Politics* (16),[7] incongruously enough, inasmuch Geuss's calls for us to proceed responsibly.

Where Sanderson aims to mitigate failure as much as possible by monitoring failure as it occurs and continuously adapting to it, Little simply endorses failing. Neither approach seriously questions the business of public policy and instead seeks to acknowledge its inevitable failure, in the belief that acknowledging this makes its consequences less serious than ignoring it, increasing the chances of success by adapting to failures as they happen in Sanderson's case, and trying out more options more quickly in Little's. Both options seem to continue the paradigm of evidence-based policymaking, differing from the conventional "evidence-based" policy only in that rather than gathering evidence from examining what has worked elsewhere, policymakers are now encouraged to turn their own dominion into a laboratory. This basic idea unites Sanderson and Little, and has the advantage over gathering evidence from elsewhere that our evidence is immanent, more immediately relevant.

These suggestions seem to me to have more or less the same problem, if perhaps on a different scale, as Rawls's position does for Geuss: there is no route for them to affect policymaking other than simply being "adopted" by policymakers, and it seems unlikely that any politician is going to want to be the first to admit failure, hence suggestions for better policymaking of this type must be suspected of being a reform discourse that supports the status quo by supporting the basic mechanism of top-down policymaking.

I would suggest, in any case, a different and more radical conclusion from the failure of policymaking, namely, to make it more immanent than even Little suggests through a democratization of policy that would allow for a more immediate feedback as to its results, with decision making from below rather than above, immanent to the processes over which decisions are made, and the effects they have. I do not propose this through the assertion of democracy as norm, even if doubtless the existence of this norm in our political society influences me to suggest such a thing, but as the negation of public policy as it exists today, in favor of the kind of delegate model of politics and administration advocated by Lenin in *State and Revolution*. On such a model, policy is controlled directly by those that it affects, and, in turn, can be almost immediately rescinded by them should it fail—the structures of endemic failure would be removed, and the determination of the norm of what counts as a success or failure placed in the hands of those it concerns. This is not to say this will issue in a problem-free utopia, only that it could negate specific vicissitudes of politics as it exists today. We can't anticipate the problems that would come from such a change, because of social complexity, but this is not to say that I am advocating this change as a matter of experimental policymaking at a meta level. Rather, I advocate the abolition of the domination of the political caste, not a positive public policy experiment, but a negative one, the abolition of public policy as such. Making public policy flexible (Sanderson) or defeasible (Little) does not promise such an abolition. This abolitionism moreover provides a different answer to how this new situation is to arise: while Sanderson and Little must hope for adoption, or perhaps advocacy through existing channels, I hope for change via grassroots struggle from below. It might be argued that this is less realistic, but I think it is impossible to assess accurately how realistic it is: wholesale change in this arena might in fact be more readily achievable than a kind of cultural shift within the existing set-up.

Here, I can and will invoke Foucault (2000, 370):

> We must transform the field of social institutions into a field of experimentation, in order to determine which levers to turn and which bolts to loosen in order to bring about the desired effects. It is indeed important to undertake a campaign of decentralization, for example, in order to bring the users closer to the decision-making centers on which they depend, and to tie them into the decision-making process, avoiding the type of globalizing integration that leaves people in complete ignorance about the conditions of particular judgments. We must then multiply these experiments wherever possible on the particularly important and interesting terrain of the social,

considering that an entire institutional system, now fragile, will probably undergo a restructuring from top to bottom.... For the moment, we lack completely the intellectual instruments to envisage in new terms the framework within which we could achieve our goals.

It's true that Foucault, when asked, did directly give public policy recommendations to the French government. However, these were generally simply in a negative direction, namely, that rules should be relaxed: he proposed that the age of consent be lowered, to give a specific example (Foucault 1988a, 285). Making negative policy recommendations is quite different to proposing new ways of doing things: while abolishing x or y may have all kinds of unforeseen knock-on effects, it will at least get rid of specific effects we do not like in the present, though the flow-on effects are unforeseeable. Still, there is a single, proximal, comprehensible effect that an abolition will have, namely, the absence of the thing abolished. This makes it possible to will it without being completely mistaken as to what one is doing. Critique has effects and plays a social role not anticipated nor even in principle foreseeable by its practitioners. The difference is that these unintended and unforeseen effects are not self-defeating: critique does not in itself aim at determinate effects, and any production of determinate effects is a matter for tactical reconsideration of the critique, an ongoing work of criticism of a fluctuating political reality.

Foucault did consider taking up bureaucratic posts, but that's something quite different again: I am here with Foucault delineating the role of an intellectual in relation to politics, not arguing that it is somehow imperative to be an intellectual. Still, while an intellectual, Foucault was on a commission to reform higher education. But again, this is what academics in the United States call "service," acting as an administrative functionary, not as part of his intellectual function. While there may be some blurring at the edges between intellectual and administrative functions, Foucault does not make public policy pronouncements in his books: they are not a component of his genealogical or archaeological methods. Just as he may have had moral prejudices, these are things bracketed from his thought.

For Foucault (1991, 172), political choice is ultimately a matter for the masses. The intellectual has the correlative function of exposing complexity: "I dream of the intellectual who destroys evidence and generalities, the one who, in the inertias and constraints of the present time, locates and marks the weak points, the openings, the lines of force, who is incessantly on the move, doesn't know exactly where he is heading nor what he will think tomorrow for he is too attentive to the present" (Foucault 1988a, 124). He proposes

> to raise questions in an effective, genuine way, and to raise them with the greatest possible rigor, with the maximum complexity and difficulty. . . . I take care not to dictate how things should be. I try instead to pose problems, to make them active, to display them in such a complexity that they can silence the prophets and lawgivers, all those who speak for others or to others. In this way, it will be possible for the complexity of the problem to appear in its connection with people's lives; and, consequently, through concrete questions, difficult cases, movements of rebellion, reflections, and testimonies, the legitimacy of a common creative action can also appear (Foucault 2000, 288).

It has been suggested that Foucault is a complexity theorist *avant la letter* (Olssen 2008). I think this is half-true: Foucault certainly accounts for complexity independently of complexity theory. But he does not seek to theoretize complexity; while complexity theory seeks to expand systems theory to account for complexity, Foucault sees complexity as the limit of theory.

8

Foucault
The Lure of Neoliberalism

This final chapter is the only one of the book to focus on Foucault. This is the logical end point of a trajectory in which I have tended to come closer and closer to Foucault's own position as the book progressed. This focus on Foucault, however, is refracted through the lens of another figure, Paul Patton, an Australian scholar of French philosophy who was one of the first to write about Foucault in English (Morris and Patton, 1979).[1] Unlike the previous chapters, there is no contrast here between Foucault and a non-Foucauldian alternative, but rather a contestation of the interpretation of Foucault.

Patton's early work on Foucault is directly seminal to my interpretation of Foucault as non-normative, which grounds this entire book. However, Patton has lately read Foucault normatively. Patton presents his two perspectives as compatible, because the first was a reading of a particular phase of Foucault's work as in specific respects non-normative, and his more recent readings are of later works of Foucault's as normative. I will argue here that the second reading is wrong, however, and that Foucault's non-normativity persists through his career. In so doing, I join the debate that has erupted in recent years around Foucault's relationship with neoliberalism.

Patton's earlier position is articulated primarily in two articles: his 1989 "Taylor and Foucault on Power and Freedom," and his sole piece on Foucault of the 1990s, "Foucault's Subject of Power." His later position was initially developed in print in two articles on Foucault and rights—"Power and Right in Nietzsche and Foucault" (2004) and "Foucault, Critique and Rights" (2005)—though its apogee in print to date is perhaps "Foucault and Normative Political Philosophy" (2010).

In what follows, I will first explain my interpretation of Foucault's position; second, detail criticisms of Foucault that emerged from critical theorists outside France in the early 1980s; third, examine Patton's defense of Foucault against one of these critics, Charles Taylor; fourth, examine Patton's work on Foucault and rights; and last, deal with recent work on Foucault's relation to neoliberalism, including by Patton.

Foucault's Position

Foucault's principal works give accounts of historical phenomena and their development—madness, medicine, the human sciences, the prison, sexuality—which vary between dry description and excoriatory critique. Some readers have seen normative connotations in his vocabulary, but I would argue that these connotations are either nonexistent or at least not intended by Foucault. In particular, both Nancy Fraser (1995, 143) and Jon Simons (1995, 42) have seen something pejorative in Foucault's notion of "biopower." I would argue that this word has no ineluctably negative overtone (though I think some—specifically, Giorgio Agamben and Hardt and Negri—have taken it up as a pejorative term in Foucault's wake), and that Foucault is not opposed to biopower—at least, there is no clear indication whatsoever that he is, and the most he ever suggests practically in relation to it is not abolishing biopower per se, but trying to decouple it from racism (Foucault 2003, 263). Even "racism," which has clear negative connotations as a term in contemporary parlance, and is a phenomenon that Foucault opposes in the form that is commonly meant by the term, is a word that Foucault uses not in order rhetorically to condemn, but as a matter of descriptive accuracy. As Patton (1985, 71) says in one of his earliest pieces on Foucault, "there is no denunciation. . . . The texts do not display on their surface any values."

Foucault (1980, 212) pointedly refuses to engage in polemic. Instead, he engages only in critique. In his genealogical works of the 1970s, Foucault's critique primarily means the analysis of power relations. He enjoins us not to "ask, is power good or is it evil, legitimate or illegitimate, a question of right of morality? Rather, simply, try to rid the question of power of all the moral and juridical overtones that we have previously given it, and ask this question naïvely, which hasn't been posed that often, even if effectively a number of people have been posing it for a long time: what do power relations essentially consist of?" (Foucault 1994c, 540). This question calls for a purely descriptive answer, without a normative component, beyond the trivial extent to which normativity might be said to be necessary for language to function.

Foucault does nonetheless in his published work voice a wish to oppose such things as sexuality and racism, domination and normalization, in the sense of advocating action against them. He does not suggest a normative basis for this opposition, however. Rather, the opposition follows from analyses of power relations. In all these cases, Foucault opposes concealed realities exposed by his analyses. Now, Foucault has no basis to prescribe opposition to these things, nor even does he engage in an explicit negative evaluation of them, but he clearly does oppose them, and it is hard to see how anyone agreeing with his analysis could not, since he has effectively exposed the hypocrisy of power. This portrays his work as functioning somewhat like immanent critique, though a non-normative form: where conventional immanent critique upholds the values of a society against the reality that fails to conform to norms, Foucault's critique condemns both norm and reality as two sides of a structural whole that conceals the complicity of apparently contradictory discourses. Power is hypocritical when it involves a subterfuge about its own nature, and Foucault (1998a, 86) indeed holds that this is inevitable—"power is tolerable only on condition that it mask a substantial part of itself"—hence we can conclude that critical unmasking is inimical to such power. We cannot continue to will sexual liberation in the same way after reading Foucault's *Will to Knowledge*, if we agree with his factual claims, because he shows that this liberation is not what we thought it was—indeed, not a liberation at all: where we thought we were sexually repressed and that we could free ourselves by talking about sex, he shows that it is through our talking about it that sexuality has ensnared us. It is not necessary for us to have a negative normative evaluation of being ensnared for us not to like this: the logic of sexuality is exploded, and to the extent that we are convinced by Foucault's critique we cease to believe in that logic—even if this effect is difficult to sustain in the context of imbrication in the regime of sexuality in our everyday lives. Similarly, once Foucault in *Discipline and Punish* shows us that the prison in fact regularly produces criminality as its first effect, our belief in this form of punishment is fundamentally disturbed, unless we reject or ignore Foucault's empirical thesis. To say an institution does not serve its purported purpose is a devastating criticism in itself. Foucault's (1994c, 540–541) method is extraordinarily simple, viz. "to make visible precisely what is visible, which is to say, to take what is so close, what is so immediate, what is so intimately connected to ourselves that we cannot perceive it, and make it apparent."

Foucault's critiques only undermine and cannot by themselves destroy the machinations of power they describe. He never suggests in more than the most allusive terms, specifically in terms of the negation of the status quo through resistance to the existing order, to man and to sexuality for example, what the alternative would be, and hence never assumes any positive stance.

The Reaction to Foucault

A number of similar criticisms of Foucault have been made by those who believe that political thought and practice require a normative ground. I believe these are based on an inadequate understanding of Foucault's genealogical method, although this is explained in part by the inadequacy of his methodological explanations in his major published genealogies, where he is more concerned with engaging in the project of critical genealogy rather than examining its bases. To understand his position, therefore, we must have recourse to his interviews and short articles, which have been slow to appear in English. Two of the quotations I give above, for example, which I believe go some distance to explaining his position, are from materials still not available in English translation.

Foucault's critics do not in any case seriously consider how it might be possible to engage in political criticism non-normatively, so when faced with his non-normative thought, they either condemn it as incoherent or posit normative values that they see at work in his thought. Foucault's interest in ethics and subjectivity in his late work appears in this light as a belated recognition of the purported normative deficit in his thought and an attempt to correct it.

Patton (1985, 71) points out that the objectivity of Foucault's analyses encourages readings of him as lacking any interest in political change, which is to say, essentially, as a conservative. Patton cites Richard Rorty (1984) and Edward Said (1983, 247) as examples of such readings. Both these two writers accurately see Foucault's prose as neutral and dispassionate, but for them this seems to betoken a lack of genuine political commitment. These reactions echo an earlier reaction to Foucault in France from the humanist left, which cast Foucault's anti-Marxist historical relativism about truth in the human sciences as conservative. His critical reception outside France was, by contrast, coming later after his genealogical work, marked by a concern with his relativism concerning normativity. As Patton points out, however, Foucault's apparent neutrality is coupled with committed political activism.

I would explain the relation of Foucault's activism to his thought by saying schematically that his thought is for him another form of political activism. As Foucault says in conversation with Deleuze, "theory does not express, translate, or serve to apply practice: it is practice" (Deleuze and Foucault 1977, 213). Foucault's writing (which in this context can be considered "theory"—he is here using this word that Deleuze introduced into the discussion with the caveat "in this sense") is for him a specific form of activist intervention—and it is my contention that part of its specificity lies in its distinction from politics, lack of normativity, and non-theoreticism. I do not believe that for Foucault it either seeks to find an expression in practice nor is it supposed to be an expression of practices other than itself. Here I am at odds with Marcello Hoffman's (2013) recent reading of Foucault as crucially influenced in his conceptual development by his activist experiences. While of course these experiences cannot but have some influence on his thought and vice versa, I consider Hoffman's argument wholly meretricious (Kelly 2014a). Foucault's thought is a parallel and complementary, but nonetheless quite distinct, activity to his activism in the more literal sense. We should be careful here to distinguish Foucault's activist statements, for example, statements he allegedly authored but which were signed by a group or an organization, from his own position: when he wrote as a spokesman, he is not simply giving his views, but rather in fact engaging in a rather different practice.

Still, the notion that Foucault's thought is a form of practice might seem to confirm what many have alleged—that Foucault in fact does have a left-wing normative political position but fails to acknowledge it explicitly in his work. This is broadly the position of Nancy Fraser (1995), Jürgen Habermas (1987, 272–276), and Charles Taylor (1984), to name only the most prominent political thinkers who argue that Foucault's work is (in Habermas's phrase) "cryptonormative." Taylor's "Foucault on Freedom and Truth" is particularly important for our purposes, since Patton's 1989 piece was a direct response to it, and I think it can serve as an exemplary case of the general tendency in Foucault commentary. This article of Taylor's mostly consists of a critical reading of the first volume of Foucault's *History of Sexuality*. In the final section of his article, Taylor (1984, 175) argues that Foucault is lost without a normative basis for his inquiries, but that his inquiries do presuppose such a basis, in the form of a fidelity to freedom and truth, which Foucault disavows because of his "Nietzschean relativism." Taylor implies that Foucault does think that disciplinary power is bad and that liberation from power is good, that Foucault's own analyses of these phenomena are true, and that truth can set us free. That is, Foucault is really an Enlightenment humanist, fighting for truth and justice, who refuses to accept this status, but this refusal is untenable, causing confusion for himself and his readers in the process.

Foucault (1998a, 60) for his part denies that truth is on the side of freedom or error on the side of enslavement, but, as we have seen, he claims at the same time that power needs to mask itself to exist, himself trying to expose power by showing us its operation. The compatibility of these positions is a matter of elementary logic, however. Though Foucault does think that power uses ignorance to shield itself, and that the truth can be useful in setting us free from power, this does not imply that truth *in general* serves to set us free from power, nor that ignorance always plays into power's hands. In all kinds of ways, power does work via the truth. All truth is selective; *pace* Hegel, there is no possibility of absolute knowledge, since humans lack the capacity for omniscience. The truth as we understand it will always be partial. Thus truths that are articulated always leave a space of concealment in which power may operate. There will therefore always be a task to point out truths that expose specific strategies of power, though never any possibility of exposing the entirety of ubiquitous social power.

Patton's Defense of Foucault

Patton's (1989) challenge to Taylor consists largely in explaining how Foucault's vocabulary works. Foucault uses the terms "power," "truth," and "freedom" in different ways to their use by normative humanists who see power as simply a bad thing to be opposed and truth and freedom as goods to be affirmed. In particular, where "power" and "freedom" are binary opposites from Taylor's conventional point of view, for Foucault the latter is merely a modality of the former. For Foucault, any and all human interaction implies power relations, so the idea of opposing power as such is nonsense: we can only oppose particular instances or forms of power. "Freedom" for Foucault thus simply refers to a condition of relatively loose power relations, where agents can contest arrangements by exerting influence on one another. He is not absolutely in favor of this arrangement, moreover.

All three terms, "truth," "power," and "freedom," for Foucault refer to historically variable forms. There is no historically transcendent truth, no power without resistance, no ultimate freedom toward which we strive. Patton in his early work argues that these concepts in Foucault are not merely historically relative, but non-normative, that Foucault's use of the terms "freedom," "power," and "truth" are not "evaluative" at all, but rather only descriptive (Patton 1989, 260). That is, they are for Foucault only a grid of analysis, only regimes of truth, strategies of power, and practices of freedom.

This explains how Foucault uses apparently normative terms without their usual normative connotations, but does not explain what the basis for the orientation of his work is if it is not a normative one. Thus, in his reply to Patton, Taylor (1989) continues to push the claim that Foucault has a hidden normative agenda. Patton (1998) in turn provides a deeper explanation of the non-normativity of Foucault's position in his next major intervention, his main piece on Foucault of the 1990s, "Foucault's Subject of Power." Where Patton's debate with Taylor had centered on *Discipline and Punish* and the first volume of Foucault's *History of Sexuality*, works published a year apart from one another in the mid-1970s, Patton now discusses Foucault's extraordinary late essay, "The Subject and Power," first published in 1982. Patton's account here completes his earlier account of Foucault on power, much as, I have argued elsewhere, Foucault's "Subject and Power" completed Foucault's account of power itself (Kelly 2009, 77).

Foucault in this essay revisits the question of power and resistance he previously raised in his work of the mid-1970s. His humanist critics tend to argue that the only way to differentiate resistance from power is via normative evaluation, but Foucault now provides a value-neutral basis for a differentiation of resistance from power per se, and also for considering resistance as prior to power. This last element seems particularly surprising, since putting resistance before power seems to imply a normative valorization of it. Patton explains to us how it does not, however. This is the core of his argument:

> In the attempt to exercise their capacity for autonomous actions, those subject to relations of domination will inevitably be led to oppose them. It is not at all a question of advocating such resistance, of praising autonomy or blaming domination as respective exemplars of a good and evil for all, but simply of understanding why such resistance does occur. Foucault does not think that resistance to forms of domination requires justification. To the extent that it occurs, such resistance follows from the nature of particular human beings. It is an effect of human freedom. (Patton 1998, 73)

Power is a force that supervenes on our actions, and our actions therefore always already produce resistance—as Foucault (1997b, 167) himself puts it, "resistance comes first." There is no need to assert normatively that we should be on the side of resistance, since we are already on the side of resistance: we are essentially resistant entities. Patton characterizes this as part of a Foucauldian notion of human nature. Foucault (1997, 109) himself "mistrusts" the idea of a human nature per se, because of its essentialist, universalist connotations, but Patton's conception of human nature is that our nature is precisely to defy any attempt to ascribe to us any specific natural qualities, much like the Feuerbachian conception of human nature I ascribed to Marx in Chapter 1.

As I have argued elsewhere, this explains in turn the force of Foucault's critique (Kelly 2009, 125). First, it explains how critique can be motivated even in the absence of normativity: the critic herself encounters forms of power such as discipline and sexuality and is motivated to oppose them automatically, as it were, without the need for any moral framework. Second, it explains critique's effect on readers: we recognize these ubiquitous strategies of power in our own lives and are moved by the description of them to resist them (or we fail to recognize or relate to them, in which case we are left cold by the critique).

Patton on Foucault and Rights

Patton's next engagement with Foucault, in the following decade, took place around a tangential issue, namely Foucault's attitude to rights. Patton (2004, 45) uses Foucault as an important inspiration in the development of what he calls a "naturalistic account of rights."

Foucault invoked the concept of rights only late in his life, but did so enthusiastically. For Patton (2004, 43), Foucault in this moment "appears to rely without embarrassment upon normative concepts for which his own discourse not only does not provide any foundation but rather seems to undermine the very possibility of foundation, at least in the terms in which this has traditionally been provided."

Patton's position here is broadly similar to that taken by Foucault's critics twenty years before, inasmuch as Patton now sees Foucault as using a normative vocabulary that is apparently in contradiction with his meta-ethical position. However, Patton does not criticize Foucault for this, but holds that Foucault's position can coherently incorporate normativity. In doing so, Patton seems to be going against the logic of his previous defense of Foucault, inasmuch as that seemed to take Foucault to be rigorously non-normative. That said, Patton's earlier defense of non-normativity was specifically confined to the issues of power, resistance, freedom, and truth, and did not deal with the question of rights—hence there is no necessary contradiction. Nevertheless, I will argue that Patton's claim that Foucault's invocation of rights is normative is incorrect, and that Foucault is on the contrary consistently non-normative.

Patton (2004) argues, following Nietzsche, that rights may be seen as a kind of formalized structure of power relations. This explains for him how rights can in Foucault's schema be real elements of an historical configuration. Patton's naturalism about rights means a view of rights that is realist and historically relative: the concept of rights emerges in a particular context, and different rights will be appropriate in different historical contexts. On Patton's (2004, 57) view this means that rights are grounded normatively in an historically contingent, but nonetheless real, normative framework. Patton proceeds in an article the following year, "Foucault, Critique and Rights," to read Foucault directly as espousing an historically relative normativity. This work on rights, then, becomes the basis of a more general claim by Patton (2010, 204) about Foucault, viz. that Foucault "makes frequent and explicit normative recommendations, especially in interviews and occasional texts in support of particular causes." Patton's cited evidence for this assertion consists entirely of Foucault's advocacy of rights, with Patton (2010, 221) explicitly referring to four instances of Foucault's rights discourse in an endnote in support of this claim. This list includes three of four instances of Foucault's use of rights in Patton's (2004, 43) earlier article on Foucault and rights. Putting the two lists together, we have a list of five instances in which Foucault uses the language of rights, which Patton believes are all (the) instances evincing Foucault's normativity:

1. "In a 1984 speech he gave in support of non-governmental organizations attempting to protect Vietnamese refugees being attacked by pirates in the Gulf of Thailand, he spoke of the right of international citizens to intervene in matters of international policy hitherto reserved for governments and suggested that the suffering of individuals "founds an absolute right to stand up and speak to those who hold power" (Foucault 2000, 474–475)" (Patton 2004, 43; cf. Patton 2010, 221).

2. "In a 1983 interview on "The Risks of Security," he endorsed the idea of a right to the "means of health" and also a right to suicide (Foucault 2000, 365–381)" (Patton 2010, 221).

3. "In a 1982 interview on the issue of gay rights, he advocated the creation of new forms of relational right that would recognize same sex relationships (Foucault 1997b, 157–162)" (Patton 2004, 43/Patton, 2010, 221).

4. "In a 1977 interview on the extradition of Klaus Croissant, lawyer for the Red Army Faction, Foucault referred to the "rights of the governed," including the right to be properly defended in a court of law, and described these as "more precise, more historically determined than the rights of man" (1994c, 362)" (Patton 2010, 221).

5. "Earlier, in a 1976 lecture, he suggested that the struggle against disciplinary power called for a new articulation of right which would be 'emancipated from the principle of sovereignty' (Foucault 2003, 40)" (Patton 2004, 43).

I would point out that each of these five invocations of rights by Foucault is a call for rights only qua limitations on power. In the specific cases listed above:

1. Foucault suggests a right of individuals to object to the actions of others specifically in relation to the actions of

pirates: it is a right of counter-power. Foucault sees non-governmental organizations here as innovating and pursuing such rights. This constitutes an appeal to governments, but only in the limited sense of a right "to stand up and speak to those who hold power" (Foucault 2000, 475). It is not a policy recommendation, but a refusal to allow governments a monopoly on action. This right is not a new norm so much as an objection. It is "absolute" not in the sense of being universal or transcendental, but rather in that sense that those who demand it authorize themselves to do so outside of any legal or moral framework. For Foucault (1994d, 708), the demand is "founded" in the people's "misfortune" (*malheur*—the published translation speaks of it being "grounded" in their "suffering," which would be somewhat different; Foucault, 2000, 475). This could be taken to imply a normative grounding, via a claim that no one should be allowed to experience adversity, that adversity is a bad thing. Foucault is not saying this, however, but rather only that this is factically the ground in which the demand springs up, qua the site of emergence of resistance. If "suffering" were being posited as a normative grounding, it would ground a right to an absence of any unpleasantness, but Foucault only posits a right to speak up against oppression.

2. Here, a similarly absolute demand is raised toward the state, a pure counter-power demand, implicitly posed diametrically against the contemporary Western biopolitics that, according to Foucault (2003, 241), "makes live" and "lets die." Against this, we demand that power neither let people die, nor force them to live against their will, albeit without demanding the rescindment of biopolitics's assistance to those who want to live.

3. In this interview, Foucault (1997b, 157) is directly asked in the opening question about "rights" as such, to which he responds by suggesting that the legal framework of rights is inadequate to deal with the problem of discrimination against homosexuals, which is so deep-rooted in behavior. He does not here simply advocate a right of homosexuals

to marry, but a form of recognition of all kinds of relationships that would greatly open up the possibilities for people to relate to one another, beyond the paradigm of marriage, which Foucault finds constraining. His positive invocation of rights here is relatively minor, and is only to advocate an explosion of the limits of contemporary legality, a profusion of rights vis-à-vis the limited ones we have at present, thus an act of negation of limits, not a normative proposal.

4. What Foucault has to say in relation to the case of Croissant, a lawyer charged with aiding his terrorist clients, is in a basically descriptive register, though Foucault asserts the importance of the right to legal representation. This instance, more than any of the others, resembles Patton's notion of supporting existing real rights. Unlike in the previous examples, there is no demand for a new right here, only a discussion of the real importance of an existing legal right. The importance of this well-established right to legal advocacy is as a form of protection against the power of the state. This protection was effectively under attack in the Croissant case, with a lawyer persecuted for helping his clients (albeit in possibly illegal ways). Such a right requires the state to exist to assure it, but the right itself only limits the state's power, by not allowing the state to punish without due process. Now, I would contend that this right can play into the hands of power where powerful interests confront the state: the right of unlimited legal representation to the rich and to corporations allows them to run rings around poorly resourced public prosecutors. But the right to legal representation per se is not the right to such stupendous legal resources. In any case, Foucault here does not normatively call for justice to work in a certain, idealized way. Rather, he simply intervenes in support of existing rights of defendants in a particular context. This does not preclude denunciation of the legal system more generally.

5. Foucault's statement here is strictly hypothetical, about what we would need to do if we want to resist discipline,

not calling absolutely for a new form of right on categorical, normative grounds. I will expand on this case in more detail below, since it plays a peculiarly important role in Patton's later commentary.

In Foucault's 1979 piece in *Le Monde* reacting to the co-option of the Iranian Revolution by the Ayatollah Khomeini, "Useless to Revolt?," Foucault spells out why rights are important for him: "The rules that exist to limit [power] can never be stringent enough; the universal principles for dispossessing it of all the occasions it seizes are never sufficiently rigorous. Against power one must always set inviolable laws and unrestricted rights" (Foucault 2000, 453). In this guise, rights are an expression of resistance, negative, belonging to private individuals or to the masses, not to the powerful. Not all rights work this way, however, and Foucault's calls are, I will argue, constructed so as to avoid falling into the trap of power, though one may certainly argue that they have not always been successful in this regard. Any right—indeed, any statement—can be incorporated into a strategy of power relations, and indeed this is true of resistance too: all resistance is apt to be reincorporated within power's emergent intentionality. This does not mean that resistance is futile, defeated from the start, only that resistance is a matter of continual reinvention, and that there is no form that is resistant in all contexts, including the language of rights. Patton is entirely correct to point out that rights are for Foucault historically relative, but this is not because they must be in accordance with the mores of the time, but rather just the opposite: rights for Foucault are useful only insofar as they actively challenge the status quo. While Foucault might have agreed with Patton's naturalist position as an understanding of the operation of existing, legally established rights, I would argue, against Patton's reading, that Foucault's own invocation of the language of rights as an activist works in a rather different way. Foucault raises the banner of rights only in such instances as it escapes the old logic of defined, individual rights; he does so in order to demand new rights that challenge existing power structures. Ben Golder (2015) has, in a contribution with which I agree in almost every detail, pointed out a number of instances in which Foucault contemporaneously avoids the notion of rights in contexts in which it was not tactically helpful. The fact that these rights may then be taken up as a discourse of power is no contraindication, since there is no form of resistance that is immune from such a colonization.

Foucault and Liberalism

The limitation of power by rights has historically been synonymous with liberalism. Patton (2010) has in his more recent published work on Foucault argued, starting from this evidence of normativity given by Foucault's invocation of rights, that Foucault is at least sympathetic to liberalism. The mainspring of this claim is a reading of Foucault's 1979 Collège de France lecture series, *The Birth of Biopolitics*, which deals with the history of neoliberalism.

Patton is not the first to read *The Birth of Biopolitics* as showing signs of sympathy with its subject matter. Foucault's own sometime assistant, François Ewald, had long before turned Foucauldian thinking to the service of neoliberalism, though it is only recently that Ewald (2012, 5) has explicitly declared that Foucault himself found "a solution" in neoliberal thought. Eric Paras (2006) was perhaps the first to read these lectures explicitly this way, on the basis of tape recordings, before they were ever published. In Paras's wake, Michael Behrent (2009) has read Foucault more concertedly as a liberal. Most recently the allegation of Foucault's neoliberalism has been aired through a widely shared online translation of an interview with Daniel Zamora (2014), editor of a book on the topic of Foucault and neoliberalism. Though in his essay on the topic, Zamora (2016) is more strident than Patton in proclaiming Foucault's neoliberalism, he produces no arguments not introduced previously by Patton, nor does he approach Patton's sophistication, apparently indeed being quite ignorant of Patton's work.

I would suggest that Patton's, and others', reading of *The Birth of Biopolitics* as sympathetic to neoliberalism can be accounted for by reference to the profound ambiguity of the work: *The Birth of Biopolitics* is more ambiguous than most of Foucault's work, since it is really just a matter of an immediate re-presentation of Foucault's then-most-recent reading, rather than anything resembling an archaeological or genealogical analysis.

Behrent, Paras, and Zamora all cast Foucault as shifting in the milieu of the late 1970s away from Marxism toward liberal normativity. I agree that this is the general trajectory of Foucault's interests and vocabulary at this time, although only to the extent of taking normative perspectives as objects of analysis, rather than subscribing to them himself. Foucault (2010, 3) talks about studying "normative frameworks of behavior," but this is precisely to take them as the object of critical study only, not to articulate new ones: "I tried to pose the question of norms of behavior first of all in terms of power" (4). Here there is an extraordinary footnote to an undelivered manuscript remark in which Foucault (5) refers to his position (uniquely) as "negativism." I do not accept that there is any serious change in his underlying political or philosophical orientation, only an engagement with the new realities around him on the basis of an ongoing ethos of critical resistance.

Foucault never makes any direct statement of sympathy with any variety of liberalism. Such an alignment with an ideology would indeed be at odds with Foucault's intellectual project of the critical analysis of historical discourses. One might suggest there is a difference because Foucault's canonical books deal with discourses for the most part relatively distant to the present, whereas *The Birth of Biopolitics* is uniquely contemporary in its concerns. Yet, Foucault's historical works are all, he says, "histories of the present," targeted at finding the genealogical roots of current discourses and practices.

Behrent (2009, 546) sees Foucault as attracted to neoliberalism rather than classical liberalism because its economism meant he could embrace it without adopting rights-based humanism. However, Foucault says things much more directly supportive of rights discourse than he does of neoliberal discourse, so Behrent's argument seems to have things backward here. I believe with Patton that if Foucault is liberal at this time, this would have to be connected to his occasional contemporaneous use of the vocabulary of rights.

Behrent (2009, 562), despite having argued that neoliberalism attracts Foucault because of its difference from classical liberalism, goes on to argue that Foucault is attracted to classical utilitarianism, and that, because classical liberalism was concerned to prevent there being too much government, liberalism is in general consonant with Foucault's project of cutting the head off the king. Such an argument is specious: Foucault's (1978, 88–89) metaphor of cutting off the head of the king in political theory in his *Will to Knowledge* is about ridding us of a conception of power that sees power as hierarchically organized around the state, not about any reduction of the power of the state. Liberalism's demand for the limitation of state-power in fact is thus the opposite of cutting the head off the king, since it involves thinking about power primarily in terms of the state. Relatedly, in *The Birth of Biopolitics* Foucault (2008, 76) cautions us to avoid an attitude he calls "state phobia." State phobia is the belief that the state is essentially evil, a "cold monster," to use a phrase of Nietzsche's that Foucault quotes. State phobia is one way of failing to cut the head off the king in political theory by viewing power negatively as centered on the state. It also involves the belief that the state naturally tends toward totalitarianism. This form of suspicion is extraordinarily widespread: it is animated by a fear of totalitarian regimes, but itself also animates totalitarian ideologies themselves, most obviously Marxism with its aim of the "withering away of the state," but also Nazism, insofar as the Nazis wanted to replace the state with the *Volk* (Foucault 2008, 111).

Foucault mentions this phobia in the context of an exploration of neoliberalism because neoliberalism is a contemporary example of the state-phobic tendency Foucault criticizes. We should note here that, for Foucault (2008, 78), there are "two main forms" of contemporary neoliberalism, the German and the American, though they share European roots and are closely interrelated in theory and in practice. He spends five lectures of *The Birth of Biopolitics* dealing mostly with the former, then four dealing with the latter. The American form is the more state-phobic of the two: it tends to cast the state as simply a bad thing to be combated in favor of the market. The German form, "ordoliberalism," by contrast, sees the state as necessary to create the market, but is nonetheless state phobic, since it casts the state as a problem to be limited. Foucault (2008, 189) adduces as an example of state phobia German neoliberal Wilhelm Röpke's analysis of William Beveridge's plan for the post-war British social welfare state. Röpke argues that the increase of the state sector will inevitably lead in a totalitarian direction. Such state phobia was, according to Foucault (2008, 106), animated by the experience of Nazism, which was taken to have revealed the insidious tendencies of all statism.

Foucault rejects state phobia in favor of taking seriously the specificity of different modes of government. However, by the same token, he might seem to have an affinity with neoliberalism's ultimate intention of limiting power. The demand for reduced government is a commonality between Foucault and liberalism, as Patton notes. Foucault (1997c, 29) defines critique as "the art of not being governed quite so much," hence we can interpret his entire critical enterprise, and in effect his life's work, as being about limiting government through criticism, which, as Foucault (28) argues here, is a matter of producing objections to certain forms of government. However, for Foucault "being governed" is not synonymous with "government" as it is understood by liberals, that is, with the state. Rather it refers to many forms of unequal power relations. Foucault is concerned with the state to an extent, but adamant that we should not see that as the main focus of resistance. Moreover, even in the domain in which liberals do oppose power, viz. state power, they aim to produce a stable but minimal state power, where Foucault would accept no such horizon to resistance: liberals aim to establish a positive, optimal minimum of government, where Foucault simply aims to reduce government with no particular goal in sight. In relation to the original growth of liberal governmentality, Foucault (2008, 62) indicates that, while liberalism is centered on the concept of freedom, this does not imply that its adoption as a governmental rationality led to an increase in freedom in practice.[2] Neoliberals hold that freedom is correlative to the size of the state, at least ceteris paribus, and that to increase one is to reduce the other. Foucault (62–63), however, does not believe it is possible in principle to quantify freedom. Even to the extent one could, moreover, there's no reason to believe that there is a simple negative relation between size of the state and freedom: some measures taken by states may increase freedom, as liberals allow is true of the basic functions of the state in safeguarding life and liberty.

However, does Foucault's wish not to be governed so much not imply precisely a quantification of freedom? Foucault's aim I think is rather different from an idea of minimizing a quantum of government. Rather, his point is that critique attacks determinate forms of government. There is unfortunately no guarantee that getting rid of one form of power will not open the door to something else more aggressive appearing in its place—we can't see that far ahead due to social complexity. However, the abolition of forms in itself constitutes an objective reduction. We do not necessarily become "more free," but we are to this extent governed less, at least immediately thereafter.

Where Foucault is mistrustful and critical of the state, the (neo)liberal approach is a technocratic, overall limitation based on a specific, positive construction of a governmental order. Yet Patton (2010, 213) argues that Foucault is attracted to precisely the public policy stances of neoliberalism, specifically "the neo-liberal theory of criminality" that he claims Foucault "appears to endorse." But Foucault (2008, 253) in fact merely discusses this and gives no indication of approving of it.

Patton, at least in more recent writings on the topic (e.g., Patton 2013, 176), distances himself from the most strident associations (e.g., Behrent 2009) of Foucault with neoliberalism, that is, from claims that Foucault is simply a convinced neoliberal. Patton nonetheless claims that Foucault sympathizes with neoliberalism, or at least with certain neoliberal positions. Patton's contention is based on connecting Foucault's (2008,

207) assessment that the neoliberal alternative is "less . . . disciplinary" with a comment made by Foucault (2003, 39–40) in *Society Must Be Defended* that, if we are to resist discipline, "we should be looking for a new right that is both antidisciplinary and emancipated from the principle of sovereignty" (Patton 2010, 214), the fifth on our above list of Foucault's invocations of rights. Patton pairs these two remarks to infer that in neoliberalism, in 1979, Foucault found what he had been looking for in 1976: a post-disciplinary form of right.

Foucault does indeed think that neoliberalism is less disciplinary than the forms of governmentality that preceded it. For him, neoliberalism's attitude toward punishment in particular is something new: where the previous governmentality saw incarceration as a form of rehabilitation that grasped the individual physically and psychically, detailed by Foucault in *Discipline and Punish*, neoliberalism conceives punishment as an economic disincentive. That Foucault recognizes neoliberalism as less disciplinary does not amount to an endorsement of it, however. While he may be looking for some new right that is anti-disciplinary and non-sovereign, this does not imply that he must endorse any right that fits this bill. Patton argues that we can only adopt a new right that we find already available to us, and neoliberalism is the best available candidate. Here, Patton effectively takes up a position discussed at length above in relation to Richard Rorty, which I argued is not Foucault's position. Patton's (2010, 214–215) evidence that this is Foucault's position seems to be that Foucault only gives as his example of counter-conducts and resistances movements that really exist. However, to conclude from this that we as actors in an unfolding present must try to use only concepts already available to us seems to invalidly rule out the possibility of radical innovation: we can use a neoliberal conception of rights because it already exists, but this conception of rights presumably itself had to be formulated, hence one can formulate a new conception of rights. As useful contrast, here is provided Foucault's position on socialist governmentality, which is, as Patton (2013, 176) glosses it elsewhere, that "if there was such a thing as socialist governmentality, it remained to be invented." That is, there's no guarantee that there is or ever will be anything that fits this bill.

More to the point, perhaps, in any case, I do not accept that neoliberalism is either anti-disciplinary and non-sovereign, nor that Foucault thinks it is: "less disciplinary" is not "non-disciplinary"; indeed, it implies precisely that neoliberalism is still disciplinary, just not as disciplinary as what came before. In Foucault's terminology, neoliberalism is a governmentality, whereas discipline is a technology of power. However different its rationale for and conception of punishment, neoliberal punishment remains disciplinary about shaping human behavior. Here, Patton's position is reminiscent of Deleuze's in positing a form of post-disciplinary society, and my refutation of Deleuze's in Chapter 4 applies.

Patton (2010, 214) is right that Foucault's critiques do sometimes point in the same direction as neoliberal discourse, most notably Foucault's position in a late interview that current social security arrangements have become untenable and should be abandoned in favor of a social security system that frees us from subjugation (Foucault 2000, 366). Zamora (2016, 74) similarly leans on this interview as evidence for his interpretation of Foucault as neoliberal.[3] While Foucault's position here is consonant with the neoliberal commonplace that beyond a certain point welfarism harms the market economy, it is equally compatible with a Marxist diagnosis that capitalism's ability to supply welfare to the workers is limited and that it is thus capitalism, not welfarism, that must be superseded. Foucault actually gives neither gloss. He rather simply baldly states that in an era where there is no upper limit to how much might be spent on medical care, for example, due to the proliferation of expensive treatments and research possibilities, rationing becomes necessary (Foucault 2000, 367–368). Neoliberals' solution to this is to use markets to allocate resources efficiently. By contrast, Foucault (2000, 370) posits "the objective of an optimal social coverage joined to a maximum of independence." Some neoliberals might accept this phrasing as describing their intention, but all brands of liberalism will tend to emphasize independence over coverage, which Foucault does not. Similarly, he calls for "decentralization," and while it's possible for neoliberals to conceive of their agenda in this way, it's hardly their standard jargon. Foucault does seem to be endorsing a different normative vision, which is in itself problematic for my reading of him. One must note the context, however, viz. that this is an interview in which Foucault is directly asked whether he agrees with certain objectives, and assents that he does. He then notes that the objectives (quoted above) are "clear enough." Here, I think Foucault expresses a personal preference, as well as describing what is demanded by society at large today. In any case, here, in 1983, years after the *Birth of Biopolitics*, Foucault (2000, 370) still says that he does not believe that the appropriate solution has been found—since he clearly knows about neoliberalism, this implies he does not think neoliberalism is capable of addressing the problem.

While the critical aspect of neoliberalism might coincide with some of Foucault's criticisms, its positive aspect has nothing in common with Foucault's *soi-disant* negativism. One could say that Foucault sympathized with neoliberalism because it was not yet clear what neoliberalism would mean in practice, and argue, as Behrent does, that Foucault was swept up in a contemporary enthusiasm for neoliberalism in France—but there is only circumstantial evidence for this, in particular Foucault's association with the explicitly liberal Nouveaux Philosophes, which does not imply thoroughgoing agreement with them. By contrast, Foucault (2008, 20) identifies Valéry Giscard d'Estaing as introducing neoliberalism in France already from 1972, first as economics minister and then as president from 1974, and who was still in the Élysée Palace when Foucault gave his lectures in 1979, but there is no indication of any enthusiasm on Foucault's part for Estaing.

Unlike Foucault's thought, neoliberalism is utopian and normative: it proposes measures, and holds up a utopia of the market, either through the simple restriction of state intervention in the case of American neoliberalism, or through state intervention to construct a market in the case of ordoliberalism. The Foucauldian approach to neoliberalism is to ask, qua discourse, how it operates within strategies of power. Neoliberalism in practice slots into a disciplinary society, producing little more than the marketization and privatization of disciplinary mechanisms.

Patton (2010, 208) implies that Foucault has a moral position that accords with that of neoliberalism, on the basis of a remark of Foucault's (2008, 186) that he is studying neoliberalism for "a reason of critical morality." This is an ambiguous phrase: Patton takes Foucault to be saying that neoliberalism itself is a form of "critical morality," that is, a moralism that incorporates critique; I would contend contrariwise that Foucault means to say that his own critical ethos is what makes he brings to bear in studying neoliberalism. As Foucault (1988b, 1) says in an interview the following year, "I am a moralist, insofar as I believe one of the tasks, one of the meanings of human existence—the source of human freedom—is never to accept anything as definitive, untouchable, obvious, or immobile." Such a morality is the opposite of "morality" as it is ordinarily understood. Patton's normativity is a compromise, a search for historically located specific grounds for action. Foucault's only normative stance, by contrast, was to refuse any kind of static conception of the human that could ground normativity more generally. Neoliberalism's conception of man as *homo oeconomicus* is just the kind of normalization that Foucault consistently rejected.

In more recent work, Patton (2014) associates a triad composed of neoliberalism, the thought of John Rawls, and Foucault's *Birth of Biopolitics* suggestion that socialists need to formulate a "socialist governmentality." Zamora (2016, 76) also in passing notes "socialist governmentality" as a possible connection to neoliberalism. While Patton is merely suggestive in this regard and does not posit any particular interrelations within this triad, I think any suggestion that either Rawls's thought or neoliberalism can provide a governmentality for socialism is prima facie implausible inasmuch as both viewpoints are usually understood to be alternatives to socialism. Patton (2014, 146) seeks to associate French socialism of the 1970s with neoliberalism via the former's enthusiasm for workers' self-management, but the sole thing this has in common with neoliberalism is that both point away from direct management of the economy by the state. Foucault's complaint about socialism in the relevant passage of *The Birth of Biopolitics* is precisely that because it lacks a distinctive governmentality of its own it is forced to adopt one from elsewhere, which is to say either the totalitarian party governmentality that is shared with fascism (as in the *soi-disant* socialist governments of Eastern Europe), or a governmentality that it shared with Western liberalism (as in the occasional government of Western nations by *soi-disant* socialist parties). Patton's suggestion doesn't break this bind at all, but rather simply commends Western socialists to continue to govern like liberals of one stripe or another.

Patton (2014, 147) reads Foucault's phrase "governmentality appropriate to socialism" as raising a normative question of what real governmental practice would operate in an ideal socialist society. This interpretation has no particular grounding in anything Foucault says, however. I believe Foucault means by "socialism" any and all real movements that describe themselves as "socialist"—in line with a rant of his in a 1977 interview against those who refuse to acknowledge that "socialism" in any of its practical applications is really socialist, in favor of a pure vision of a "socialism" that has never actually been realized (Foucault 1980, 136). Foucault does not himself endorse an alternative socialist governmentality, but rather simply analyzes socialism as having a problem in its lack of a distinctive governmentality.

Conclusion

What Now?

> If philosophy is construed as a kind of politics, one in which the educative function is especially marked, a certain amount of repetition need not necessarily be a serious deficiency.
>
> —Geuss 2016, xi

Though I have traced a trajectory of anti-normative thought that I in a sense see ending with Foucault, most of the book consists in dealing with things said after his death. In this much, I see the work of the present, the work I am trying to do here, as a matter of catching up with Foucault. I feel somewhat surprised at the extent to which Foucault's revolution in political thought has been ignored, even more so because it has been so noisily ignored by commentators who cite Foucault everywhere, but are determined to rehabilitate him to old ways of thinking, or at best use him as a partial jumping-off point into new ways of thinking that aren't his (I am thinking here of the peculiar trajectory of the thought of Judith Butler, which I think is primarily Derridean though also influenced by Foucault, and has turned Foucault to the service of the construction of new sexualities, away from the radical opposition to sexuality as such that he actually intended).

Even major French philosophers who were close to Foucault by my lights remain sub-Foucauldian in some sense in their continuing commitment to normativity, politics, and/or theory. I am thinking in particular of the aging generation of "post-Althusserian" philosophers who were friends of colleagues of Foucault and who were clearly and profoundly influenced by him, specifically Jacques Rancière, Alain Badiou, and Étienne Balibar.

Badiou was perhaps the least influenced by Foucault, being rather closer to him in age than the others, and is clearly concerned—like Deleuze, albeit in different ways and in a somewhat different direction—to theoretize and metaphysicalize politics. This allows him to resist politics and normativity as usual, but only via the hypostatization and hyperbolization of the possibility of change into a grand cause. While Badiou resists any straightforwardly normative ethics in favor of the notion of fidelity to events, the determination of politics in terms of fidelity to the event constitutes a theoretical meta-norm. If I may allow myself the license in this conclusion to say such things without substantiation, I think if one ignores his voluminous metaphysical apparatus, there is little if anything there to disagree with—but there is also simply not very much there that is radically novel.

Removing Badiou's metaphysics indeed would make his thought rather similar to Rancière's, who I think is the closest of the three to Foucault's position. I have tended to think of Rancière's political thought as a kind of "Foucault lite," very simply propounding an anti-political (or, as he idiosyncratically terms it, anti-"police") line. Nevertheless, Rancière subscribes to a kind of theoreticism (or "theoreticism lite," one might even say), that also makes him describable even as a kind of "Badiou lite," with the role of mathematics reduced to a question of "counting." In any case, however, Rancière's schematization of the political field dyadically in terms of a police/politics binary is normative. It resembles Foucault's general opposition of resistance to power, but Foucault does not simply support all resistance and condemn all power; Rancière effectively is the anarchist that commentators such as Rorty accuse Foucault of being (on Rancière's anarchism, see May 2008; for a reading of Foucault as anarchist, see May 1994).

For his part, Balibar resists the temptation of high theory, and indeed does not enjoy the same attention lavished on Rancière and Badiou perhaps because of his lack of a system. He falls for politics, however. The history of his thought, which I plan to write about at length elsewhere, is a history of an attempt to sketch a via media between the politics of compromise represented by real existing political parties and the aloof politics of abstract refusal represented by Badiou and Rancière. This via media I think is untenable, however, amounting to a compromise that is inadequately determined, which insists, somewhat similarly to Rawls, on being "realistically utopian" (or, as Balibar puts it, demanding a "possible impossible"). Balibar's focus on unlikely but not completely abstract demands may have a superficial attraction, but in the end it has no innate difference or superiority over either full utopianism or the politics of the possible: from a Foucauldian perspective, all such attempts to positively determine the goals of politics are unnecessary and put intellectuals at the disposal of power.

Of course I should and do acknowledge the utter tendentiousness of my reading every other thinker as a lesser echo of Foucault. Clearly by the lights of other thinkers, it is Foucault's thought that will seem inadequate. It seems to me, however, that we are all, myself included, sub-Foucauldian. There is in principle the possibility of someone carrying Foucault's insights beyond Foucault, but I am not aware of anyone yet doing this. The effect of Foucault's revolution in political thought and action is yet to be thought. We still have yet to cut off the head of the king in political theory—and indeed I think this also remains to be carried out, metaphorically if not literally, in political action. Though kings have been decapitated, we remain in thrall to a hierarchical model of power that has been challenged only at the margins. Attempts to move beyond this have been utopian, a matter of abstract radical egalitarianism more than acknowledging and working within the reality of networked power. In this much, we still remain in a state of self-incurred tutelage, as Kant put it, in thrall to heteronomous principles like "history" and the market. Increasingly, the very survival of humanity, and of most other species of life, depends urgently on the radical assumption of our ability to think, act, and live differently. We are up against a ticking clock.

The connection of this urgency to act in the face of environmental cataclysm to my call to evacuate the normative content from political thought surely seems tenuous. Indeed, it might seem that we need our normative resources more than ever to denounce and fight ecocide. However, I would contend that the abstract demonstration that environmental destruction is "bad" is useless. I believe most people do want *ceteris paribus* to preserve the environment, that most who apparently do not are confused about the factual danger the ecosphere faces, and that anyone who has genuine contempt for our natural environment is extremely unlikely to be convinced by normative pleading. I thus maintain that the role of political thought in the face of the threat can only be to analyze and thereby try to destabilize the strategies of power relations that are coordinating ecosphere destruction and which produce the complacency and contempt that enable this. This as an extremely—and ultimately incalculably—complex question, but pointing out associations and alliances hiding in plain sight is the best we can do. I am not optimistic about the prospects for such an effort in the face of the prodigious apparatuses of propaganda and disinformation arrayed before us, apparatuses that encompass much of the private and even public sectors such that enormous energies of people, even of those who notionally are horrified by the current situation, are devoted toward reproducing the impression that all is fundamentally well with our civilization.

It seems to me that we are thus still caught in the old Enlightenment problematic, formulated famously by Kant (1997), taken up by Foucault (1997), and formulated perhaps most clearly and extensively by Cornelius Castoriadis, who puts it in terms of a struggle of autonomy against heteronomy. To save ourselves we have as a species to take on the task of saving ourselves—we cannot merely hope for salvation to come from another quarter. It seems to me that normativity and theoreticism are in the end ways of not taking up the challenge of autonomy. Of course, Kant intended the opposite, namely, that autonomy be expressed precisely through the rational formulation of morality, but in such a reference to morality there remains a reference to God and to a supervening universal force of morality that in the end is seen as the cure to humanity's ills. We have yet in politics fully to reckon with the death of God and understand that politics is contingent and produced by humans, rather than being something the final nature of which is diagnosable through study. We can see in recent political history a series of attempts by people to subordinate themselves ideologically to heteronomous principles, whether it be a subordination to History itself in a certain kind of Marxism, or to the market today in still-ascendant neoliberalism. Such principles allow us blithely to ignore the emergent catastrophe around us on the basis that we are following the only possible path. Such habits of thought are surely comforting but are extremely dangerous. The attempt to utilize norms implicit in our society can lead us into the trap of constraining the horizons of our actions. To be sure, such a Critical-Theoretic perspective may involve positing autonomy itself as a norm, but even this I want to suggest is dangerous: once autonomy, or freedom, is elevated to the status of a norm, it can be and is rampantly invoked as a justification for continuing the destruction of the natural environment on the basis that stopping this would amount to oppression. Of course, we may argue that destroying the natural environment is ultimately invidious to freedom, but then normativity comes to be a football fought over within a rule-governed discursive game, when the point is that politics only has such rules as we give it. I see Foucault's methodological rejection of norms as, if not the final, then perhaps the maximum extent of autonomous thinking yet achieved.

The failure of the response to Trump I read precisely as a failure that amounts to a normative, political, theoretic response. The normativity is overwhelming: Trump clearly says and does things that are normatively wrong by the standards of pretty much everyone—his opponents pounce on these wrong actions triumphantly, shouting about them with the greatest possible sanctimony, to little avail, because Trump's appeal is not normative rectitude. They denounce his lack of experience and appropriateness within the paradigm of statecraft, and again this doesn't work, because he's supported largely precisely as an anti-political candidate. Last, there is the resort to theory: psephological and political theory that says how you win elections and defeat rivals. Unfortunately, all of this theory is vacuous, or works only within a highly constrained set of variables that do not include Trump. Most vacuous and irritating in its simplisticness is the approach to politics shared by almost everyone that one simply has to "struggle" to win and that every effort concatenatingly contributes to this "struggle," every protest, etcetera, etcetera, building "pressure" on Trump, a preposterous mechanical analogy that does not begin to acknowledge the complexity of the forces involved. Strictly speaking, this is not really a theory per se so much as a suppressed premise.

Now, I do not pretend to have an alternative scheme for action today, but I think action urgently needs a new strategic analysis of power relations to inform it.

Notes

Introduction

1. My translation; for an alternative English translation see Habermas 1973, 113. Habermas (1996, xli) says that this "civil war" is now over—which I dispute.

Chapter 1

1. Engels, by contrast, does use the word "evil" in an apparently normative way late in life, e.g., in 1881: "it is not the lowness of wages which forms the fundamental evil, but the wages system itself" (ME 24, 387). Engels uses the word far more frequently than Marx overall.

2. Philip J. Kain (1988, 24) points out that in Marx's very early thought (i.e., before March 1843 and his *Contribution to the Critique of Hegel's Philosophy of Right*), he has a different understanding of alienation, as a thing's failure to live up to its essence, leading to moral evil. At this point in his career, Marx understands the human essence to be something that develops historically (Kain 1988, 25). For a contradictory account of human nature in Marx, see Geras 1983.

3. There are simpler non-normative explanations of this adjective, however—for example, simply that capitalism is a system that has more in common with a machine than human consciousness.

4. The standard English translation here is "fair distribution" (ME 24, 83), but the German adjective is actually *gerecht*, "just."

5. Robert Nozick (1974, 159–160), without referring to Marx or his slogan explicitly, even takes "to each according to his _____" to be the generic formula for any account of distributive justice.

6. Peffer (1990, 150) incidentally agrees with me here that wage labor is literally a form of slavery. He does not examine how this fact sits alongside his contention that "slavery" is a term of normative condemnation, however.

Chapter 2

1. By contrast, in the Russian Revolution, unlike in Paris, the police were replaced by armed workers' militia, which indeed led to the situation in which the police in Russia are to this day called "militia."

2. Alfred B. Evans surveys a wide range of views on *State and Revolution*: while there is unanimity that it is atypical in Lenin's corpus, there is disagreement about whether this is because it represents an aberration or because it represents an element of Lenin's thought that he rarely talks about, namely, the communism he aims for rather than the requirements of the concrete situation he finds himself in.

3. Slavoj Žižek (2004, 9) claims contrary to this that Lenin does renounce *State and Revolution*, as "utopian" no less, despite that it is not a utopian work. Zizek however offers no evidence for this claim.

4. The democratic centralist model has been adopted by parties with quite different objectives, such as the Chinese Kuomintang, which was organized on strict Leninist lines during a phase of Soviet sponsorship, but has spent most of its history, while retaining the organizational model, as a pointedly anti-communist movement.

5. Evans (1987, 16) points to the same passage as having "exceptionally rich political implications."

6. In the Russian, the identification is slightly less clear-cut, with the "i.e." being interpolated by the translator to make a somewhat ambiguous identification utterly unambiguous.

7. Cf. Engels's 1847 statement in a letter that in Germany "the proletarians, small peasants and urban petty bourgeoisie . . . constitute the 'people'" (ME 6, 294).

8. The closest Marx comes are a couple of references to certain nations' proletariats as constituting the vanguard of international struggle—rather than of the struggle within their respective nations—in the preface to the 1882 edition of the *Manifesto* and an early draft of *The Civil War in France*.

9. Trotsky later resiled this criticism in favor of adherence to Lenin, but it was revived by the Trotskyist Tony Cliff (1960) to explain the Russian Revolution's trajectory.

10. On the very troubled history of this commissariat and the lack of workers' control in Bolshevik Russia in general, see Perrins 1980.

11. On the controversy surrounding this aspect of *What is to Be Done?*, see Draper 1999.

12. This is a mark of Draper's residual Trotskyism, despite Draper's scathing comments on Trotsky in the same work—Trotsky (1930, 320) himself refers to Trotskyism as "the conception according to which the Russian proletariat, having come to power, would not be able to build a national socialist society with its own forces alone."

Chapter 3

1. Accounts differ on the exact timing of Foucault's departure from the PCF: Defert's chronology has him leaving in October 1952 (see Foucault 1994a, 20), and Macey (1993, 40) has him leaving in 1953 after the Doctors' Plot.
2. On class, see Foucault's extensive use of class categories such as "bourgeoisie" during his 1970s output, and his explicit positing of class domination as a general phenomenon at Foucault 1997, 292–293.
3. On Foucault's complex attitude toward revolution, see Kelly 2013c.

Chapter 4

1. For more detail on this point, see Grace 2009.
2. It appeared originally, in French, in the relatively obscure *L'autre journal* (Deleuze 1990), before being translated into English and appearing in *October* (Deleuze 1992). The text was later published in English, in a different translation, in Deleuze 1995, 177–182.
3. Both published translations of the "Postscript" get this wrong: the earlier is slavishly literal, giving us "analogical"–"numerical" (Deleuze 1992, 4); the more recent renders *numérique* as "digital," but oddly counterposes it to "analogical" (Deleuze 1995, 178).

Chapter 5

1. For a detailed account of Foucault's influence on Rorty, see Małecki 2011, 108.
2. On the question of Hegelianism here, see Williams 1999, 114–115.
3. Cutrofello argues that Foucault is not an "antiutopian," which, given Rorty's use of "utopia," would mean a hostility to any structure for society. Foucault is indeed not so extreme. Foucault's analysis is critical, but Rorty is wrong to think that this means this equates to an equivocal rejection of all social forms as such.
4. In point of fact, I do think Foucault does want to abolish social norms as such—but Foucault views the "norm" as an historically localized recent form, whereas I think Rorty understands "social norms" in the conventional contemporary way to refer to any form of cultural more whatsoever.

Chapter 6

1. My translation; for published English translation, see Foucault 1972, 231.

2. The same remark appears in the German version (Foucault 1971a, 15).
3. On the significance of this term, see Kelly 2013b.

Chapter 7

1. Hubert Dreyfus (1987) and Richard Marsden (1999) have argued that Foucault is a realist with reference specifically to the philosophy of science. Mark Olssen (2008, 105) uses the adjective to describe Foucault without clearly explaining its sense, albeit describing Foucault's position accurately. Foucault (2001, 171–172) does at least at one point employ the vocabulary of the real and reality positively, and express his positive concern with the relation of thought to reality as such, but he does not think this relation as a matter of correspondence between the two. I argue elsewhere, in relation to the law (Kelly 2009, 53), and in relation to the subject (ibid. 86), that Foucault is a realist, meaning that he asserts the essential historical reality of the law and subject, rather than taking either them to be transcendental or reducible to material factors.

2. Kwame Anthony Appiah, Richard Bellamy, William Connolly, John Dunn, Stephen Elkin, Raymond Geuss, John Gray, Stuart Hampshire, Geoffrey Hawthorne, Bonnie Honig, Chantal Mouffe, Glen Newey, Philip Pettit, Mark Philp, Judith Shklar, Quentin Skinner, Bernard Yack, Iris Marion Young, Jeremy Waldron, Bernard Williams.

3. The largest single group of realists Galston (2010, 386) lists are a "British" contingent comprising "Bernard Williams, Stuart Hampshire, John Dunn, Glen Newey, Richard Bellamy, Geoffrey Hawthorne [sic], Raymond Geuss, and John Gray." Of these eight, six have an association with Cambridge. This association is clearly shared by another group Galston lists on the same page, "Quentin Skinner and the 'Cambridge historical school,'" whose membership Galston does not further enumerate. Galston also names Appiah, who was educated at Cambridge. An extraordinary document in relation to the significance of Cambridge here is a roundtable discussion between political thinkers, including Geuss, at the University of Cambridge across many disciplines, under Skinner's aegis (Skinner et al. 2002).

4. It is worth noting in fairness to Young that she defines "justice" very different from the sense in which it is rejected by Foucault and Marx. However, her justification for using the term, viz. the use of the word concept in real struggles, places her closer to Rortyian ethnocentrism than Foucauldian or Marxian radicalism, inasmuch as the latter two prefer to dispose of old concepts rather than work with them. Her redefinition of "justice" is moreover normative, couched in terms of liberation.

5. Geuss (2008, 45) effectively makes this point, arguing that the existence of the state requires a conceptual framework.

6. As Robert Geyer and Samir Rihani (2010, 27) point out, however, this "incrementalist" approach to public policy in fact dates back to the 1950s.

7. Though Little misstates the title of Geuss's book.

Chapter 8

1. Scholarship on Foucault in English prior to this date consisted almost entirely of translations of French work (e.g., Lecourt 1975); the one piece of earlier original Anglophone Foucault scholarship I am aware of is a single comparative journal article on Foucault and Sartre (Silverman 1978).

2. This Foucauldian suspicion of the notion of freedom in relation to liberalism has been extended by Nikolas Rose (1999) in relation to neoliberalism.

3. Indeed, this interview is the only evidence Zamora adduces for reading Foucault as neoliberal, besides a misreading of secondary literature, specifically, falsely reading Colin Gordon (Donzelot and Gordon 2008, 52) as saying that Foucault was a precursor of Tony Blair's "Third Way," which is not what Gordon says. Gordon (2015) has since pointedly rejected Zamora's interpretation of him.

Bibliography

Abbreviations

The following three abbreviations when they appear in references are always qualified with a number referring to the volume of the collection being cited.

L   V. I. Lenin, *Collected Works*. Moscow: Progress.

ME   The *Collected Works of Karl Marx and Frederick Engels*. New York: International Publishers.

MEW *Marx-Engels-Werke*. Berlin: Dietz.

Althusser, Louis. 1969. *For Marx*. London: Allen Lane.
———. 1970. "Foreword to the Italian Edition." In *Reading Capital*. London: NLB.
———. 1971. "Ideology and Ideological State Apparatuses." In Louis Althusser, *Lenin and Philosophy and Other Essays*. Translated by Ben Brewster. London: NLB.
———. 1993. *The Future Lasts Forever*. Translated by Richard Veasey. New York: The New Press.
———. 2006. *Philosophy of the Encounter*. Edited by François Matheron and Olivier Corpet. Translated by G. M. Goshgarian. London: Verso.
Badiou, Alain. 2012. *The Adventure of French Philosophy*. London: Verso.
Balibar, Étienne. 1977. *On the Dictatorship of the Proletariat*. London: New Left Books.
———. 2007. *The Philosophy of Marx*. London: Verso.
Barbour, Charles. 2012. *The Marx Machine*. Lanham, MD: Lexington.
Becker, G. S., F. Ewald, and B. E. Harcourt. 2012. "Becker on Ewald on Foucault on Becker: American Neoliberalism and Michel Foucault's 1979 'Birth of Biopolitics' Lectures." Working Paper No. 614. Coase-Sandor Institute for Law and Economics.
Behrent, M. 2009. Liberalism without Humanism: Michel Foucault and the Free-Market Creed, 1976–1979. *Modern Intellectual History*, 6(3): 539–568.

Bourdieu, Pierre. 1991. *The Political Ontology of Martin Heidegger*. Cambridge: Polity.
Brovkin, Vladimir N. 1987. *The Mensheviks after October: Socialist Opposition and the Rise of the Bolshevik Dictatorship*, Ithaca: Cornell University Press.
Burroughs, William S. 1978. "The Limits of Control." *Semiotext(e): Schizo-Culture* 3(2): 38–42.
Carr, E. H. 1950. *The Bolshevik Revolution, Vol. I*. London: Macmillan.
Carver, Terrell. 1998. *The Postmodern Marx*. University Park, PA: Pennsylvania State University Press.
Cliff, Tony. 1960. "Trotsky on Substitutionism." Accessed at http://www.marxists.org/archive/cliff/works/1960/xx/trotsub.htm
Colapietro, Vincent. 1998. "American Evasions of Foucault." *The Southern Journal of Philosophy* 36: 329–351.
Connolly, William. 2011. *A World of Becoming*. Durham, NC: Duke University Press.
Cutrofello, Andrew. 1993. "'Young Hegelian' Richard Rorty and the 'Foucauldian Left.'" *Metaphilosophy* 24: 136–146.
Davidson, Arnold I., ed. 1997. *Foucault and His Interlocutors*. Chicago: University of Chicago Press.
Deleuze, Gilles. *Lectures de Cours sur Michel Foucault (1985–1986)*, 8 April 1986. Accessed at http://www2.univ-paris8.fr/deleuze/article.php3?id_article=477
———. 1988. *Foucault*. Translated by Seán Hand. Minneapolis: University of Minnesota Press.
———. 1990. "Post-scriptum sur les sociétés de contrôle." *L'autre journal* 1.
———. 1992. "Postscript on the Societies of Control." *October* 59, 3–7.
———. 1995. *Negotiations*. Translated by Martin Joughin. New York: Columbia University Press.
———. 1997. "Desire and Pleasure." In Davidson, *Foucault and His Interlocutors*, 183–193.
———. 2007. "What is a *Dispositif?*" In *Two Regimes of Madness*. New York: Semiotext(e), 338–348.
Deleuze, Gilles, and Michel Focuault. 1977. "Intellectuals and Power." In Focuault, *Language, Counter-Memory, Practice*.
Deleuze, Gilles, and Félix Guattari. 1983. *Anti-Oedipus: Capitalism and Schizophrenia*. Translated by Robert Hurley, Mark Seem, and Helen R. Lane. Minneapolis: University of Minnesota Press.
———. 1994. *What is Philosophy?* Translated by Hugh Tomlinson and Graham Burchell. New York: Columbia University Press.
Deranty, Jean-Philippe. 2004. "Injustice, Violence and Social Struggle: The Critical Potential of Axel Honneth's Theory of Recognition." *Critical Horizons* 5(1): 297–322.
———. 2009, *Beyond Communication: A Critical Study of Axel Honneth's Social Philosophy*. Leiden: Brill.

Deranty, Jean-Philippe, and Emmanuel Renault. 2007. "Politicizing Honneth's Ethics of Recognition." *Thesis Eleven* 88: 92–111.
Donzelot, Jacques, and Colin Gordon. 2008. "Governing Liberal Societies—the Foucault Effect in the English-speaking World." *Foucault Studies* 5: 48–62.
Dosse, François. 2010. *Gilles Deleuze & Félix Guattari.* New York: Columbia University Press.
Draper, Hal. 1987. *The "Dictatorship of the Proletariat" from Marx to Lenin.* New York: Monthly Review Press.
———. 1999. "The Myth of Lenin's 'Concept of the Party': Or What They Did to What Is to Be Done?" *Historical Materialism* 4(1): 187–213.
Dreyfus, Hubert. 1987. "Foreword to the California Edition." In Michel Foucault, *Mental Illness and Psychology*, vii–xliii. Berkeley: University of California Press.
Dreyfus, Hubert, & Paul Rabinow. 1982. *Michel Foucault: Beyond Structuralism and Hermeneutics.* Chicago: Chicago University Press.
Elden, Stuart. 2001. *Mapping the Present: Heidegger, Foucault and the Project of a Spatial History.* London: Continuum.
Eribon, Didier. 1991. *Michel Foucault.* Translated by Betsy Wing. Cambridge, MA: Harvard University Press.
Evans, Alfred B. 1987. "Rereading Lenin's State and Revolution." *Slavic Review* 46(1): 1–19.
Foucault, Michel. 1969. *L'archéologie de savoir.* Paris: Gallimard.
———. 1970. *The Order of Things.* London: Tavistock.
———. 1971a. *Die Ordnung der Dinge.* Frankfurt: Suhrkamp.
———. 1971b. "Orders of Discourse." Translated by Rupert Swyer. *Social Science Information* 10(2): 7–30.
———. 1972. *The Archaeology of Knowledge.* Translated by A. M. Sheridan Smith. London: Tavistock.
———. 1975. *Surveiller et punir.* Paris: Gallimard.
———. 1976. *La volonté de savoir.* Paris: Gallimard.
———. 1977. *Language, Counter-Memory, Practice.* Edited by Donald F. Bouchard. Ithaca, NY: Cornell University Press.
———. 1979. *Discipline and Punish: The Birth of the Prison.* Translated by Alan Sheridan. London: Penguin.
———. 1980. *Power/Knowledge: Selected Interviews and Other Writings, 1972–1977.* Edited by Colin Gordon. Brighton: Harvester Wheatsheaf.
———. 1982a. "On the Genealogy of Ethics." In Dreyfus and Rabinow, *Michel Foucault*, 229–252.
———. 1982b: "The Subject and Power." In Dreyfus and Rabinow, *Michel Foucault*, 208–226.
———. 1983. Preface to Deleuze and Guattari, *Anti-Oedipus*, xi–xiv.

———. 1984. "Politics and Ethics: An Interview." Translated by Catherine Porter. In *The Foucault Reader*, 373–380. Edited by Paul Rabinow. New York: Pantheon.

———. 1988a. *Politics, Philosophy, Culture*. London: Routledge.

———. 1988b. "Power, Moral Values and the Intellectual." *History of the Present* 4(1–2): 11–13.

———. 1990. "Nietzsche, Freud, Marx." Translated by Alan D Schrift. In *Transforming the Hermeneutic Context*. Edited by Gayle L. Ormiston and Alan D. Schrift. Albany, NY: SUNY Press.

———. 1991. *Remarks on Marx*. Translated by R. James Goldstein and James Cascaito. New York: Semiotext(e).

———. 1994a. *Dits et écrits I, 1954–1969*. Edited by Daniel Defert and François Ewald in collaboration with Jacques Lagrange. Paris: Gallimard.

———. 1994b. *Dits et écrits II, 1954–1969*. Edited by Daniel Defert and François Ewald in collaboration with Jacques Lagrange. Paris: Gallimard.

———. 1994c. *Dits et écrits III, 1954–1969*. Edited by Daniel Defert and François Ewald in collaboration with Jacques Lagrange. Paris: Gallimard.

———. 1994d. *Dits et écrits IV, 1954–1969*. Edited by Daniel Defert and François Ewald in collaboration with Jacques Lagrange. Paris: Gallimard.

———. 1996. *Foucault Live*. Edited by Sylvère Lotringer. New York: Semiotext(e).

———. 1997a. *Ethics*. Translated by Robert Hurley et al. Edited by Paul Rabinow. New York: The New Press.

———. 1997b. "Human Nature: Justice and Power." In Davidson, *Foucault and His Interlocutors*, 107–145.

———. 1997c. *The Politics of Truth*. New York: Semiotext(e).

———. 1998a. *The Will to Knowledge: The History of Sexuality, Vol. I*. Translated by Robert Hurley. London: Penguin.

———. 1998b. *Aesthetics, Method, and Epistemology*. Edited by James D. Faubion. New York: The New Press.

———. 1998c. "Truth, Power, Self: An Interview with Michel Foucault." In *Technologies of the Self*, 9–15. Edited by Luther H. Martin, Huck Gutman, and Patrick H. Hutton. Amherst: University of Massachusetts Press.

———. 2000. *Power*. Edited by James D. Faubion. London: Penguin.

———. 2001. *Fearless Speech*. Los Angeles: Semiotext(e).

———. 2002. *The Order of Things*. London: Routledge.

———. 2003. *Society Must Be Defended*. Translated by David Macey. London: Allen Lane.

———. 2004. *Sécurité, territoire, population*. Paris: Seuil.

———. 2005. *Hermeneutics of the Self*. Translated by Graham Burchell. New York: Palgrave Macmillan.

———. 2007a. *Security Territory, Population*. Translated by Graham Burchell. Basingstoke: Palgrave Macmillan.

———. 2007b. "The Meshes of Power." Translated by Gerald Moore. In *Space, Knowledge and Power*. Edited by Jeremy W. Crampton and Stuart Elden. Aldershot: Ashgate.

———. 2008. *The Birth of Biopolitics*. Basingstoke: Palgrave Macmillan.

———. 2010. *The Government of the Self and Others*. Basingstoke: Palgrave Macmillan.

———. 2011. *The Courage of the Truth*. Basingstoke: Palgrave Macmillan.

Fraser, Nancy. 1995. "Foucault on Modern Power: Empirical Insights and Normative Confusions." In *Michel Foucault: Critical Assessments, Vol. V*. Edited by B. Smart. London: Routledge, 133–148.

Fukuyama, Francis. 1989. "The End of History?" *National Interest* 16.

Galston, William A. 2010. "Realism in Political Theory." *European Journal of Political Theory* 9: 4.

Geras, Norman. 1983. *Marx and Human Nature*. London: Verso.

———. 1984. "The Controversy about Marx and Justice." *New Left Review* 47.

Geuss, Raymond. 2005. *Outside Ethics*. Princeton, NJ: Princeton University Press.

———. 2008. *Philosophy and Real Politics*. Princeton, NJ: Princeton University Press.

———. 2010. *Politics and the Imagination*. Princeton, NJ: Princeton University Press.

———. 2014. *A World Without Why*. Princeton, NJ: Princeton University Press.

———. 2016. *Reality and Its Dreams*. Cambridge, MA: Harvard University Press.

Geyer, Robert, and Samir Rihani. 2010. *Complexity and Public Policy*. Abingdon: Routledge.

Gledhill, J. 2012. "Rawls and Realism." *Social Theory and Practice* 38(1): 55–82.

Golder, Ben. 2015. *Foucault and the Politics of Rights*. Stanford, CA: Stanford University Press.

Gordon, Cordon. 2015. "Colin Gordon, Foucault, Neoliberalism etc." *Foucault News*. Accessed at http://foucaultnews.com/2015/01/15/colin-gordon-foucault-neoliberalism/

Goshgarian, G. M. 2003. "Introduction." In *The Humanist Controversy and Other Writings*. Edited by François Matheron. London: Verso.

Grace, Wendy. 2009. "*Faux Amis*: Foucault and Deleuze on Sexuality and Desire." *Critical Inquiry* 36: 1.

Graham, Keith. 1992. *Karl Marx Our Contemporary*. Hemel Hempstead: Harvester Wheatsheaf.

Habermas, Jürgen. 1973. *Theory and Practice*. Translated by J. Viertel. Boston: Beacon.

———. 1978. *Theorie und Praxis*. Frankfurt: Suhrkamp.

———. 1987. *The Philosophical Discourse of Modernity*. Cambridge: Polity.

———. 1996. *Between Facts and Norms*. Translated by William Rehg. Cambridge, MA: MIT Press.

Hallward, Peter. 2000. "The Limits of Individuation, or How to Distinguish Deleuze and Foucault." *Angelaki* 5:2.

Hardt, Michael, and Antonio Negri. 2000. *Empire*. Cambridge, MA: Harvard University Press.

Hartmann Martin, and Axel Honneth. 2006. "Paradoxes of Capitalism." *Constellations* 13:1.

Heidegger, Martin. 1977. "The Word of Nietzsche: 'God Is Dead.'" Translated by William Lovitt. In *The Question Concerning Technology*, 53–112. New York: Garland.

Honneth, Axel. 1991. *Critique of Power*. Boston: MIT Press.

———. 1995. "Foucault and Adorno: Two Forms of the Critique of Modernity." In *The Fragmented World of the Social: Essays in Social and Political Philosophy*. Albany, NY: SUNY Press.

———. 1995. *The Struggle for Recognition*. Cambridge: Polity.

———. 2007. "Pathologies of the Social." In *Disrespect*. Cambridge: Polity.

———. 2011. "Rejoinder." In *Axel Honneth: Critical Essays*. Edited by Danielle Petherbridge. Leiden: Brill.

Kain, Philip J. 1988. *Marx and Ethics*. Oxford: Clarendon.

Kant, Immanuel. "*Was ist Aufklärung?*" In Foucault, *The Politics of Truth*.

Kelly, Mark G. E. 2009. *The Political Philosophy of Michel Foucault*. New York: Routledge.

———. 2013a. "Foucault, Subjectivity, and Technologies of the Self." In *A Companion to Foucault*. Edited by Christopher Falzon, Timothy O'Leary, and Jana Sawicki. Oxford: Blackwell.

———. 2013b. *Foucault's History of Sexuality, Vol. I: The Will to Knowledge*. Edinburgh: Edinburgh University Press.

———. 2013c. "Revolution." In *The Cambridge Foucault Lexicon*. Edited by Leonard Lawlor and John Nale. Cambridge: Cambridge University Press.

———. 2014a. "Against Prophecy and Utopia: Foucault and the Future." *Thesis Eleven* 120(1): 104–118.

———. 2014b. *Foucault and Politics*. Edinburgh: Edinburgh University Press.

Korsgaard, Christine. 2009. *Self-Constitution: Agency, Identity, and Integrity*. Oxford: OUP.

Lance, Mark, and May, Todd. 1994. "Two Dogmas of Post-Empiricism: Anti-Theoretical Strains in Derrida and Rorty." *The Philosophical Forum* 25: 273–309.

Lecourt, Dominique. 1975. *Marxism and Epistemology: Bachelard, Canguilhem and Foucault*. Translated by Ben Brewster. London: NLB.

Leiter, Brian. 2011. "Nietzsche's Moral and Political Philosophy." In *The Stanford Encyclopedia of Philosophy*. Summer 2011 ed. Accessed at http://plato.stanford.edu/archives/sum2011/entries/nietzsche-moral-political/

Lewin, Moshe. 1969. *Lenin's Last Struggle*. London: Faber.

Little, Adrian. 2012. "Political Action, Error and Failure: The Epistemological Limits of Complexity." *Political Studies* 60: 3–19.

Lukács, Georg. 1971. *History and Class Consciousness*. Cambridge, MA: Merlin.
Lukes, Steven. 1985. *Marxism and Morality*. Oxford: Clarendon.
Macey, David. 1993. *The Lives of Michel Foucault*. London: Hutchinson.
Małecki, Wojciech. 2011. " 'If happiness is not the aim of politics, then what is?': Rorty versus Foucault." *Foucault Studies* 11: 106–125.
Marchand, Roland. 1998. *Creating the Corporate Soul*. Berkeley: University of California Press.
Marcuse, Herbert. 2002. *One-Dimensional Man*. Abingdon: Routledge.
Marsden, Richard. 1999. *Marx after Foucault: The Nature of Capital*. New York: Routledge.
May, Todd. 1994. *The Political Philosophy of Poststructuralist Anarchism*. University Park, PA: Pennsylvania State University Press.
———. 2008. *The Political Thought of Jacques Rancière: Creating Equality*. Edinburgh: Edinburgh University Press.
Mayer, Robert. 1996. "The Status of a Classic Text: Lenin's *What Is To Be Done?* After 1902." *History of European Ideas* 22(4): 307–320.
———. 1997. "Lenin, the Proletariat, and the Legitimation of Dictatorship." *Journal of Political Ideologies* 2(1): 99–102.
Menke, Christoph. 2010. "Neither Rawls Nor Adorno: Raymond Geuss' Programme for a 'Realist' Political Philosophy." *European Journal of Philosophy* 18(1): 137–147.
Miliband, Ralph. 1970. "Lenin's the *State and Revolution*." *Socialist Register* 11.
Miller, James. 1993. *The Passion of Michel Foucault*. London: HarperCollins.
Montag, Warren. 1995. "The Soul Is the Prison of the Body: Althusser and Foucault. 1970–1975." *Yale French Studies* 88.
Morris, Meaghan, and Paul Patton. 1979. *Michel Foucault: Power, Truth, Strategy*. Sydney: Feral.
Nail, Thomas. 2016. "Biopower and Control." In *Between Deleuze and Foucault*. Edited by Nicolae Morar, Thomas Nail, and Daniel W. Smith. Edinburgh: Edinburgh University Press, 247–263.
Nietzsche, Friedrich. 2002. *Beyond Good and Evil*. Cambridge: Cambridge University Press.
Nozick, Robert. 1974. *Anarchy, State, and Utopia*. New York: Basic Books.
Olssen, Mark. 2004. "Foucault and Marxism: Rewriting the Theory of Historical Materialism." *Policy Futures in Education* 2: 3–4.
———. 2008. "Foucault as Complexity Theorist: Overcoming the Problems of Classical Philosophical Analysis." *Educational Philosophy and Theory* 40(1).
Paras, Eric. 2006. *Foucault 2.0: Beyond Power and Knowledge*. New York: Other Press.
Patton, Paul. 1985. "Michel Foucault: The Ethics of an Intellectual." *Thesis Eleven* 11: 71–80.
———. 1989. "Taylor and Foucault on Power and Freedom." *Political Studies* XXXVII: 260–276.

———. 1998. "Foucault's Subject of Power." In *The Later Foucault*, edited by Jeremy Moss. London: Sage.

———. 2004. "Power and Right in Nietzsche and Foucault." *International Studies in Philosophy* XXXVI(3): 43–61.

———. 2005. "Foucault, Critique and Rights." *Critical Horizons* 6(1): 267–287.

———. 2010. "Foucault and Normative Political Philosophy." In *Foucault and Philosophy*. Edited by Timothy O'Leary and Chris Falzon. Oxford: Blackwell.

———. 2013. "From Resistance to Government: Foucault's Lectures 1976–1979." In *A Companion to Foucault*. Edited by Chris Falzon, Timothy O'Leary, and Jana Sawicki, 172–188. Oxford: Blackwell.

———. 2014. "Foucault and Rawls: Government and Public Reason." In *The Government of Life*. Edited by Vanessa Lemm and Miguel Vatter. New York: Fordham.

Pavliuchenkov, Sergei. 1997. "Workers' Protest Movement against War Communism." In *The Bolsheviks in Russian Society*. New Haven, CT: Yale University Press.

Peffer, Rodney G. 1990. *Marxism, Morality, and Social Justice*. Princeton, NJ: Princeton University Press.

Perrins, Michael. 1980, "Rabkrin and Workers' Control in Russia 1917–34." *European History Quarterly* 10(225): 225–246.

Petherbridge, Danielle. 2013. *The Critical Theory of Axel Honneth*. Plymouth: Lexington.

Pirani, Simon. 2008. *The Russian Revolution in Retreat, 1920–24: Soviet Workers and the New Communist Elite*. New York: Routledge.

Pogge, T. 1989. *Realizing Rawls*. Ithaca, NY: Cornell University Press.

Rancière, Jacques 1999. *Disagreement*. Translated by Julie Rose. Minneapolis: University of Minnesota Press.

———. 2011. *Althusser's Lesson*. Translated by Emiliano Battista. London: Verso.

Rawls, John. 1971. *A Theory of Justice*. Cambridge, MA: Harvard.

Rorty, Richard. 1984. "Habermas and Lyotard on Postmodernity." *Praxis International* 4(1): 32–44.

———. 1989. *Contingency, Irony, and Solidarity*. Cambridge: CUP.

———. 1991a: "Moral Identity and Private Autonomy: The Case of Foucault." In *Essays on Heidegger and Others*, 193–198. Cambridge: CUP.

———. 1991b: *Objectivity, Relativism and Truth*. Cambridge: CUP.

———. 1993. "Paroxysms and Politics." *Salmagundi* 97: 61–68.

———. 1995. "The End of Leninism and History as Comic Frame." In *History and the Idea of Progress*. Edited by A. M. Melzer, J. Weinberger, and M. R. Zinman, 211–226. Ithaca, NY: Cornell University Press.

———. 1997. *Truth, Politics and "Post-modernism."* Assen: Van Gorcum.

———. 2000: "The Overphilosophication of Politics." *Constellations* 7: 128–132.

Rose, Nikolas. 1999. *Powers of Freedom*. Cambridge: Cambridge University Press.

Said, E. W. 1983. *The World, the Text, and the Critic*. Cambridge, MA: Harvard University Press.
Sanderson, Ian. 2009. "Intelligent Policy Making for a Complex World: Pragmatism, Evidence and Learning." *Political Studies* 57: 699–719.
Sayers, Sean. 1994. "Moral Values and Progress." *New Left Review* 204.
Searle, John. 2012. "Foucault and Bourdieu on Continental Obscurantism." YouTube video, 5:53, excerpt, posted by "theorrhea," December 18, 2012. Accessed at https://www.youtube.com/watch?v=yvwhEIhv3N0
Simons, Jon. 1995. *Foucault and the Political*. London: Routledge.
Skinner, Quentin et al. 2002. "Political Philosophy: The View from Cambridge." *The Journal of Political Philosophy* 10(1): 1–19.
Sleat, Matt. 2010. "Bernard Williams and the Possibility of a Realist Political Theory." *European Journal of Political Theory* 9(4).
Sokal, Alan, and Jean Bricmont. 1998. *Intellectual Impostures*. London: Profile.
Taylor, Charles. 1984. "Foucault on Freedom and Truth." *Political Theory*, 12(2): 152–183.
Trotsky, Leon. 1904. *Our Political Tasks*. Accessed at http://www.marxists.org/archive/trotsky/1904/tasks/ch03.htm
———. 1930. *The History of the Russian Revolution, Vol. III*. Accessed at http://www.marxists.org/archive/trotsky/works/download/hrr-vol3.pdf
Wood, Allen. 1979. "Marx on Right and Justice: A Reply to Husami." *Philosophy & Public Affairs* 8(3): 267–295.
———. 1984. "Justice and Class Interests." *Philosophica* 33.
Wood, Allen. 1990. "Marx against Morality." In *A Companion to Ethics*. Edited by Peter Singer. Oxford: Blackwell.
Williams, Bernard. 2005. *In the Beginning Was the Deed: Realism and Moralism in Political Argument*. Princeton, NJ: Princeton University Press.
Williams, Howard. 1999. "The Ends of History." *International Journal of Philosophical Studies* 7: 102–118.
Young, Iris Marion. 1990. *Justice and the Politics of Difference*. Princeton, NJ: Princeton University Press.
Zamora, Daniel. 2014. "Can We Criticize Foucault?" *Jacobin*. Accessed at https://www.jacobinmag.com/2014/12/foucault-interview/.
———. 2016. "Foucault, the Excluded, and the Neoliberal Erosion of the State." In *Foucault and Neoliberalism*. Cambridge: Polity.
Žižek, Slavoj. 2004. "Introduction: Between Two Revolutions." In *Revolution at the Gates*. London: Verso.

Index

Adorno, Theodor, 110, 117, 120, 139
Agamben, Giorgio, 148
Allen, Amy, 119
Althusser, Louis, 13–15, 21–22, 24, 44, 59–73, 92
America, United States of, 20, 82, 88, 95–99, 106, 128, 131
anarchism, 8, 23, 41, 103, 170
Aristotle, 34–35

Badiou, Alain, 169–170
Balibar, Étienne, 19, 50–51, 54, 57, 169–171
Baudrillard, Jean, 79
Behrent, Michael, 160–161
Bentham, Jeremy, 83
Bauman, Zygmunt, 79
biopolitics/biopower, 80–81, 88, 104, 122, 148, 157
Burroughs, William, 91
Butler, Judith, 169

Carr, E. H., 47, 51
Castoriadis, Cornelius, 172
Cliff, Tony, 41, 44, 54, 55
communism, 8, 21–22, 27, 35–37, 40–41, 44–45, 53, 56–57, 67, 101
Colapietro, Vincent, 106
Connolly, William, 142
Cutrofello, Andrew, 101, 107

Deleuze, Gilles, 15, 62, 73–93, 151
Deranty, Jean-Philippe and Emmanuel Renault, 116
Derrida, Jacques, 6–7
Draper, Hal, 41, 48, 54

egalitarianism, 130
Engels, Friedrich, 23, 43, 48
Ewald, François, 160

Foucault, Michel, 1, 3–16, 18, 23, 30, 33–36, 41–42, 56–57, 59–62, 65–93, 96, 98–124, 126, 132, 135–138, 140, 143–167, 169–172
Fraser, Nancy, 148, 151
French Communist Party, 19, 60–67, 72
Freud, Sigmund, 75
Fukuyama, Francis, 98

Galston, William, 126
Geras, Norman, 25, 31–32
Geuss, Raymond, 125–141, 143
Gledhill, James, 130
Golder, Ben, 159
Goshgarian, G. M., 72
governmentality, 41–42, 56–57, 81, 86, 132, 163–164, 167
Graeber, David, 83
Graham, Keith, 32

191

Guattari, Félix, 83, 91

Habermas, Jürgen, 1–2, 95, 100, 109–110, 112, 116, 120, 123, 151
Hallward, Peter, 76, 91
Hanssen, Beatrice, 119
Hardt, Michael, 81, 148
Hegel, G. F., 19–21, 34, 60–63, 92, 98, 115–116, 152
Heidegger, Martin, 6–7
history, 19, 30, 36, 62, 67–68, 83, 98, 100, 112, 117, 123, 141, 172
Hobbes, Thomas, 116, 131
Hoffman, Marcello, 151
Honig, Bonnie, 126
Honneth, Axel, 14–15, 109–124
Horkheimer, Max, 110

Iran, 71, 159

Kafka, Franz, 88
Kant, Immanuel, 19–21, 127, 171–172
Kelsen, Hans, 133
Koopman, Colin, 119

Lacan, Jacques, 24
Lance, Mark, 107
Lenin, Vladimir, 9, 14–15, 47–60, 63, 70, 92, 132, 144
Little, Adrian, 143–144
Lukács, György, 33
Lukes, Steven, 33

Małecki, Wojciech, 107
Marcuse, Herbert, 102
Marx, Karl, 4–7, 13–14, 17–37, 39–44, 48, 53, 56, 58–63, 65, 68–71, 92, 115–117, 126–127, 131, 138
Marxism, 2–3, 8, 17–22, 37, 39–44, 47–48, 54, 58–63, 65–71, 75, 85–86, 92, 97, 99–101, 140, 162

May, Todd, 107, 170
Mauss, Marcel, 83
Mayer, Robert, 52
Menke, Christoph, 139
Mensheviks, 45, 53
Miliband, Ralph, 47, 52–54, 57
Miller, James, 104
Mouffe, Chantal, 126

Nail, Thomas, 81
Negri, Antonio, 83, 85–86, 148
Nepal, 42
New Philosophers, 71
Nietzsche, Friedrich, 4–7, 62, 68, 74, 92, 113, 117, 119, 132, 135–136, 138, 155, 161

Olssen, Mark, 146

Paras, Eric, 160
Paris Commune, 53, 57
Patton, Paul, 147–148, 150–156, 158–167
Peffer, Rodney, 29
Petherbridge, Danielle, 115, 119
Pirani, Simon, 46, 51, 55
Pogge, Thomas, 130
power, 4–6, 8–9, 11, 33, 40, 42–45, 49–52, 55, 66, 69, 71, 75–83, 86–88, 90–92, 103, 105–107, 112, 114, 117, 121–124, 149–150, 152–154, 156–7, 159, 173
Putin, Vladimir, 98

Rancière, Jacques, 20, 63, 169–170
Rawls, John, 2, 20, 101, 126–131, 167
Rorty, Richard, 14–15, 95–108, 119, 150

Said, Edward, 150
Sanderson, Ian, 142–144

Santanyana, George, 141
Simons, Jon, 79, 148
Sleat, Matt, 133–134
Sokal and Bricmont, 88
Spinoza, Baruch, 62–63, 66

Taylor, Charles, 119, 151–153
Trotsky, Leon, 41, 50–51, 54–56
Trump, Donald, 173

Virilio, Paul, 79

Weber, Max, 132–133
Williams, Bernard, 126, 133–134
Wood, Allen, 32, 34

Young, Iris Marion, 126

Zamora, Daniel, 160, 165, 167